Lord

of All

the Dead

Lord

of All

the Dead

A Nonfiction Novel

———— ∞∞∞ ————

Javier Cercas

TRANSLATED FROM THE SPANISH BY
Anne McLean

Alfred A. Knopf
New York | 2020

THIS IS A BORZOI BOOK
PUBLISHED BY ALFRED A. KNOPF

www.aaknopf.com

Knopf, Borzoi Books, and the colophon are registered
trademarks of Penguin Random House LLC.

Library of Congress Cataloging-in-Publication Data
Names: Cercas, Javier, 1962– author. | McLean, Anne,
1962– translator.
Title: Lord of all the dead : a nonfiction novel / by Javier
Cercas ; translated from the Spanish by Anne McLean.
Other titles: Monarca de las sombras. English
Description: First edition. | New York : Alfred A. Knopf,
[2019] | "A Borzoi book"—Title page verso. |
Identifiers: LCCN 2019016660 (print) |
LCCN 2019981499 (ebook) | ISBN 9780525520900 (print) |
ISBN 9780525520917 (ebook)
Subjects: LCSH: Cercas, Javier, 1962—Family—Fiction. |
Ibahernando (Spain)—History—20th century—Fiction. |
Spain—History—Civil War, 1936–1939—Fiction. | GSAFD:
Biographical fiction. | Historical fiction.
Classification: LCC PQ6653.E62 M6613 2019b (print) | LCC
PQ6653.E62 (ebook) | DDC 863/.64—dc23
LC record available at https://lccn.loc.gov/2019016660
LC ebook record available at https://lccn.loc.gov/2019981499

Jacket photograph of Manuel Mena,
courtesy The Cercas Mena Family Archives
Jacket design by Janet Hansen

Printed in the United States of America

First Edition

For Raül Cercas
and
Mercè Mas

For Blanca Mena

Dulce et decorum est pro patria mori.

How sweet and honourable it is
to die for one's country.

—HORACE, *Odes*, III.2.13

Lord
of All
the Dead

His name was Manuel Mena, and he died at the age of nineteen in the Battle of the Ebro. It was September 21, 1938, towards the end of the Spanish Civil War, in a Catalan village called Bot. He was an enthusiastic supporter of Franco, or at least an enthusiastic Falangist, or at least he was at the beginning of the war: that was when he enlisted in the Third Bandera of the Cáceres Falange, and the following year, having recently attained the rank of provisional second lieutenant, he was posted to the First Tabor of Ifni Riflemen, a shock unit belonging to the Corps of Regulars. Twelve months later he died in combat, and for years he was the official hero of my family.

He was my mother's uncle on her father's side, and she has told me his story countless times since I was a boy, or rather his story and his legend, so often that even before I was a writer I thought I would have to write a book about him one day. I discarded the idea as soon as I became a writer; the reason is that I felt that Manuel Mena was the exact paradigm of my family's most onerous legacy, and telling his story would not only mean taking on his political past but also the political past of my whole family, which was the past that most embarrassed me. I did not want to take that on, I did not see any need to, and much less to discuss it at length in a book: it was enough to have to learn to live with it. Besides, I wouldn't have even known how to start telling that story: should I have stuck strictly to reality, to the truth of events, supposing that such a thing were possible and that the passing of time had not opened impossible-to-fill gaps in Manuel Mena's story? Should I have mixed reality and fiction, to plug up the holes inevitably left by the former? Or should I have invented a fiction out of reality, even though everyone might believe it was true, or in order for everyone to believe it was true? I had no idea, and my ignorance of the form seemed to be an endorsement of my decision on the content: I should not write the story of Manuel Mena.

A few years ago, however, that old refusal seemed to enter into a crisis. By then my youth was far behind me. I was married and had a son; my family was not going through a great time: my father had died after a long illness and, after five decades of marriage, my mother was still having difficulty adjusting to the thankless stage of widowhood. My father's death had accentuated my mother's natural propensity to melodramatic, resigned, and catastrophic fatalism ("Oh, son," was one of her most well-worn maxims, "may God not send quite as many sorrows as we're able to bear"), and one morning a car struck her on a crosswalk; the accident was not particularly serious, but my mother got a bad scare and found herself forced to remain seated in an armchair for several weeks with her body covered in bruises. My sisters and I urged her to leave the house, took her out for meals and excursions and took her to her parish church for Mass. I won't forget the first time I went with her. We had walked the hundred yards between her house and the Sant Salvador parish church, and, when we were about to cross the street at the crosswalk, she squeezed my arm.

"Son," she whispered, "blessed are those who believe in crosswalks, for they shall see God. I was just about to."

During that convalescence I visited more frequently than usual. I often even stayed overnight, with my wife and son. The three of us would arrive on Friday afternoon and stay until Sunday evening, when we went back to Barcelona. During the day we talked or read, and in the evening we watched films or television programmes, especially *Big Brother*, a reality show my mother and I loved. Of course, we talked about Ibahernando, the village in Extremadura from which my parents had moved to Catalonia in the sixties, as so many people from Extremadura did in those years. I say, "of course," and I understand I have to explain why I say that; it's easy: because there is no event as significant in my mother's life as emigration. I say there is no event as significant in my mother's life as emigration, and I understand I should also explain why I say that; this is not so easy. Twenty years ago I tried to explain it to a friend by saying that overnight my mother went from being the privileged daughter of a patrician family in small-town Extremadura, where she was everything, to being not much more than a proletarian or a little less than a petit-bourgeois housewife overwhelmed with children in a Catalan city, where she was nobody. As soon as I had formulated it, the answer struck me as valid but insufficient, so I wrote an article titled "The Innocents," which still seems the best explanation I know how to give of this matter; it was published on December 28, 1999, Feast Day of the Innocents and thirty-third anniversary of the date my mother arrived in Gerona. It goes like this:

The first time I saw Gerona was on a map. My mother, who was very young then, pointed to a faraway spot on a paper and said that was where my father was. A few months later we packed our bags. There was a very long trip, and at the end a rustic, crumbling station, surrounded by sad buildings wrapped in a mortuary light and mistreated by the pitiless December rain. My father, who was waiting for us there, took us out for breakfast and told us that in that impossible city they spoke a language different from ours, and he taught me the first sentence I ever spoke in Catalan: "M'agrada molt anar al col·legi" (I really like going to school). Then we all piled into my father's Citroën 2CV and, as we drove to our new home through the hostile desolation of that foreign city, I am sure that my mother thought and did not say a phrase she thought and said every time the anniversary of the day we packed our bags came around: "¡Menuda Inocentada!" (What a dirty trick!) It was the Feast Day of the Innocents, Holy Fools' Day, and she must have felt like a practical joke had been played on her, thirty-three years ago.

The Tartar Steppe is an extraordinary novel by Dino Buzzati. It is a slightly Kafkaesque fable in which a young lieutenant named Giovanni Drogo is posted to a remote fortress besieged by the steppe and the Tartars who inhabit it. Thirsting for glory and battles, Drogo waits in vain for the arrival of the Tartars, and his whole life is spent waiting. I've often thought that this hopeless fable is an emblem of the fates of many of those who packed their bags. As many did, my mother spent her youth waiting to go home, which always seemed imminent. Thirty-three years went by like that. As for others among those who packed their bags, things weren't so bad for her: after all, my father had a salary and a fairly secure job, which was much more than many had. I think that my mother, all the same, never accepted her new life and, shielded by her all-consuming work of raising a large family, lived in Gerona doing as much as possible not to notice that she lived in Gerona, rather than in the place where she'd packed her bags. That impossible illusion lasted until a few years ago. By then things had changed enormously: Gerona was a cheerful and prosperous city, and its station a modern building with very white walls and immense windows; apart from that, some of my mother's grandchildren barely understood her language. One day, when none of her children lived at home anymore and she could no longer protect herself from reality behind her all-consuming work as a housewife, nor evade the evidence that, twenty-five years later, she was still living in a city that even now was foreign to her, she was diagnosed with depression, and for two years all she did was stare dry-eyed and silently at nothing. Perhaps she was also thinking, thinking of her lost youth and, like Lieutenant Drogo and like many of those who packed their bags, of her life used up in futile expectation and perhaps also—she, who has not read Kafka—that all this was a huge misunderstanding and that this misunderstanding was going to kill her. But it didn't kill her, and one day when she was beginning to emerge from the pit of the years of depression and was going to see the doctor with her husband, a gentleman opened a door and held it for her, saying, "Endavant," which means "after you" in Catalan. My mother said: "To the doctor." Because my mother had understood

"¿Adónde van?," "Where are you going?" in Spanish. My father says that at that moment he remembered the first sentence that, more than twenty-five years earlier, he had taught me to say in Catalan, and also that he suddenly understood my mother, because he understood that she had spent twenty-five years living in Gerona as if she were still living in the place where she had packed our bags.

At the end of *The Tartar Steppe* the Tartars arrive, but illness and old age prevent Drogo from satisfying his long-postponed dream of confronting them. Far from the combat and the glory, alone and anonymous in the dingy room of an inn, Drogo feels the end approaching and understands that this is the real battle, which he had always been waiting for unwittingly; then he sits up a little and straightens his military jacket a little, to face death like a brave man. I don't know if those who pack their bags ever go home again; I fear not, among other reasons because they will have understood that return is impossible. I don't know either whether they sometimes think that life has passed them by as they waited, or that this has all been a terrible misunderstanding, or that they've been deceived or, worse, that someone has deceived them. I don't know. What I do know is that in a few hours, as soon as she gets up, my mother will think and maybe say the same phrase she's been repeating for thirty-three years on this same day: "¡Menuda Inocentada!"

That's how my article ended. More than a decade after it was published my mother still hadn't left Ibahernando even though she was still living in Gerona, so it is logical that our foremost pastime during the visits we paid her to alleviate her convalescence consisted of talking about Ibahernando: more unexpected was that on one occasion our three foremost pastimes converged into one and the same. It happened one night when we all watched *L'Avventura,* an old Michelangelo Antonioni film. The film is about a group of friends on a yacht trip, during which one of them goes missing; at first everyone searches for her, but they soon forget about her and the excursion goes on as if nothing had happened. The static density of the film quickly defeated my son, who went to bed, and my wife, who fell asleep in her chair in front of the television; my mother, however, outlasted the almost two and a half hours of black-and-white images and dialogues in Italian with Spanish subtitles. Surprised by her endurance, when the film ended I asked her what she'd thought of what she'd just seen.

"It's the film I've most enjoyed in my whole life," she said.

If it had been anyone else, I might have thought it was a sarcastic answer; but my mother does not do sarcasm, so I thought the lack of incidents and endless silences of *Big Brother* had trained her perfectly to enjoy the endless silences and lack of incidents of Antonioni's film. What I thought was that, since she was accustomed to the slowness of *Big Brother, L'Avventura* had seemed as frenetic as an action movie. My mother must have noticed my astonishment, because she hurried to try to dispel it; her clarification did not entirely belie my conjecture.

"Of course, Javi," she explained, pointing to the television. "What happened in that film is what always happens: someone dies and the next day nobody remembers him. That's what happened to my uncle Manolo."

Her uncle Manolo was Manuel Mena. That very night we

talked about him again, and the following weekends we barely changed the subject. As long as I can remember I've heard my mother talk about Manuel Mena, but only during those days did I come to understand two things. The first is that Manuel Mena had been much more than an uncle for her. According to what she told me then, during her childhood she had lived with him in her grandmother's house, a few feet from the house of her parents, who'd sent her there because their first- and second-born daughters had died of meningitis and they harboured a reasonable fear that the third would catch the same illness. It seems my mother had been very happy in that big, bustling widow's house belonging to her grandmother Carolina, accompanied by her cousin Alejandro and spoiled by a boisterous army of bachelor uncles. None of them spoiled her as much as Manuel Mena; for my mother, none could compare to him: he was the youngest, the most cheerful, the liveliest, the one who always brought her gifts, the one who made her laugh most and the one who played with her most often. She called him Uncle Manolo; he called her Blanquita. My mother adored him, so his death represented a devastating blow to her. I have never seen my mother cry; never: not even during her two years of depression, not even when my father died. My mother, simply, does not cry. My sisters and I have speculated a lot about the reasons for this anomaly, until one of those nights after her accident, while she was telling me for the umpteenth time about the arrival of Manuel Mena's body in the village and she remembered she'd spent hours and hours crying, I thought I found the explanation: I thought that we all have an allotment of tears and on that day hers ran out, and since then she simply had no tears left to shed. Manuel Mena, in short, was not just my mother's uncle: he was like an older brother to her; he was also her first death.

The second thing I understood in those days was something even more important than the first. As a boy I didn't understand why my mother talked to me so much about Manuel Mena; as a youth I thought, secretly horrified and ashamed, that she did so because Manuel Mena had been a Francoist, or at least a Falangist, and during Franco's regime my family had been Francoists, or had at least accepted Francoism with the same uncritical meekness with which most of the country accepted it; as an adult I've understood that this explanation is trivial, but only during those nocturnal conversations with my convalescing mother did I manage to decode the exact nature of that triviality. What I understood then was that Manuel Mena's death had been seared into my mother's imagination in childhood as what the ancient Greeks called *kalos thanatos:* a beautiful death. It was, for the ancient Greeks, the perfect death, the death of a pure and noble young man who, like Achilles in *The Iliad,* demonstrates his nobility and purity by risking his life for all or nothing while he fights in the front line for values greater than himself or that he feels are greater than himself, and falls in combat and leaves behind the world of the living in the fullness of his beauty and his vigour and escapes the usury of time and does not find out about the decrepitude that ruins men; this eminent young man, who renounces worldly values and his own life for an ideal, constitutes the Greeks' heroic paragon and reaches the apogee of their ethics and the only form of immortality possible in that world without God, which consists of living for ever in the precarious and volatile memory of humanity, as happens to Achilles. For the ancient Greeks, *kalos thanatos* was the perfect death, which is the culmination of a perfect life; for my mother, Manuel Mena was Achilles.

That double discovery was a revelation, and for several weeks a suspicion worried me: perhaps I had been wrong to refuse to write about Manuel Mena. Of course, I still thought more or less what I'd always thought about his story, but I wondered if the fact that it was a shameful story for me was reason enough not to tell it and to continue to keep it hidden; at the same time I told myself I still had time to tell it, but that, if I really wanted to tell it, I should get down to work immediately, because I was sure that there would be barely a trace of documentary evidence of Manuel Mena in archives and libraries and that, seventy-odd years after his death, he would be little more than the shreds of a legend in the eroded memories of a diminishing handful of elderly people. Anyway, I also understood that if my mother understood Antonioni so well, or Antonioni's film, it was not only because the aphasic slowness of *Big Brother* had prepared her for it, but that, even though she still inhabited a world with God (a world that had already been extinguished and that Manuel Mena had thought he was fighting to defend), as a girl she had been perplexed to learn and had suffered as an outrage the fact that precarious and volatile human memory spurned her uncle, unlike its treatment of Achilles. Because the truth is that oblivion had begun its demolition job immediately after Manuel Mena's death. In her own house a dense and incomprehensible silence, or one that my mother as a girl judged incomprehensible, fell over him. Nobody investigated the circumstances or precise causes of his death and everyone made do with the hazy version of it given by his orderly (a man who accompanied his body to the village and stayed for a few days in his mother's house), nobody was interested in speaking with his fellow officers or the commanders who had fought at his side, nobody wanted to investigate the vicissitudes of his war, which fronts he'd fought on or the unit he'd belonged to, nobody bothered to visit Bot, that distant Catalan village where he'd died and which I'd always thought was called Bos or Boj or Boh, because, since Spanish has no words that end in *t*, that's how my mother always pronounced it. A few months after Manuel Mena's death, in short, his name was already almost never mentioned in the family, or mentioned only when there was no way not to mention it, and, a few years after his death, his mother and his sisters destroyed all his papers, mementos, and belongings.

All except for one photograph (or at least that's what I always thought): a military portrait of Manuel Mena. After his funeral, the family made seven enlarged copies; one of them presided over his mother's dining room until her death; the other six were distributed among his six siblings. That relic vaguely unsettled the summers of my cold immigrant childhood, when we returned in the holidays to the warmth of the village. Happy to leave behind for a few months the inclemency and confusion of exile and recover my cosy status as the progeny of one of the patrician families of Ibahernando, I settled into my maternal grandparents' house and saw the portrait of the dead man hanging on the unprivileged wall of a dressing room where trunks full of clothing and shelves full of books accumulated; and it unsettled my adolescence and youth even more, when my grandparents died and the uninhabited house was closed up all year and opened only when my parents and my sisters returned in the summers and I tried to get used to the cold of the outdoors and the confusion of the uprooting and tried to emancipate myself from the false warmth of the village by visiting it as little as possible, keeping myself as far apart from that house and that family and that ominous portrait that watched over the room full of trunks alone in the winter, afflicted by a vague shame or guilt the roots of which I preferred not to investigate, the shame of my theoretical hereditary condition of village patrician, the shame of my family's political origins and actions during the war and Franco's regime (unknown to me or almost unknown), the diffuse, parallel, and complementary shame of being tied by an unbreakable bond to that lost and needy little one-horse town that wouldn't quite disappear. But most of all Manuel Mena's portrait has unsettled me in maturity, when I haven't stopped feeling ashamed of my origins and my inheritance but have in part resigned myself to them, have in part accepted being who I am and having the bonds I have and coming from where I come from, have grown accustomed for better or worse to the rootlessness and to being out in the open and to feeling unsettled, and have understood that my patrician condition was illusory and have often returned to the village with my wife and son and my parents (never or almost never with friends, never or almost never with people outside the family) and have stayed in that house that's crumbling away where Manuel Mena's portrait has been collecting dust in silence for more than seventy years, converted into the perfect, mournful and violent symbol of all the errors and responsibilities and guilt and shame and misery and death and defeats and fright and filth and tears and sacrifice and passion and dishonour of my ancestors.

Now I have it in front of me, in my office in Barcelona. I don't remember when I brought it back from Ibahernando; in any case, it was years after my mother recovered from her accident and I made a resolution about Manuel Mena's story.

The resolution was that I would not write it. The resolution was that I would write other stories, but as I wrote them I would gather information about Manuel Mena, even if it was just between one book and the next or in my spare time, before all traces of his brief life vanished completely and disappeared from the precarious and worn-out memories of those who had known him or from the volatile order of archives and libraries. In this way Manuel Mena's story or what was left of Manuel Mena's story would not be lost and I could tell it if I one day got the urge to tell it or felt able to tell it, or I could give it to another writer so they could tell it, supposing some other writer might want to tell it, or I could simply not tell it, turn it forever into a void, a hole, into one of the thousands and thousands of stories that will never be told, perhaps into one of those projects that some writers are always expecting to write and never write because they don't want to take on the burden or because they fear they'll never be equal to the task and prefer to leave them in the state of mere possibility, converted into their radiant, never-written masterpiece, radiant and masterly precisely because it will never be written.

That was the decision I made: not to write Manuel Mena's story, to continue not writing Manuel Mena's story. As for his portrait, since I brought it to my office I haven't stopped gazing at it. It is a studio portrait, taken in Zaragoza: the city's name appears in the bottom right corner, in white, almost illegible letters; time has deposited stains and scrapes on the paper, has cracked its edges. I don't know the exact date it was taken, but there is a clue on Manuel Mena's uniform that lets me fix an approximate date. On the left-hand side of his jacket our man displays, sure enough, a Suffering for the Nation Medal—the equivalent of an American Purple Heart—and above it a ribbon

with two stripes; both decorations mean that, at the moment the photograph was taken, Manuel Mena had been wounded in combat twice by enemy fire, which could not have happened before the spring of 1938, when he had gone into combat only once with the First Tabor of Ifni Riflemen, but also no later than the middle of the summer, when the Battle of the Ebro broke out and he barely returned to the rearguard again. The portrait must have been taken, therefore, between the spring and early summer of 1938, during Manuel Mena's second or third stay in Zaragoza or in the vicinity of Zaragoza. At that time he was about to turn or had just turned nineteen, and in a few months he would die. In the photograph, Manuel Mena wears the dress uniform of the Ifni Riflemen, with his tilted white-and-black peaked cap and his immaculate white jacket with gold buttons and black chevrons, on each of which shines a second lieutenant's star. The third star is on his cap; immediately above it, on the white background, is the insignia of the infantry: a sword and an arquebus crossed over a bugle. The insignia is repeated on the lapels of the jacket. Under the right lapel, blurrier, part of it almost invisible, the insignia of the Ifni Rifle Company can be distinguished, an Arabic crescent moon on which can be read or intuited, in capital letters, the word IFNI, and in the semicircle of which fits a five-pointed star with two crossed guns. Under the left lapel, the Suffering for the Nation Medal and the ribbon with two stripes stand out against the white cloth of the military jacket. The top two buttons of the jacket are left undone, as is the right breast pocket; this deliberate carelessness allows a better view of the white shirt and black tie, both similarly spotless. It is striking how thin he is; in fact, his body seems unable to fill out his uniform: it is the body of a child in the clothing of an adult. The position of his right arm is also striking, with his forearm crossed in front of his abdomen and his hand clutching the inside of his left elbow, in a gesture that does not seem natural but dictated by the photographer (we might also imagine the photographer suggesting the jaunty angle of the peaked cap, which casts a shadow over Manuel Mena's right eyebrow). But what is most striking is the face. It is, unmistakeably, a childish face, or at most adolescent, with his newborn complexion, without a single wrinkle or any trace of whiskers, his tenuous brows and his virgin, half-open lips, between which peek out teeth as white as his jacket. He has a straight and slender nose, his neck is also slender, and his ears stick quite far out from his head. As for his eyes, the black-and-white photography has robbed them of their colour; my mother remembers them as green; they do look light. They are not looking at the camera, in any case, but to his right, and they don't seem to be looking at anyone in particular. I have been looking at them for a long time, but I have not managed to see in them any pride or vanity or thoughtlessness or fear or joy or ambition or hope or discouragement or horror or cruelty or compassion or delight or sadness, not even the hidden imminence of death. I have spent a long time looking at them and I am unable to see anything in them. Sometimes I think those eyes are a mirror and the nothing I see in them is me. Sometimes I think the nothing is the war.

Manuel Mena was born on April 25, 1919. Back then Ibahernando was a remote, isolated, and miserable village in Extremadura, a remote, isolated, and miserable region of Spain, over towards the border with Portugal. The name of the place is a contraction of Viva Hernando; Hernando was a Christian knight who in the thirteenth century contributed to conquering the Moors of the city of Trujillo and incorporating it into the possessions of the King of Castile, who presented his vassal with the adjoining lands as payment for services rendered to the crown. Manuel Mena was born there. His whole family was born there, including his niece, Blanca Mena, including Blanca Mena's son, Javier Cercas. Some maintain that the family arrived in the region with Hernando's Christians, dragged by the medieval impetus of the Castilian conquest. Maybe so. But it could also be that they arrived earlier, because before the impetuous Christians settled in Ibahernando the pithy Iberians and the reasonable Romans and the barbarous Visigoths and the very civilised Arabs had settled there. The fact might surprise people, because it's not a gentle land but a bleak plateau of freezing winters and torrid summers, extensive uncultivated land out of the dry surface of which jut craggy stretches like the shells of gigantic buried crustaceans. Whatever the case, if the family did settle in the village with Hernando and his Christians, the impetus or desperation that brought them that far must have soon extinguished, because not a single one of its members carried on with the Castilian monarchs in the invasion of the rest of the Iberian peninsula, or with the conquistadors in search of the gold and women of the Americas, and all remained in the vicinity, as still as holm oaks, putting down roots so powerful that in spite of the mid-twentieth-century diaspora, which practically emptied the village, few have been able to pull them up entirely.

Manuel Mena could not even try to. At the moment of his arrival on earth, Ibahernando was further from the twentieth century than it was from the Middle Ages; to put it a better way: it's possible that it hadn't entirely emerged from the Middle Ages. Back then, after the expulsion of the Muslims by the Christians, the village formed part of the crown land of Trujillo, which was accountable directly to the king, but all its lands were in the hands of noblemen with the power of life and death over their serfs, whom they kept in a state of semi-slavery. Eight centuries later, at the beginning of the twentieth, things had barely changed. The country had not heard of the Renaissance or the Enlightenment or the liberal revolutions (or had only half-heard of them), the region did not know the meaning of industry or what the bourgeoisie was, and, although in the middle of the nineteenth century Trujillo was no longer crown land and Ibahernando had emancipated itself from the auspices of the distinguished city and established itself as a humble independent municipality, most of its territory continued to be in the hands of aristocrats with bombastic names who lived in Madrid and who nobody had ever seen around those parts—the Marquis of Santa Marta, the Count of La Oliva, the Marquis of Campo Real, the Marchioness of San Juan de Piedras Albas—while the inhabitants of the village starved to death trying to produce wheat, barley, and rye from those thankless, stony fields, and grazing with great difficulty flocks of scraggy sheep, swine, and cattle, which they sold for low prices in the nearby markets.

But the fact that the conditions of medieval servitude had barely changed since antiquity for the inhabitants of Ibahernando doesn't mean that they hadn't changed at all or weren't starting to change, at least in part or for some. Still, in the middle of the nineteenth century, a renowned geographical dictionary written by a renowned Spanish liberal contained a disconsolate portrait of the village; according to him, Ibahernando was an inclement corner reached by neither the highway nor the postal service and where one thousand two hundred and five souls were crammed into a hundred and eighty-nine lamentable houses, with a primary school, a parish church, a public fountain, and a municipal government so poor it could not attend to even the most basic and urgent needs of its residents. Only a few years on from that description, at the end of the nineteenth century or the beginning of the twentieth, the Spanish liberal's portrait would still have been an accurate etching of that dark part of Spain, but perhaps it might have been a little different. By that time, just before the birth of Manuel Mena, some enterprising agricultural labourers were inspired to rent the lands of the absent aristocrats. The arrangement supposed a fragile and unequal alliance between aristocrats and labourers or, to be specific, between some aristocrats and some labourers; it also supposed a small mutation that had various entwined consequences. The first is that the enterpris-

ing labourers began to prosper, first thanks to the profits from
their exploitation of the rented lands and later thanks to the
profits from the exploitation of the small farms they began
to acquire thanks to the profits from the exploitation of the
rented lands. The second consequence is that those labourers
with land turned into foremen or delegates of the interests of
the aristocrats and began to relegate their own interests and to
confuse them with those of the aristocrats, some even began
to want to look at themselves from a distance in the unreach-
able mirror of patrician customs and ways of life and to think
that, at least in the village, they could become patricians. The
third consequence is that the labourers with land began to give
work to the landless labourers and the landless labourers
began to depend on the labourers with land and to consider
them rich or as the patricians of the village. The fourth and
final consequence—the most important—is that the village
began to incubate a fantasy of basic inequality according to
which, while the landless labourers had not stopped being poor
or being serfs, the labourers with land had turned into rich
patricians, or were on their way to doing so.

It was pure fiction. The reality was that the landless labourers were still poor although less and less so, and that, although
there were more and more of them, the labourers with land
were not rich: it was simply that some of them were no longer
poor, or they were at least beginning to emerge from centuries
of poverty; the reality is that no matter that all of them believed
what they believed, the labourers with land were not patricians
and were still serfs, but the landless labourers could turn into or
were already turning into serfs of serfs. In short: until then the
interests of the villagers had been essentially identical, because
they were all serfs and they all knew they were; from then on,

however, the artificial mirage began to take over that in the village there were serfs and patricians, and the interests of its inhabitants began to diverge, artificially.

Manuel Mena had been born into a family that was part of this ascendant minority of illusory patricians and real serfs that began to prosper at the beginning of the twentieth century in Ibahernando. It wasn't the richest of those families, or the poorest. Manuel Mena's father was named Alejandro and, like almost everybody in the village, he earned his living working in the fields: he ran the only farm the family possessed, a few acres of unirrigated land known as Valdelaguna, where he grew grain crops and raised sheep and cattle; Manuel Mena's mother's name was Carolina and she ran a tobacco shop. They had seven children. They could not allow themselves even the tiniest luxury, but they did not go hungry. A few years after Manuel Mena's birth, his father died, and his three older brothers—Juan, Antonio, and Andrés—took over running Valdelaguna. Almost nothing is known about this initial stage of his life; most of what happened in it has been lost with the memories of those who knew him, and what remains is barely an imprecise legend out of which we can only rescue for real history a general image of his character and two concrete anecdotes. The image is clear, unanimous, and confirmed; it is also two-sided: on the one hand, the cordial image of a restless, cheerful, extroverted, quick-witted, and gleefully irresponsible boy who got along well with his mother and his brothers and sisters and knew how to make friends; on the other, the sharp image of a spoiled youngest son of a big family, with a limitless selfishness, pride verging on arrogance, and an unrestrained propensity to explosions of bad temper. As for the two anecdotes, they are both still recalled with improbable exactitude by two almost hundred-year-old women whom Javier Cercas has known since he was a boy without ever knowing they had gone to school with Manuel Mena, and whom he began to frequent when he found out they had. One was his aunt Francisca Alonso, widow of a cousin of his parents; the other, Doña María Arias, was the village teacher for decades.

When Javier Cercas began to visit them, both women still lived in Ibahernando, in two big houses, surrounded by other big houses, which were deserted except in summer; they had been friends for a lifetime and continued to see each other every day. In spite of being two or three years younger than Manuel Mena, for some time, each had shared a desk with him in the best school in the village; both remembered it well. They remembered a damp, frosty, pokey little unlit room in the back of the church where a teacher tried to inculcate a few basic notions of mathematics, history, and geography into them. They remembered that those rudiments were enough to satisfy the intellectual needs of children destined to lifetimes of servitude, but not to pass the public exams in the capital, or only enough for them to try and then return to the village with an irreparable burden of failure and discouraging humiliation. They remembered that this educational calamity seemed natural to them, or at least it didn't feel unusual, because back then Ibahernando was a population of serfs and an illiterate community that in its entire history had barely known the modest pride of being the birthplace of a university graduate. They remembered their teacher, a man with a thorny character named Don Marcelino, who in class parcelled out slaps, pinches, and knocks on the head and lacked not only any teacher's qualification but also the slightest pedagogical vocation, though he did not lack a political one (they remembered he left the school as soon as the recently proclaimed Second Republic offered him the post of secretary of the municipality, around 1932). And they remembered that, in this ragged and unstimulating school, Manuel Mena was a rascal who invested his time in collecting trading cards, tormenting his classmates by singing softly and making a racket while they were trying to work, and laughing at the girls or mocking them with offensive gossip.

Thus far the memories of the two elderly ladies converge; from this point on they diverge. Doña María Arias remembered—this is the first of the two anecdotes—that one morning, after a night of torrential rain, Don Marcelino's students found a huge mud puddle on the way into the school, and that Manuel Mena proposed to take advantage of the mess to organise an engineering game; all the children joined in with the proposal, so during recess the whole class worked together to construct, out of mud and water, a labyrinth of dams, canals, and streams outside the door to the building. One of those children was named Antonio Cartagena. He was the illegitimate son of the village doctor and his maid, but in time his father had erased the stigma by marrying the boy's mother and recognising his son. He was a weak-willed child without any malice; his peers made fun of him by calling him the Dodo. And that morning, once the game was finished and before returning to the tedium of the classroom, Manuel Mena decided to christen the recently constructed mud works one by one, until he arrived at the most successful or most spectacular of them and, amid the whistles and jeers of his classmates, named it the Dodo while Antonio Cartagena watched his humiliation with defenceless whimpering and the trembling lip of a mistreated little boy.

Doña María Arias remembered that first anecdote with the indulgence of a ninety-year-old teacher accustomed to children's cruelty; Francisca Alonso remembered the second, but she remembered it without indulgence, with the undiminished dismay of a horrified little girl who had witnessed the scene. It happened during an excursion to the countryside. Don Marcelino's primitive pedagogy barely considered the benefits of contact with nature, and Francisca Alonso remembered her excitement and that of her peers that morning as they gathered at the schoolroom door, impatient to enjoy the novelty and carrying tortillas and sandwiches and canteens that their mothers had prepared at home. The outward route was not far, although when they arrived at their destination they were all hungry and immediately got ready to eat their picnics. That was when it happened. At a certain moment, Francisca Alonso didn't know how or what about (or perhaps she knew and had forgotten), Manuel Mena and Antonio Cartagena got involved in an argument and were soon punching each other. It was not easy to separate them. When they were finally pried apart, Manuel Mena vented his rage, insulting his classmate by calling him a bastard, reminding him of his shameful past. Antonio Cartagena went back to the village alone crying his eyes out, and the incident left a bitter aftertaste that blighted the excursion.

Manuel Mena couldn't have been more than twelve or thirteen when he was the protagonist of that scene. A photograph of Don Marcelino's students has been preserved from that time; actually, it must be from a little earlier, when girls and boys attended separate classes (Don Marcelino taught the boys, and Doña Paca, his wife, the girls): which explains why neither Francisca Alonso nor Doña María Arias appear in the image; Antonio Cartagena does not appear either, as he did not attend

that school then. The one who does appear in the photograph
is Manuel Mena. He is just behind and to the right of the only
adult in the group, who is Don Marcelino. He is standing up,
his silhouette stands out against the tacky cardboard backdrop,
which doesn't manage to cover the stone wall behind it, and is
wearing a tight, striped, buttoned-up blazer, a white shirt with
a wide collar, and a rebellious curl of fine, fair hair on his forehead; it is easy to recognise the features and slimness of the late
adolescent or premature adult who appears in the only photograph of him alone that we still have, wearing his Ifni Riflemen
second lieutenant's uniform, and it is possible to discern in his
direct gaze and the circumflex shape of his mouth an unpleas-
ant glimpse of the haughtiness of a heartless brat. Apart from
Manuel Mena, it is possible to recognise in that image other
relatives of Javier Cercas; sitting on the floor at the bottom right,
for example, wearing the same blazer and same shirt as Manuel
Mena, is his uncle Juan Cercas: Francisca Alonso's husband.

One last observation about Manuel Mena's childhood also pertains to that photograph. Javier Cercas's mother was unaware of it until her son discovered it in a book about the village published just a few years ago. Cercas remembers that, when he showed his mother the photograph, she was recovering from a traffic accident, and she identified Manuel Mena and most of the boys in it without any difficulty; he also remembers that he and his mother didn't even need to guess that they were all dead: they took it for granted. Months later, however, Cercas spent a week in the village, and one day he happened to talk about the photograph with José Antonio Cercas, the only one of his cousins who still lives there, who assured him that he was wrong: not all the boys with Manuel Mena in that photograph were dead; the second boy from the right in Manuel Mena's row, with the black suit, black hair, and white shirt front, was still alive, he explained. Javier Cercas was startled by the news. At that time he did not yet know that his aunt Francisca and Doña María Arias had also been classmates of Manuel Mena's in Don Marcelino's school, and he found it extraordinary that there could still be a living witness to Manuel Mena's childhood. According to what his cousin told him, the survivor of the photograph was named Antonio Ruiz Barrado, although everyone knew him as El Pelaor, the Shearer, and he spent long periods of time in the village, although he wasn't there at that moment. What his cousin didn't tell him, because he didn't know it, was that one night at the end of August 1936, when the war had just broken out and Manuel Mena had not yet left for the front and was still in Ibahernando, the Shearer's father had been dragged out of his house by Francoists and murdered on the outskirts of the village.

❦ 3 ❦

"Are you really going to write another novel about the Civil War? Come on, are you really such a dickhead, or what? Look, the first time it worked because you caught everyone off guard; nobody knew you back then so everybody could use you. But now it's different: they're going to beat the shit out of you, kid, right down to your ID card! Whatever you write, some will attack you for idealising the Republicans, for not denouncing their crimes, and others will accuse you of revisionism or of massaging Francoism to present Francoists as normal, everyday people and not as monsters. That's how it is: nobody is interested in the truth; haven't you realised that? A few years ago it seemed they were interested, but it was a mirage. People don't like truth: they like lies; it's best not to talk about politicians and intellectuals. Some get nervous every time the subject comes up because they still think Franco's coup was necessary or at least inevitable, although they don't dare say so; and others have decided that it's playing along with the right if you don't say that all Republicans were democrats, including Durruti and La Pasionaria, and that not a single priest was killed here and no fucking churches were burned down ... Besides, haven't you noticed that the war is no longer the in thing? Why don't you write a post-postmodern version of *Sex or No Sex* or *What a Delightful Divorce!* I promise I'll make a film of it. We'll make a bundle."

In November 2012 I phoned David Trueba and asked him to come with me to Ibahernando to videotape an interview I wanted to conduct with the last witness to Manuel Mena's childhood (or with the person I then thought was the last witness), and I was still explaining who Manuel Mena was when he interrupted me with that tirade I've just summarised.

I would be lying if I said it surprised me. Years ago David had adapted a novel of mine for the cinema that was about the Spanish Civil War; unexpectedly—because the normal thing in these situations is for the novelist and director to end up hating each other's guts—we became friends. David maintained that our friendship was based on the fact that we were very similar; the truth is it's based on the fact that we're nothing at all alike. He had been a prodigal child who wrote scripts for television shows and films at an age when I was still playing with marbles, so, even though I'm seven years older than he is, when we met he had accumulated much more experience than me, had travelled much more than me, and knew many more people than I did. Actually, at times he resembled my father. Now I remember an anecdote. It happened at the end of the televised gala during which the Spanish Cinema Academy presents the Goya Awards every year. David's film based on my novel had eight nominations, including best picture and best director, and, when the news was announced, David asked me to come to the awards ceremony. The request surprised me, but I accepted and went to the gala with my wife. It was a catastrophe: of the eight Goya awards the film was up for, it won only one consolation prize, for best cinematography. When the ceremony ended, David's face was a sight: as soon as I began to sense the debacle I had been searching desperately for a consoling phrase, but in the end it was he who consoled my wife and me. "You don't know how sorry I am to have made you come all this way for this, kids," he said as soon as the lights came up, setting a hand on each of our shoulders. "I would have loved to dedicate a prize to you both. But as I always say: when it comes to making movies, apart from sex and money, don't expect anything."

David loved to pretend to be a commercial director capable of selling his soul to whoever it took for a blockbuster, but the truth is he had never directed anything commissioned by someone else, producers considered him an ultra-intellectual director, and his films were often militantly anti-commercial. He's from Madrid and lives there and, even though I live in Barcelona, when all the echoes of the film had died down we continued to see each other often. That was when the constituent imbalance of our friendship began to be glaringly obvious, because I didn't stop asking him for advice and he didn't stop giving me advice, recommending what I should and shouldn't do and trying to sort out my life, as if he were my manager or my literary agent or as if he saw me as a child lost in a wolf-infested wood. Then, for a while, the tables turned or seemed to turn or I tried to turn them, to back him up in return. It was when he and his wife separated. Although never in my life have I seen such an amicable split, David suffered a lot because of it; from one day to the next he subsided, his hair started to be interwoven with white, he aged. I'm not sure the word *split* is quite the right one: the fact is that his wife left him for someone the paparazzi call a Hollywood star; he was actually something much worse: a Hollywood star who resists being a

Hollywood star tooth and nail, which turns him into a Hollywood star squared, one of those guys all women rightly dream of. My friend tried to take it with the utmost dignity; in fact, my impression is that he was too dignified about it. I never asked him about the matter, because I remembered the phrase of an old actor David was fond of quoting ("I never tell my friends my troubles: let their fucking mothers entertain them!") and because he barely mentioned it; however, the few times he did I was struck by the fact that he spoke of his broken marriage with the equanimity of a relationship psychologist, but most of all that he didn't seem to express the slightest reproach against his wife and seemed much more worried about her than he was about himself. Until one day, while he was telling me that he'd just seen her to talk about their children, as they often did, he went to pieces and tears began to run down his cheeks. Feeling powerless to help, I let him cry; then I told him angrily that he was mistaken and it was one thing to be a gentleman and quite another to be an idiot. "Worry about yourself, for fuck's sake," I told him furiously. "Forget that woman. And let off some steam. It doesn't matter. Call her a witch and him a scumbag. Come on, say it with me: Scum-bag! You see? Easy. Two little syllables: Scum-bag! Try it, you'll see, you'll feel much better." "I wish I could, Javier," he answered, nodding while trying to wipe away his tears. "But I just can't. You don't understand: it's normal for the guy to be really good-looking and super-rich and even have blue eyes; of course, for you and me, it's totally abnormal, but that's the way it is . . . The problem is that as well as a son of a bitch he's a great guy, a really good person, and a brilliant actor. How do you expect me to curse the guy?" "Well, at least curse your wife!" I shouted. "The mother of my children?" he answered, horrified. "How could I? Besides, deep down it's all my fault: I practically persuaded her that she was in love with that bastard and should take off with him!" Anyway . . . after a while David seemed to begin to accept his new situation. I'm not sure my advice was much help to him, but I do know his work helped; he was doing better than ever, was writing nonstop in the press, had successfully published a novel, had successfully broadcast a television series and premiered a film, and was getting ready to shoot another one. At that time we started seeing each other frequently again and our friendship recovered its natural imbalance.

So, after discovering, thanks to an old school photograph and a comment from my cousin José Antonio Cercas, that there was a witness to Manuel Mena's childhood still living, I called David and, overcoming my embarrassment about taking friends to Ibahernando, asked him to go to my village with me under the pretext of needing him to film my conversation with that person; in part it was true, but only in part: the other reason was that I didn't want to interview him alone. David's first reaction was predictable, but I didn't attempt to dispel his fears because I felt that it was too difficult to explain over the phone why I wanted to go to Ibahernando and talk to the last witness of Manuel Mena's childhood (or the person I thought was its last witness) even though I wasn't going to write a novel about Manuel Mena. His second reaction was also predictable.

"When should we go?" he asked.

The morning after I took part in a literary festival that November in Madrid, David drove over to pick me up from the hotel beside the Retiro Park where I was staying. It was Saturday and my friend had both his children with him: Violeta and Leo. We dropped Violeta off at a dance academy and Leo at a soccer field in the Casa de Campo, and it was noon before we left the city on the road to Extremadura. For quite a while we were talking about the film he was working on at the time, in which he told me he wanted to tell the story of a teacher who used Beatles songs to teach English in Spain in the 1960s and who, when he finds out John Lennon is in Almería shooting a film, decides to go and meet him; he had the screenplay written, he told me, and was completely immersed in finding the money and the actors to film it. Past Talavera de la Reina, near Almaraz, or maybe Jaraicejo, we stopped at a gas station, filled up the tank, and, as we were drinking coffee beside big windows overlooking the scant traffic on the highway, David said:

"By the way, I've been thinking about your Civil War book."

"Oh yeah?"

"Yeah, and I've changed my mind: I think it's a great idea. Do you know why?" Intrigued, I shook my head. "Very simple: I now understand that in *Soldiers of Salamis* you invented a Republican hero to hide the fact that your family's hero was a Francoist."

Soldiers of Salamis was the title of the novel David had made into a film. I said:

"More like a Falangist."

"Okay, a Falangist. The thing is that you hid an ugly reality behind a pretty fiction."

"That sounds like a reproach."

"It isn't one. I'm not judging; I'm describing."

"And?"

"Now it's time to face reality, no? That's how you can close the circle. And that's how you can stop writing once and for all about the fucking war and Francoism and all the rest of that shit that tortures you so much." He gulped down the rest of his coffee. "You'll see," he added. "You're going to come out with a hell of a book."

"Well, I'm not going to write it."

David looked at me as if he'd just noticed me standing there beside him at the bar.

"Don't fuck around."

We walked back to the car and, as we went on our way, I explained my reasons for not writing the book about Manuel Mena and reminded him of the ones he'd outlined over the phone, or the ones he'd scolded me with. I also told him that I'd already written a novel about the Spanish Civil War and I didn't want to repeat myself. Trying to anticipate his objections, I added that, if I was going to talk to a witness to Manuel Mena's childhood anyway, it was because I wanted to collect as much information as possible on Manuel Mena before it all vanished.

"And then?" he asked. "When you have all the information, I mean."

"I don't know," I admitted. "Then I'll think about it. Maybe I'll give it to someone less involved in the story, so they can tell it. Maybe I'll leave it untold. Or maybe, who knows, I might change my mind and end up telling it myself. We'll see. In any case, if I did finally decide to tell it I wouldn't bind myself only to the truth of events. I'm sick of true tales. I don't want to repeat myself on that score either."

David nodded several times, although he didn't seem too satisfied with my explanations. I told him so.

"The truth is I'm not," he admitted.

"Why not?"

"I don't know: I have the impression you're less worried

about your novel than about what people are going to say about your novel."

"You're not going to tell me that's not a reproach."

"Not this time," he admitted again. "Look, what I mean is that it's not books that should be at the service of the writer, but the writer who has to be at the service of his books. What's this about not wanting to repeat yourself? If you start worrying about your literary career, what suits or doesn't suit your literary career, what critics are going to say and stuff like that, you're dead, man; worry about writing and forget the rest. All Kafka's novels are more or less the same, and all of Faulkner's as well. And who gives a fuck? A novel is good if it comes out of a writer's guts; nothing else: the rest is rubbish. And as far as not wanting to take on Manuel Mena's story, it's laughable: we go on and on about how this country needs to accept its past as it was, once and for all, with all its complexity and as harsh as it was, without sweetening or embellishing or sweeping it under the carpet, and the first thing we do when the time comes to take on our personal past is exactly that: sweep it out of sight. Fucking unbelievable."

After a while we caught sight of Trujillo, with its medieval fortress perched on top of Cabeza de Zorro and the city stretching out around it. We passed the city centre and shortly afterwards left the highway and parked in front of La Majada, a restaurant set between the highway and the old Madrid-to-Lisbon road, very close to Ibahernando by then. On the patio of La Majada there were three tables set with checked tablecloths, but only two of them were occupied by diners who were defying the November weather with the help of a hard, bright sun. We sat at the free one and, as soon as a waiter appeared, ordered two urgently needed glasses of beer. Then we ordered a salad; a double portion of *moraga,* a local dish of grilled pork; and a bottle of red wine. It was half past two; our appointment in Ibahernando was at five: we had no need to rush our meal.

When they brought the bottle of red, David noticed the label.

"*Habla del Silencio,* speak of silence," he read. "Nice oxymoron."

"It's local. The wine, I mean. My grandfather Juan used to make it at home; it was terrible, but there wasn't any other back then."

David tasted the wine.

"Well, this is good," he said.

"We've learned how to make it," I admitted. "The problem wasn't the land: it was us."

"Your grandfather Juan was Manuel Mena's brother?"

"He was the oldest of the siblings. Manuel Mena was the youngest."

We were sitting across from each other, with our coats on, him facing the restaurant and a farm that blocked the view of the highway, and me facing the old Ibahernando road, along which not a single car passed. The air was dry, vibrant. Around us spread a green and silent plain, out of which rose dusty holm oaks, stone fences, and huge boulders; above us the sky was a uniform, cloudless blue. The waiter brought us the salad and the double portion of *moraga,* and while we ate I told David about the history of Ibahernando, of its secular dependence on Trujillo and its importance in the region until emigration decimated its population in the fifties and sixties and in a very short space of time it went from having three thousand inhabitants to having five hundred; I also put him in the picture about the man we were going to interview: I told him his name was

Antonio Ruiz Barrado but everyone knew him as El Pelaor, because his job had always been to shear the sheep, told him he had always been a neighbour of my family in the village, talked to him about the school photograph where he appears together with Manuel Mena, told him that, although he lived between Cáceres, Bilbao, and Valladolid, where his three children had moved to, he was spending a few days in Ibahernando with his youngest daughter, explained that I hadn't talked to him on the phone but to his older daughter, who at first gave me little reason to hope that he might want to speak to me, because, she assured me, she had never heard her father speak of the war, and for whom it was a surprise when the Shearer agreed to the interview. We had almost finished off the salad and pork when David brought up the subject of my novel again.

"I can't believe you've given up the idea."

"Well, it's true," I said. I repeated the arguments I'd used last time, perhaps I added one or two. "Besides," I concluded, "I've never written about my village: I wouldn't even know how to."

"Why not by writing about Manuel Mena?" he asked. "After all, you didn't choose this subject: the subject chose you. And those are always the best subjects."

"You might be right, but this case is different. I'm not saying I'm not interested in Manuel Mena. The truth is he always interested me. I mean, I always wanted to know what kind of man he was. Or what kind of adolescent, rather . . . I always wanted to know why he went off to war so young, why he fought with Franco, what he did at the front, how he died. Those kinds of things. My mother has spent her whole life telling me about him, and I suppose it's natural: a little while ago I discovered that she was more like his little sister than his niece, she was living in his house when he died, for her he was the greatest, the brave young man who had saved the family, who had sacrificed everything for her. And the strangest thing is that, even though I've heard people talk about him for my whole life, I still don't know him as a character, I can't imagine him, can't see him . . . I don't know if I've explained it very well."

"Perfectly."

"Of course I'm sure my mother doesn't know him either. What she knows is just an image, a few anecdotes: the legend of Manuel Mena, more than his story. And yes, the truth is I've always been intrigued that there is truth and there are lies in that legend."

"Are there papers, letters, things like that?"

"There's nothing left."

"How many times does his name appear on the Internet?"

"As far as I know, twice. Once in an article I wrote about him and once on some forum where some guys take me to task for having written that article."

David smiled: he'd finished eating. He ran a hand through his hair, which was long, messy, and streaked with grey, like the three days' growth of stubble on his chin.

"Time buries everything," he pronounced with disappointment. "And seventy-four years is an eternity." All of a sudden he seemed to brighten up. "Can you imagine if you found a recording of Manuel Mena, a home movie or something like that, with Manuel Mena moving and speaking and smiling? Then you could see him, couldn't you? Just as you'll be able to see the Shearer after I film him."

Half-closing my eyes and shaking my head, I ruled out the mere possibility of such a miracle. David shrugged and added:

"I don't know. Maybe you're right and not writing the book

is for the best. But it's a shame: I'm sure your mother would have liked to read it. Me too."

The waiter took our plates and we ordered coffee and a couple of shots of *orujo* and asked for the bill. It was almost half past four. The sun was much less warm by then, and although it wasn't cold, we were the last diners on La Majada's patio; there was just over half an hour until our appointment with the Shearer: we had to start thinking about leaving the table.

A waitress brought our coffees and the shots, David let me pay the bill, and, when we were left alone again, I thought of what my friend had just said about my mother and drained my glass in one swallow. David didn't know my mother, or only superficially, but while he was talking, I don't remember about what now, I was distracted thinking that perhaps the best reason not to write a book on Manuel Mena was that my friend was right: my mother would have loved to read it. *I write to not be written*, I thought. I don't know where I had read that sentence, but it suddenly dazzled me. I thought my mother had spent her whole life telling me about Manuel Mena because for her there was no better or higher destiny than Manuel Mena's, and I thought, in an instinctive or unconscious way, that I'd become a writer to rebel against her, to avoid the destiny she had wanted to confine me to, so that my mother couldn't write me or not to be written by her, in order not to be Manuel Mena.

"Hey, Javier, there's one thing that intrigues me," David said, jolting me out of my reverie.

"What's that?"

"Do you feel guilty for having had a fascist uncle?"

Now it was me who smiled.

"An uncle, no," I specified, a little drunkenly. "The whole family."

"Yeah right: more or less like half this country. Did I ever tell you that my father also fought on Franco's side? And totally convinced he was doing the right thing . . . Besides, even those who didn't fight for Franco during the war put up with him for forty years. No matter what they say, here, apart from four or five guys with guts, for most of the time Francoism lasted almost everyone was a Francoist, by commission or omission. What else could they do? By the way, aren't you going to answer my question?"

"Hannah Arendt would say I shouldn't feel guilty, but I should feel responsible."

"And what do you say?"

"That Hannah Arendt is most likely right, don't you think?"

David stared at me for a second, finished drinking his liqueur, and, leaving the empty glass on the table, said:

"What I think is that you shouldn't feel guilty of anything, because guilt is the supreme form of vanity, and you and I are already vain enough."

I laughed.

"That's true." I pointed to my watch and said: "Shall we go?"

As we turned a corner I saw in the distance the first houses of the village rising up white against the blue sky, with the yellow mass of the silo in the foreground, and as usual I thought of my mother. *The fatherland,* I thought. Also as usual, I remembered that passage in *Don Quixote* almost at the end of the book when Don Quixote and Sancho Panza return to their village after a long absence and, catching sight of it on the horizon, the squire falls to his knees and gives free rein to his emotions on recovering his fatherland. Then I thought that my mother's fatherland was the same as Sancho Panza's, but also that this lowercase fatherland was not the uppercase Fatherland that Manuel Mena had died for, although they both had the same name.

I was still thinking about my mother, Sancho Panza, and Manuel Mena as we passed the silo and Civil Guard barracks on the right and the new cemetery and the lake on the left. Then we left the highway and drove into the village. There the silence was total; not a soul was to be seen on the white and very clean streets. There was barely a car parked in the square, but the bar was open, or seemed to be. As we drove down towards the Pozo Castro I asked David to stop the car at a corner. I pointed to a plaque. "Calle Alférez Manuel Mena," it read.

"Here's our hero," David said. "Steadfast and true."

We crossed the Pozo Castro, drove up as far as calle de Las Cruzes, and parked in front of the entrance to my mother's house, a big wooden door protected by a wrought-iron gate closed with a padlock. The house was only inhabited in August, but it didn't look abandoned, in part because not long before we'd whitewashed the façade and in part because the rest of the year some relatives and friends looked after it, among them Eladio Cabrera, a neighbour who for years had worked as a tractor driver for my family. Now Eladio acted as the informal guard of the house, and my mother had told me to ask him for the keys to take a look inside. I was intending to do so, but not before doing what I had come to Ibahernando to do.

So David and I arrived at the Shearer's house, which my mother had told me was almost directly across the street from Eladio's, and we knocked on the door. The metal knocker clattered noisily in the quiet of the village, but nobody opened the door. Although we looked left and right up and down the street, we didn't see anyone except an old man sitting on the steps of a distant house, one arm leaning on a crutch, watching us with the brazen curiosity that village people reserve for strangers (or that was the impression he gave me). I wondered in silence if at the last moment the Shearer had regretted granting me an interview, and had decided to remain faithful to his habit of not talking about the war; David asked me out loud if I was sure that was where the Shearer lived. Since I wasn't sure, we knocked on Eladio Cabrera's door. Eladio himself soon opened it and celebrated our appearance with huge displays of happiness and regret that his wife, Pilar, wasn't there, as she'd gone to visit her sister. I asked him about the Shearer. Eladio confirmed that his house was the one I thought it was, told us he was spending some time in the village with his daughter Carmen, supposed that he must have gone out for a walk and bet he would be back soon; in turn, I proposed to David that we wait for the Shearer's return by fulfilling the task my mother had assigned me.

He accepted. Eladio offered to accompany us, and the first thing he did upon entering my mother's house was turn on the light in the entrance hall, disappear into the darkness of the living room, and open the shutters after wrestling with the latches for a few seconds: filtered by the slats of the blinds, the afternoon autumn sun invaded the living room, revealing its elaborate skirting tiles, its walls decorated with Talavera ceramics, its chairs, armchairs, and sofas of disparate styles and ages, its antediluvian television set and its sideboards full of inherited dishes and tablecloths, on their shelves family photographs and trophies from my sporty adolescence; myriad particles of dust floated in the stagnant silence of the living room. Preceded by Eladio, we walked through the ground floor in the semidarkness, the dining room, the kitchen, the bathrooms and bedrooms, with their tiled floors convex from the damp and motley confusion of furniture and wooden, china, and bronze ornaments, with their beds with their rickety bases and wardrobes of different sizes, with their still-lifes and hunting pictures and religious images hanging on walls blotted with damp patches. At the door to my mother's bedroom I said to David:

"Come here: I'm going to show you something."

We crossed the bedroom, walked into a storage room, and I switched on the light. A bare bulb shone on a shelf filled with books and a pile of old junk, including various trunks with black hinges and domed lids; on one free wall hung the framed portrait of Manuel Mena. David and I stood looking at it while Eladio opened a small window and switched off the light.

"Is that him?" asked David.

I said yes. There was silence as Eladio joined us, in front of the portrait.

"Shit," David said. "He's a kid."

"He's nineteen there," I said. "Or just about to be. It was a few months before he died."

I tried to decode the portrait for them, or rather Manuel Mena's dress uniform—the solitary second lieutenant's stars on the chevrons, and on the peaked cap, the infantry insignia on the cap and the lapels of the jacket, and the Ifni Riflemen insignia, the Suffering for the Nation Medal and the ribbon with two stripes—and Eladio told us what he'd heard about Manuel Mena. When we were on our way out of the room I thought I saw some books I'd never noticed there before and, as Eladio and David left, I stayed for a moment looking through them. Among the books was a Spanish translation of *The Iliad* and another of *The Odyssey,* published in two snug volumes; I leafed through them thinking of Achilles and of Manuel Mena. Then I closed the small window and took them with me.

We finished walking around the house (the entrance gate, the yard with its well and lemon tree, the stables and cowshed with its roof half caved in, the mangers and troughs overflowing with rubble, the empty hayloft, the old kitchen where animals were butchered), and, by the time Eladio closed the door and put the lock back on the iron gate, he and David were talking as if they'd known each other for years. In the street, before saying goodbye, Eladio warned me:

"Your mother is worried, Javi."

We looked at each other without speaking for a second. Eladio had pale eyes and skin burnt by the sun.

"Worried? Why?"

"Why do you think?" answered Eladio. "About the house. She's got it into her head that when she dies you kids will sell it."

"And what are we supposed to do?" I asked him. "My sisters live six hundred miles from here, and so do I. The village is hard to get to and none of us ever come here anymore, except with my mother, in the summer. What should we do, Eladio? Keep the house to spend one weekend a year here, if that?"

Eladio nodded sadly, with resignation.

"You're right, Javi," he conceded. "It's what I always tell Pilar: when we die, that'll be it for the village."

We said farewell to Eladio and went back to the Shearer's house; we knocked on his door again; again, nobody answered. The street was still empty, although the old man with the crutch was still watching us from afar, sitting on the steps of the house. We decided to kill time by having a coffee in the bar and, as we walked down the calle de Las Cruces and crossed the Pozo Castro, we talked about Eladio and about my mother's house; David said, if he were me, he'd keep it.

"And if I were Stephen King, so would I," I answered.

"Bullshit," he replied. "If you were Stephen King you could keep the whole village."

Aside from the owner, in the bar there were only two customers, playing dominoes. I knew all of them vaguely; we said hello and the five of us talked for a moment. Over coffee I explained to David that for many years the place had been the village cinema and dancehall, and I'd first kissed a girl and seen my first film here.

"And what film was it?" he asked.

"*The Sons of Katie Elder*," I answered.

"See how right Eladio was?" I looked at him without understanding. He explained: "A guy is from wherever he gets his first kiss and sees his first western." He paid for the coffees and added: "This isn't your parents' village, kid: this is your fucking village."

The door to the Shearer's house was ajar. I pushed it without knocking, saying good afternoon, and a slim, smiling woman in her fifties, with fair hair and a lilting voice, immediately appeared. It was the Shearer's daughter Carmen, and I recognised her straightaway, because during my childhood I'd seen her helping my aunt Sacri with the household chores every summer. Back then she was cheerful and affectionate; she still was: she gave me a big kiss on each cheek, asked after my mother and my sisters, apologised for not having been home at the agreed time, and said her father had gone out for a walk after lunch as he did every afternoon, and it was very strange that he wasn't back yet. We all looked out the door.

"Look at him," Carmen said, pointing up the street. "There he is."

It was the old man we'd seen from the start, sitting on the steps of a house and leaning on a crutch. I realised the distance had deceived me and that he hadn't been watching us with curiosity but with concern. Carmen confirmed my impression.

"He's been uneasy about the interview all week," she told us, walking up the street towards her father. "He says he doesn't know what he has to say."

We followed her. The Shearer stood up, helping himself with his crutch, and, leaning on it, waited until we reached him. When we did I shook his hand firmly (a rough and hard, but indecisive hand), introduced myself, introduced David. He was a bald, compact, and burly man, with dark, nervous eyes and rounded features, as if sculpted by his ninety-four years of age; he was wearing a very clean white shirt and polyester trousers. I had never seen him before, or I didn't remember him, which seemed strange. He was uncomfortable or scared, or both at the same time. As we walked back towards his house I tried to reassure him, and when we arrived we sat in the front hall, me on his left and across from him David, who took a small, high-definition Sony camera out of his pocket; to the right of the Shearer sat Carmen and her husband, a quiet and discreet man, somewhat older than her. Carmen must have offered us something to drink, though I don't remember. What I do remember is that before getting to the point I asked the Shearer:

"Do you mind if we film you?"

[4]

It's not true that the future modifies the past, but it is true that it modifies the meaning and the perception of the past. That's why the memory many elderly people in Ibahernando have of the Second Republic is a memory poisoned by confrontation, division, and violence. It is a false memory, a memory distorted or contaminated retrospectively by the memory of the Civil War that swept the Second Republic away. The violence, the division, and the confrontation existed, but they existed most of all at the end of the Second Republic. To begin with, it was all different.

On April 13, 1931, the day after municipal elections that had turned into a plebiscite, which the monarchy lost unreservedly in the big cities and which precipitated the immediate exile of Alfonso XIII and the immediate proclamation of the Republic, the king's last prime minister declared that Spain had gone to bed monarchist and woken up republican. I don't know if that was what happened all over the country; it is undoubtedly what happened in Ibahernando. In fact, on April 12 it wasn't even necessary to hold elections in the village, because electoral law at the time held that elections not be held in municipalities which did not have several candidates standing, and in Ibahernando only one candidate had put himself forward: the monarchist candidate. However, two months later there were more elections, this time national ones, and Alejandro Lerroux's Radical Republican Party won a convincing victory in the village that time, obtaining four hundred and forty of the five hundred votes cast. So it is probable that in April of that year the majority of the inhabitants of Ibahernando were monarchists by inertia and in June the majority were by inertia republicans. The fact is that, as in the rest of the country, that fickle majority received the Republic with hope. It was a fitting sentiment. Back then the village had not entirely assumed any fantasy of basic inequality among its inhabitants nor had it entirely entered into that fiction, and most of the locals must have intuited that although some of them were agricultural labourers with land and some of them were labourers without land, their interests were not essentially different, that they were not serfs and patricians but that they were all serfs subjugated by the remote and absentee tyranny of the aristocratic landowners in Madrid, and that they all had a common adversary against whom the new Republic could defend them, whose promise of a prosperous and emancipated future was not only seductive but plausible.

That intuition was spot on, and the first years of the new regime seemed to confirm it. It's possible that when the Second Republic was established most of Ibahernando became republican by inertia or intuition or contagion with the fever for change that inflamed a large part of the country; if that was the case, soon that heteronomous impulse turned into an autonomous one, so that the inaugural fever affected the whole village or almost all of it: the new republican and socialist ideas took a strong hold among labourers with land and labourers without land, a village hall (Casa del Pueblo) was built, parties and labour unions were created or financed linked to the Socialist Party and union, such as the Agrarian Socialist Union. This effervescence did not have a single political sign, because Ibahernando was not a divided community, but nor was it idyllic or empty of conflicts and opposing interests: even though the interests of the community were the same, they weren't identical or monolithic; the proof is that some agricultural labourers first founded a right-wing union called The Future and later another called the Society of Farmers. But, as well as political and syndicalist, the effervescence was also social and religious. At the beginning of the century a group of Protestants led by the son of a pastor of German origin had settled in the village, and in 1914 founded a church. It was the visible beginning of a profound change. As in the rest of Spain, in Ibahernando the Catholic Church had been hunkered down in a stupefying and monopolistic despotism for centuries, much less interested in the well-being of its faithful than in the preservation of its power and privileges, and the recently arrived Protestants defied that pitiless negligence by looking after the poorest and neediest, teaching them to read and write, even helping them economically. They didn't take part in politics, at least not openly, but the result of this active compassion was that by the time the monarchy fell the Protestants had become acclimatised to Ibahernando and that, along with the unheard-of republican secularism, the members of its congregation became even more dynamic and their presence ever more conspicuous.

Nothing of what happened in that time better symbolised the modernising turn of the Republic, however, than the arrival of a new doctor in town. He was named Don Eladio Viñuela. He'd been born in a village near Ávila and studied medicine in Salamanca. Thanks to his first-class qualifications, at the beginning of 1928, having just finished his degree, he received a grant from the Board of Further Study to continue his internship in Berlin, and three years later was still enjoying that prerogative earned through his hard work when his father fell ill and his mother asked him to come home as quickly as he could to shore up the threatened family finances by accepting a job offer that a group of notables of Ibahernando had made through his brother Gumersindo. That happened in 1931, a few weeks after the proclamation of the Second Republic, and that's how that brilliant young man exchanged from one day to the next his promising scientific future for a sombre present as a village doctor, and the metropolitan splendour of the capital of Europe for the shabby closed-mindedness of that godforsaken place. The reasons the prominent families of Ibahernando offered the job to Don Eladio are not entirely clear; here I'll set out the most often repeated (and most plausible) hypothesis. Don Eladio's predecessor was Don Juan Bernardo and he was a doctor of such fervent monarchist convictions that he had baptised most of his children with names of members of the royal family and had presided for years over the local committee of the Patriotic Union, the conservative party created in the 1920s to support the monarchist dictatorship of General Miguel Primo de Rivera, which had more than one hundred members in the village. Don Juan Bernardo was an enterprising and ambitious man. Years earlier, with the support of two of the men who had brought him to Ibahernando by contracting his services, he had founded a business in town to produce electricity and flour; at least one of his two associates was as ambitious and enterprising as he was: Juan José Martínez, maternal great-grandfather of Javier Cercas, a man who had risen from nothing and who, though far from being the biggest landowner in the village, had become one of its most powerful. The commercial alliance between Juan José Martínez and Don Juan Bernardo broke down after a time, and the men became enemies. Everything indicates that antagonism was the reason that the conservative doctor was removed from his position and Don Eladio Viñuela was sought to replace him; everything also indicates that Don Juan Bernardo did not take his dismissal well and that he interpreted it as a reprisal from his former associate. It is also possible that he interpreted it as an obvious sign that the strong families of Ibahernando considered him an ungovernable person and were determined to frustrate his ambitions. Conjectures apart, the fact is that from that moment on, Don Juan Bernardo forswore his former monarchism, converted to passionate republicanism, and began to claim to be a doctor who championed the poor and oppressed, and who, although the war turned him into a devoted Francoist after having underhandedly swerved to the right in the months before the conflict—when the political and social situation became embittered and the same frightened and violent prewar atmosphere of confusion was prevalent in the village as it was all over the country—for the majority of the Republican period was the ideological leader of the local leftists.

But there was still a while to go before all this would happen. In May 1931, when Don Eladio Viñuela replaced Don Juan Bernardo, the foundational optimism of the Second Republic dominated Ibahernando. Don Eladio was a cultured, secular, cosmopolitan, and liberal-minded man; he did not drink, he was not interested in the countryside, hunting, high society, or the ins and outs and intrigues of local politics, and for the fifteen years he lived in the village nobody ever knew him to practise any vices other than playing a card game every day after lunch and devoting several hours after dinner to reading: he professed a contradictory loyalty to Miguel de Unamuno and José Ortega y Gasset and the *Revista de Occidente*, his library was full of scientific publications in German and over the years he learned English in order to read George Bernard Shaw in the original. When he arrived in the village he was twenty-four years old. His mother, Doña Rosa, came with him, and the two of them moved into a house adjacent to that of Blanca Mena, mother of Javier Cercas, who in her old age remembered him as a tall, elegant, olive-skinned man with glasses, with a wise man's simplicity and a good-looking man's grace. It is not strange that his arrival in the village should have unleashed an expectant stir among the young women of marriageable age, who began to dispute the privilege of his company and lavish him with their attentions. Don Eladio did not take long to choose; his decision seemed like a declaration of principles: to the surprise of all, the fortunate one was not a rich heiress or what was considered a rich heiress in the village, but a poor, protestant, educated girl named Marina Díaz, whom Don Eladio married in a Lutheran ceremony after a long engagement and with whom he went to live near the village square.

By then the doctor had organised his own personal rebellion against the village's inveterate backwardness. As well as bringing a radio and projecting or getting the first films projected to general amazement, from the community clinic he set up in his home he instilled elemental but unknown rules of hygiene, such as regular hand washing, encouraged moderate and healthy eating habits, and introduced new ways of living, starting with taking children to the beaches of Portugal in the summers so the water and sea air would protect them for the rest of the year against illness; in the same way he battled ceaselessly against the afflictions that ravaged the village, such as malaria, tuberculosis, and high infant mortality. Don Eladio worked for the families that had hired him and assured his livelihood, but also for all those who required his services, so his silent revolution reached the furthest corner of the village, which earned him unanimous respect and admiration and encircled his name with the perpetual aura of a benefactor.

The novelties that Don Eladio introduced to Ibahernando were not only to do with health and technology; there were also educational ones. On the advice or at the instigation of his fiancée, who was studying for a degree in philosophy and letters, in the autumn of 1933 Don Eladio founded a secondary school. At first the only teachers were the two of them; Don Eladio taught the science classes and Doña Marina taught arts, including French. However, the faculty of two soon began to attract more students, first from the village and later from the neighbouring villages—from Ruanes, from Santa Ana, from Santa Cruz—and after a short time they felt obliged to increase the staff, which was soon joined by Doña Julia, Doña Marina's sister, and Don Severiano, a gentle and intelligent man who had been banished to the village for political reasons. The new school's success was predictable. Accustomed to the gruff, rustic, hopeless squalor of Don Marcelino's school, Don Eladio's students noticed a huge difference: first because they no longer had classes in the gloomy, freezing, pokey little room in the back of the church, but in a house on calle de Las Cruzes with three bright, clean, and airy classrooms, as well as a big yard where the students could go outside and play during recess; second— and especially—because Don Eladio and Doña Marina both had pedagogical vocations, a love of learning, and the ability to create a favourable atmosphere for study, not to mention that their knowledge was far greater than that of Don Marcelino. All this explains why, unlike Don Marcelino's unlucky students, Don Eladio and Doña Marina's students finished their studies in the village prepared to pass the official baccalaureate exams without difficulty, and that the school run by the young doctor and his wife produced the first university graduates in the history of the village.

Manuel Mena could have been one of them; in fact, only the outbreak of the war prevented him. Manuel Mena studied at Don Eladio's academy for barely two years, but that was enough to change him completely: he did not lose his cheerful and extroverted nature, but at the end of that time the unruly, arbitrary boy who was a bit of a know-it-all with no interest in education, victim of his badly managed pride and rough-hewn intelligence, turned into an industrious, reflective, and responsible adolescent, with a precociously clear idea of what he wanted to do with his life and with such passion for knowledge and reading that, according to what his classmates remember, he began to get up at daybreak to read and study. Nobody remembers, however, what he liked to read; his library, if he managed to accumulate one, was lost or dispersed; in July 1936, when the war turned the country upside down, he had enrolled in law school, but that signifies nothing or hardly anything. Only one thing is sure: his intellectual curiosity could have been sated by Don Eladio's library, and it does not seem adventurous to suppose that the doctor would have started him off with his favourite books and that Manuel Mena should have benefited from them. Because Don Eladio was not just a decisive teacher for him—this is also a certain fact—but perhaps the only one he had in his very short life. He was more than that: he was a *maître à penser*, who he visited at home, with whom he had conversations without time limits, who he helped with his classes and accompanied on his strolls in the countryside. He could even have been more than that: a vaguely paternal figure, a vague successor to a lost father, or perhaps, given that only twelve years separated them, the kind of older friend who guides rebellious adolescents when they feel an urgency to emancipate themselves from their childish past and immediate surroundings, the man able to fascinate with the radiant prestige of his modernity and culture, to show him that life existed beyond the village without prospects in which he'd been born, and to inculcate the desire to learn and to travel, the subversive ambition to grow to be himself. He might have been more: he might have been, apart from a teacher of knowledge, a teacher of life.

In the autumn of 1933, while Don Eladio was opening the doors of his school and Manuel Mena was beginning his providential relationship with that providential doctor, the Second Republic was falling into a crisis that two and a half years later would lead to a war, or rather a military coup, the failure of which would lead to a war that would eventually sweep it away.

The origin of the crisis went back to the origin of the new regime itself. The Republic counted on two basic supports in its euphoric beginning: on the one side the urban and rural proletariat, workers and agricultural labourers increasingly aware of the ferocious injustice that had condemned them to humiliating servitude and unending misery and increasingly anxious to rid themselves of both; on the other side, a very significant section of the middle class, the majority of the country, including an ever-growing number of land-owning labourers: this middle class rightly understood that its interests did not diverge essentially from those of the proletariat (and that the Republic could defend them), although, unlike the proletariat, they were defined by their apolitical nature and their conformism, their attachment to traditional habits and routines, their instinctive suspicion of the new, their confidence in strong authorities, and their fetishistic devotion to public order and stability. Nevertheless, the Second Republic also suffered from its first second of life from relentless harassment by the oligarchy and the Catholic Church. Wilfully entrenched in the country since medieval times, accustomed to treating it as their private property, both these forces felt their indisputable power endangered by the arrival of the new authorities and embarked on a permanent conspiracy against them. To this conspiracy was added another: it was orchestrated by a fatal historical conjunction of the country's anaemic democratic tradition with the worldwide crisis of 1929 still wreaking havoc on its battered economy, and with fascism and communism stretching their totalitarian shadows across Europe. In these circumstances the Second Republic could not permit itself the luxury of making mistakes, at least not big ones; the fact is it made quite a few, big and small: it acted with innocence, with clumsiness, sometimes with dogmatism, and almost always with more goodwill and ambition than prudence, embarking on the huge reforms the country needed simultaneously and not successively or incrementally, without realistically measuring its own strength and the strength of its opponents, and generating impossible-to-satisfy expectations among its supporters, especially among some of its supporters, the neediest and most left wing, the suffering throng of those humiliated and offended by the high-handedness of the powerful. It was a fatal error. Because, frustrated and exasperated by the slow pace of the reforms and by the solid intransigence of the right, the humiliated and offended began to mistrust the democratic methods of the Republic and started a process of radicalisation that drove them towards violent confrontation and hopeless riots, and drove the Republic to lose a huge part of the favour of the part of the middle class that, while sharing many more real interests with the humiliated and offended than with the oligarchs and the Catholic Church, shared with the Catholic Church and the oligarchy their superstitious love for order and tradition and their mortal fear of revolution.

This suicidal process began to accelerate from November 1933 onwards. On the nineteenth of that month the second general elections of the Republic were held, and won by the right. It was by then a right that barely believed in the Republic and almost didn't believe in democracy and that, as soon as it reached power, devoted its best efforts to dismantling the incipient reforms put in place by the new regime, while from its very entrails emerged organisations that imitated the fascism triumphant in Europe; the most important was the Spanish Falange, a political party that, with its ultramodern and fraudulent synthesis of granite-like patriotism and revolutionary rhetoric, was going to constitute itself into a de facto militia of reaction, into the violent emergency procedure secreted from the oligarchy to finish off a democracy that was trying to reduce its privileges and which it considered unfit to avoid a revolution. For its part, the left committed a mistake by taking to the streets with the aim of recovering there the space it had lost in parliament and by stopping the right by force, forgetting that it lacked sufficient force to do so. The revolution of October '34, and the later savage military repression, was the first big, bloody testimony of the gradual failure of a democracy that was being left without democrats: a failure that the elections of February '36 were not able to restrain. By then Spanish society had split, and although the left (grouped together as the Popular Front) won, the right did not accept the result and from that moment fed with all the fuel at its disposal a surge of disorder that created the ideal climate for the usual, powerful anti-Republicans to launch a coup d'état with the support of a traditional class horrified by the chaos and the violence, and skilfully driven by the oligarchy and the Catholic Church to the flagrant falsehood that their interests were irreconcilable with those of the proletariat and to an illusory certainty that the only way to finish off the mayhem was to finish off the Republic.

The collapse of peaceful coexistence and the crisis of faith in democracy infected the country from top to bottom, but in few places did it strike with such virulence as in Extremadura, where the majority of the population continued to live in ancestral conditions of servitude, stupefied by hunger and humiliations, and where the Republic had to confront social conflicts of a certain intensity from the start. That's what happened in the region of Trujillo, one of the poorest in the area; it's what happened in Ibahernando. As in La Cumbre, in Santa Marta de Magasca, in Miajadas, or in Trujillo itself, in Ibahernando at the end of June and beginning of July 1931, when the new regime was recently installed, numerous strikes of agricultural labourers were called with the objective of protesting the paltriness of daily wages and the use of machinery as replacement for manpower, and the Trujillo Association of Proprietors submitted repeated protests to the authorities about the threatening attitudes of striking workers who travelled the countryside disabling the irrigation machines. Two months later, at the beginning of September, there was a series of farm invasions in Ibahernando that resulted in a strike being called in which groups of labourers armed with stakes obliged a general work stoppage; as the Civil Governor of Cáceres informed the Minister of the Interior days later, "In the first hours of the night of September 10, the workers congregated in the village square and resisted the instructions of the Civil Guard, which ordered their dispersal. The guards were attacked with stones and one of them was injured; they charged several times. The groups reformed again, the workers put up resistance again, and the Civil Guards fired once into the air. The aggression came from the Workers' Centre. Several individuals were arrested and handed over to the mayor, who set them free; the doctor, Juan Bernardo, and the state schoolteacher also intervened and had an influence. I have ordered the closure of the Workers' Centre and the detention of the individuals mentioned." The Workers' Centre was actually the Casa del Pueblo, or village hall, attached to the Federation of Land Workers of the UGT, the socialist union; as for the state schoolteacher, this was not Don Marcelino, Manuel Mena's teacher, but Don Miguel Fernández, a cultured, judicious, circumspect man much appreciated in the village. The clash between the workers and civil guards resulted in a protest from the mayor and the president of the Agrarian Society, "in the name of the majority of residents, for the abuses committed by the Civil Guard on September 10," and, although some of the strikes in June and July were described by their organisers as revolutionary, the fact is that they were all short-lived (and the description decorative). So it is true that, at the beginning of the Republic, Ibahernando was not an ideal society, devoid of conflicts, and that orderly people were alarmed; but it is also true that it was not a divided or confrontational society, that conflicts were not frequent or unmanageable, and that orderly people could chalk up their natural fears in the still-intact credit side of the Republic's accounts and could resign themselves to them as a secondary effect of the beneficial advent of the new regime.

Things got worse starting in November 1933, when the right won the general elections in the village, as in the rest of Spain. A year later, during the October Revolution, with martial law imposed all over the country and the Cáceres provincial government in the hands of a military commander, these incidents multiplied. The Young Socialists of the village requested the suppression of the religious festivities of Easter week, and one day the Civil Guard arrested three people for attempting to set the church on fire; another day they arrested another five, accused of intimidating political rivals with shots from firearms, and they confiscated a rifle and a pistol. But the event that caused the deepest impression in the village featured Juan José Martínez, Javier Cercas's maternal great-grandfather, and it happened on October 7, 1934. According to the sentence passed a year later by a judge in Cáceres, that night Juan José Martínez was about to enter his house on the plaza del Pozo Castro after having spent a few hours chatting and visiting with friends; he was not alone: his wife was with him. It was ten o'clock, and Pozo Castro, which had no streetlights, was dark. At that moment someone fired at him with a hunting rifle. The shot came from forty feet away, and, although Juan José Martínez was hit by a hundred and ten pellets, forty days later the wounds had healed: the shot had hit him in the back of the legs and "the dorsal-lumbar-gluteus region"—that is to say, in the back and in the arse.

The attack caused such a commotion in Ibahernando that eighty years after it happened all the survivors of the time remember it, undoubtedly because Juan José Martínez was the boss or something very similar to the boss of the village. Five residents of Ibahernando were tried for the attack; only two were convicted and sentenced: the attacker, to twelve years and one day in prison, and the instigator, a former municipal judge, to fourteen years, eight months, and one day; both also received the additional punishment of a fine of five hundred pesetas. According to the judge's verdict, the motive of the crime was hatred, "great hatred [. . .] owing to political rivalries" that the instigator of the crime felt for Juan José Martínez. That sort of hatred rapidly began to spread throughout the village and, from the time of the elections of February 1936, transformed, there as in the whole country, into a venom the massive consumption of which nobody could or wanted to curb, and the effects of which were lethal.

In the middle of March of that calamitous year, after the victory of the Popular Front in the February elections, the new left-wing authorities dismissed all the right-wing councillors in the village, among them Javier Cercas's paternal grandfather, Paco Cercas, and his maternal grandfather, Juan Mena; the manoeuvre was an inverse reflection of that realised by the right-wing authorities after the revolution of '34, when they dismissed all the left-wing councillors and closed the Casa del Pueblo. By then Ibahernando had fully entered into the fiction, into an induced fantasy of basic inequality according to which, while the landless agricultural labourers continued to be serfs, the landowning labourers had turned into patricians and therefore the interests of the two groups diverged irremediably and their confrontation became inevitable; by then Ibahernando had already split in half: there was a bar for the right-wing people and another bar for the left-wing people, one dance for the right-wing people and another dance for the left-wing people; sometimes, right-wing young men would burst brusquely into the dances at the reopened Casa del Pueblo, protected by their servants, trying to intimidate everyone with their high-and-mighty bullying. For their part, the left-wing young men, who were increasingly well read and politicised, increasingly more prepared to assert their rights, more rebellious and better protected by their union and by the municipal authorities, contested these provocations and, unlike their fathers and grandfathers, refused to accept the abuses and faced up to the landowning labourers, who took revenge on the most turbulent of them by refusing to hire them in harvest season. "Eat Republic," spat those who four or five years earlier had all been Republicans to a man. In revenge for that revenge, the landless young labourers burned crops, damaged olive groves, stole sheep and rams, invaded farms, and intimidated right-wing people and made their lives impossible. The violence even reached the children, who set up ambushes in the streets, pelted each other with stones, or rubbed nettles on each other's legs. In the spring of 1936 a rumour spread around the right-wing families according to which some young socialists had put forward a list of names of people on the right during a meeting held at the Casa del Pueblo and had proposed taking them one by one from their houses and murdering them; according to the same rumour, the proposal had not gone any further thanks only to the socialist mayor, a man named Agustín Rosas, who had drawn on all his authority as a veteran leftist militant and all his sangfroid to put a stop to that raid, making it clear to those excitable young men that, while he was in charge of the council, nobody was going to kill anybody in that village. At another moment, more or less at the same time as that hair-raising rumour was going around, some right-wing men went to the Civil Guard asking for protection for themselves and their families; the reply from the Civil Guard was to assure them that they were not authorised to do more than what they were doing and advised them to protect themselves. It's very probable that they did so, or that they tried to do so, which would explain why some on the right—including Paco Cercas and Juan Mena, grandfathers of Javier Cercas—spent a short time in the Trujillo prison, accused of stockpiling weapons at Los Quintos farm. By that time everything was prepared for the whole country to shatter into a thousand pieces.

We might wonder how Manuel Mena experienced those months of growing anxiety: what did he do, what did he think, what did he feel as his village and his country divided into two halves pitted against each other and fuelled by a common hatred? A *literato* could answer these questions, because *literati* can fantasise, but not me: fantasy is forbidden to me. A few things, however, are certain. Or almost certain.

Manuel Mena did not spend the year before the war in Ibahernando; he spent it in Cáceres, where he was doing his final year of secondary school. He could not have been unaware of the hopes his mother and his siblings had resting on him, of the economic sacrifices they were making so that he could be the first member of the family to leave the village and study and prepare to go to university; given his character, this would oblige him to do his best at his studies, to try to be equal to his responsibility and measure up. He was living on the calle Arco de España, next to the Plaza Mayor, in the house of a Civil Guard sergeant who had become friendly with the family when he was in charge of the Ibahernando headquarters. He was named Don Enrique Cerrillo. Apart from Don Eladio Viñuela, Manuel Mena had barely any friends left in the village, because his new adolescent interests had distanced him from his childhood affiliations, but he returned frequently to see his mother and siblings, and there is no doubt he was informed of the explosive situation going on in Ibahernando, which was *mutatis mutandis* the explosive situation going on in the country; nor is there any doubt that he was informed of his brother Juan's brief stay in prison or of the family's fears. Did he devote that 1935–36 school year exclusively to his studies or, in spite of enjoying them and being interested, and his acute awareness that he should not neglect them, did the general politicisation of the country politicise him as well? There is no doubt that during the war or during most of the war Manuel Mena was a convinced Falangist—much more Falangist than Francoist, assuming he was ever really a Francoist—but was he also before the war? Or did he become a Falangist when the war started, like the majority of Falangists?

It is impossible to answer these questions. At the beginning of 1936 the Falange was still very much a minority party in Spain; in the February elections that year it won barely a seat: that of José Antonio Primo de Rivera, its leader. The party as such did not exist in Ibahernando, and its national candidates never obtained a single vote there. But none of that means that Manuel Mena could not have been attracted in Cáceres to the romantic and anti-liberal idealism, the youthful radicalism, the irrational vitality and enthusiasm for charismatic leaders and strongmen of that ideology that was all the rage everywhere in Europe; on the contrary: the Falange was a party that, with its system-bucking vocation, its jovial prestige of absolute novelty, its irresistible nimbus of semi-clandestinity, its denial of the traditional distinction between right and left, its proposal for a transcending synthesis of the two, its perfect ideological chaos, its simultaneous and impossible bet on patriotic nationalism and egalitarian revolution, and its captivating demagogy, seemed made to measure for a student fresh from his village who, at barely sixteen years of age, in that decisive historical period would be dreaming of putting a stop with one redemptive blow to the fear and poverty that stalked his family and to the hunger, the humiliation, and the injustice he'd seen daily in the streets of his childhood and adolescence, all of it without putting the social order in jeopardy and also allowing him to identify with the aristocratic elitism of José Antonio, Marquis of Estella. We do not know if Don José Cerrillo, the family friend he lived with in Cáceres, belonged to the Falange at that time; most likely he did not. But there is no doubt that at the beginning of that year Cáceres was one of the provinces of Spain with the highest number of party members; nor that Manuel Mena could have attended José Antonio's second meeting in Cáceres, on January 19, 1936, in the Norba, a theatre located on the Paseo de Cánovas. There he could have seen how the young leader of the Falange addressed a crowd of comrades come from all over Extremadura, sporting his regulation blue shirt and interrupted by the persistent thunder of ovations, with words like these: "The great task of our generation consists of demonstrating the flaws of the capitalist system, the final fatal consequences of which are the accumulation of capital in big businesses and the proletarianisation of the masses." Or like these: "The process of capitalist hypertrophy will only be ended in one of two ways: either by terminating it with a decision, even a heroic one, by some who participate in its advantages, or by waiting for the revolutionary catastrophe, which, as it burns the capitalist edifice, will set fire in passing to our immense cultural and spiritual heritage. We prefer collapse to arson." And even like these: "To block the path of Marxism it is not votes we need, but resolute chests, like those of our twenty-four fallen comrades who, by blocking the path, left their fresh lives in the streets. But there is more to do than to counter Marxism. We must create Spain. Less 'down with this,' and 'against that,' and more 'Arise Spain.' For one Spain: United, Great, and Free. For the Nation, Bread, and Justice."

All the foregoing is no more than conjecture. The only thing certain is that Manuel Mena spent the eve of the Civil War in Cáceres, preparing to enrol in the university the following year, and that the first thing he did when he returned to Ibahernando was to visit Don Eladio Viñuela. They saw each other at the doctor's house or, more often, at his school; that's what the students who were then attending it remembered. They remembered that Manuel Mena brought them his notes from his courses in Cáceres, thorough, impeccable notes written out especially for them with the aim of improving the teaching of the academy. They remembered Manuel Mena often helped Don Eladio in the classes, that Don Eladio was fond of teaching out in the countryside, in the fresh air, and that ominous spring he did so often, assisted by Manuel Mena. They remembered that sometimes, during those studious outings, Don Eladio and Manuel Mena would divide up the students, and that, once the lesson was finished, the pupils would make their own way back to the village while the teacher and his disciple would stay on their own out in the country. And they also remembered that other times Don Eladio would set them exercises and that, during the time it took to complete them, he and Manuel Mena would walk some distance away, talking. What did they talk about during those peripatetic conversations? Years later those who'd watched them would wonder, having observed them strolling with heads bent and hands behind their backs or buried in the pockets of their trousers, while the golden evenings fell in silence against the uninterrupted horizon, over the stone fences, and the empty holm-oak woods. Did Manuel Mena unburden himself of his doubts to Don Eladio? Did he tell him his anxieties, his perplexities, his fears and ambitions of a rural adolescent transplanted to the provincial capital? Did they discuss books? Or were they informing each other of what was happening in Cáceres and in Ibahernando, commenting on the dismal way reality was going? It is tempting to imagine Manuel Mena trying to persuade Don Eladio of the newest revolutionary merits recently learned from José Antonio, and Don Eladio countering Manuel Mena's fresh-faced, ardent rhetoric and the utopian spell of the Falangist ideology and its shiny new suggestion of youth and modernity with the old rationalist scepticism and the old and peaceful arguments of the old liberal ideology, which Manuel Mena would consider out of date. It's tempting to imagine or fantasise it like that. But I am not a *literato* and I cannot fantasise, I can only confine myself to facts, and the fact is we don't know whether it was like that, and it's almost certain that we'll never know. Because the past is an unfathomable pit in the blackness of which we can barely manage to glimpse hints of truth, and what we know of Manuel Mena and his story is infinitely less than what we don't know.

❦ 5 ❧

David Trueba filmed more than two hours of conversation in the front hall of the Shearer's house, but the film he put together lasted barely forty minutes. It is titled *Memories* and is divided into five chapters, each of which announces the subject it will deal with in a heading. Most of the film is a single low-angle shot of the Shearer, in which we only see, covered by a white shirt, his torso and farm worker's shoulders, still strong despite being over ninety years old, and his head, almost completely bald, his powerful, senatorial skull, with a spot on his temple and a grazed cheek; his silhouette against a backdrop of ceramic tiles with very brightly coloured floral motifs.

He remains seated throughout the entire film. The images do not show the physical presence of his daughter Carmen, or that of his son-in-law, but her voice is often heard clarifying my questions, or reinforcing or qualifying or annotating his replies. At first the Shearer is apprehensive, uneasy and suspicious; bit by bit, however, he seems to relax, although he never gives the impression of being totally relaxed; he sometimes smiles, on one occasion he even laughs (and his face turns youthful then and his eyes narrow into furrows); most of the time his expression is one of resigned and slightly absent seriousness, but each time one of the many silences that punctuate the interview opens up his eyes sink into a sadness so solid, so heavy, and so deep that it seems impossible one man alone might be able to bear it. I experienced this feeling as I conducted the interview, but while watching the film the feeling was even stronger. The Shearer always has his crutch in his hand, as if he felt orphaned or defenceless without it; sometimes he leans it against the back of a nearby chair; most of the time he rests his hand or his arm or his armpit on the top of it, moving it from one side to the other, impatiently or nervously. During a very short sequence he wears a wool cap that I didn't remember.

At the beginning of the interview we talk about his trade, which consisted of shearing the animals of Ibahernando and the surrounding villages. Then we talked about my family, my great-grandmother Carolina and her children, among them my grandfather Juan, and also the wife and daughters of my grandfather Juan, among them my mother; according to him, they were always his neighbours, he knew them all well, has fond memories of them all, which do not seem feigned. He also speaks of other people from the village; one of them is my grandfather Paco, my father's father, who he remembers with admiration because he worked very hard, he says, to send all three of his sons to university. At a certain moment, after a quick cut, a chapter titled "The Photograph" begins. It is the third, and its first image shows the Shearer putting on a pair of tortoiseshell glasses; then I am heard to ask them:

"Have you seen this photograph?"

Although the images don't show this, I have just handed Carmen a copy of an old photograph of the boys who attended Don Marcelino's school; Manuel Mena appears in the photograph and almost beside him, according to my cousin José Antonio Cercas, is the Shearer. Carmen replies in her singsong voice:

"Oh, no, I haven't. Never."

As Carmen hands the photograph to the Shearer, I can be heard insisting:

"Let's see if your father has seen it."

The Shearer takes the photograph and looks at it closely.

"No," Carmen repeats, convinced. "My father has never seen that photo."

After a few seconds of silence, during which the Shearer does not take his eyes off the image, concentrating hard on it, my nose, a lock of my hair, and my index finger break into the left edge of the shot, pointing at the photograph.

"Do you recognise anybody there?"

"I don't know," answers the Shearer; he immediately apologises, as if that were an exam and he fears that his performance was not up to the expected level: "People change so much . . ."

After a silence, trying to help, I explain:

"It's a photo of Don Marcelino's students." I add: "And I think you are one of those boys."

Then the Shearer raises his eyes from the photograph and looks to his left, which is where I am, although the image doesn't show me.

"No, that's impossible," he corrects me, visibly relieved. And he explains: "I didn't go to Don Marcelino's school. I went to Don Miguel's, a teacher who came from Santa Cruz; when Don Marcelino came to the village I was already working. That's what used to happen to us boys: as soon as we were twelve or thirteen, they'd take us out to the pastures to look after cows or lambs."

The Shearer goes on talking in the image; off-screen, I am doing my best to digest my disappointment, or that's how I remember that moment. After a few seconds, after another cut, a new chapter begins, this one titled "Manuel Mena." It begins with the image of the Shearer's face very close to my face, which has burst into the frame, and with the sound of my voice asking a question:

"Do you know this one?"

The camera tilts to bring the Shearer's hands into the foreground of the image. They are the hands of a countryman, coarse and worn, and just the fingertips hold the photograph of Don Marcelino's students while I point with a tense index finger to a boy dressed in a striped jacket and white shirt with a lock of unruly hair on his forehead, standing to the right of the teacher, and I ask again:

"Do you remember Manuel Mena?"

The Shearer looks to his left and in his filmed gaze I notice the same thing I noticed that day in his real gaze: that his daughter Antonia, with whom I had arranged that interview by telephone, had put him in the picture about its precise purpose.

"How could I not remember him?" he answers.

"And isn't this kid him?" I insist, without taking my index finger off the photograph.

The Shearer looks again; a little upset, he nods several times before saying:

"Yes. That's him."

From that moment on the direction of the conversation changes. For several minutes I try to get the Shearer to talk to me about Manuel Mena, about his relationship to Manuel Mena, but the attempt drifts into a struggle throughout which he responds to my questions in monosyllables or very succinct sentences, or simply does not respond or responds by dodging the question, uncomfortably, and moving his crutch from one side to the other. The Shearer tells us that Manuel Mena and he were more or less the same age, were neighbours and as children they had been friends, playing together in the street, the calle de Las Cruces, and in my great-grandmother Carolina's yard. I ask him if they still saw each other when they were no longer children, when they became adolescents, and he says yes, although less. I ask him if he remembers that Manuel Mena went off to war and died at the front and he says yes, of course, and that he also remembers that he was nineteen when he died and a second lieutenant in the Regulars, and that when he came home on leave he came back with his orderly, a North African who never left his side. I ask him if they saw each other when Manuel Mena came home from the front on leave, and he says yes, that they could hardly not have seen each other since they still lived next door to one another. I ask him if they talked about the war during those encounters and about Manuel Mena's life at the front and he says no. Then I ask him if he remembers the day of his funeral, which is a day all the old folks in the village remember, and he says yes, perfectly, that he saw the whole thing from the door of his house, but when I try to get him to tell me details of the event he begins to talk about a different funeral, another well-attended funeral that happened before or after or almost at the same time as Manuel Mena's, the funeral of a doctor named Don Félix, and, when I ask again about Manuel Mena or about Manuel Mena's funeral, he dodges the question again and goes back to talking about my great-grandmother Carolina and my grandfather Juan and my family. That strange back-and-forth goes on for several minutes, until I stop asking questions, undoubtedly convinced that the Shearer is refusing to budge and it's futile to carry on my interrogation from this angle.

Then, after another cut, begins the best chapter of the film, which is also the last one. It is titled "Murder in Ibahernando" and opens with the Shearer's face of unshaken sadness and my voice asking a question in a strange tone, a touch too high.

"So, your father was killed at the beginning of the war?"

It is clear (or at least it is for me) that in the film I have just reformulated as a question something the Shearer has just told us off-camera; it is also clear that I have tried to react as if the words of my interlocutor did not take me by surprise, although I don't know if I've posed the question to give myself time to take them in, to keep the Shearer from changing the subject, to ensure the camera records the news I've just heard, or for all three reasons at once. Whatever the case, the conversation changes again, and over the following minutes the Shearer sinks into ever more intense and longer silences, during which his sadness turns deeper and his expression even tenser, his eyes fixed on the invisible floor, his lips sealed. The Shearer's answer to my question consists of saying yes in a very faint, almost inaudible voice.

"He cut hair," Carmen interjects, exchanging her natural cheerfulness for genuine sorrow. "He was a barber."

At that moment, for the first and only time in the film, we hear the voice of David Trueba.

"Oh, really?" he says. "So you both worked in the same field."

He means the Shearer and his father. I don't know if David has interjected because he feels that we've arrived at the crucial moment of the interview and that I need help, but the fact is that his comment seems to inject confidence into the Shearer, as if my friend's previous silence had intimidated him (or perhaps what intimidated him was the camera). Looking me in the eye, the Shearer tells us:

"Here, at the beginning of the war, they killed a few people. A schoolteacher who was named Don Miguel."

"Your teacher?" I asked. "The one who came from Santa Cruz?"

"No," explained the Shearer. "Another one. A good man. They killed a girl too. Sara was her name. Sara García. She had a boyfriend in the Red zone. They say that's why they killed her." The Shearer falls silent again; his gaze fixes on the floor again. There are five of us in that vestibule, but the camera doesn't pick up the slightest noise. Finally the Shearer adds: "That night they killed a handful."

Then, without me or anybody else having asked, the Shearer describes the event that changed his life for ever. He does so with a lost look in his eye, with few words, which more than words seem like objects, and with a coolness that chills the blood. His mother had died years before, he tells us, and he and his father and brother were having dinner as on any other night in the dining room of their house. "Right there," he clarifies, pointing vaguely to his right. He doesn't remember what they were eating. He doesn't remember what they were talking about, if they were even talking about anything. The only thing he remembers is that at a certain point someone knocked on the door and his father asked him to answer it. The war had just broken out, but he didn't remember noticing concern in his father's voice; he doesn't remember feeling concerned himself either. He obeyed, left the table, opened the door. On the threshold, silhouetted against the hot breath of the recently fallen August night, were some men. He didn't remember how many there were or what they looked like. He didn't know any of them. The men asked if his father was home, he said yes, and several of them went in and took him. That was it. He didn't remember if his father left the house voluntarily or if he put up any resistance and the strangers had to take him out by force. He didn't remember if his father could get dressed or if he left in the clothes he was wearing. He didn't remember if his father was scared or not. He didn't remember if he said anything to him before leaving, or if he looked at him one last time. He only remembered what he'd just told us: the rest had been erased from his memory, or never registered. He was eighteen, a year older than Manuel Mena, and he never saw his father alive again.

When the Shearer finishes speaking, a stony, imposing silence ensues, which only Carmen dares to break.

"That's the first time I've heard my father talk about this," she says in a voice without perplexity, without even sorrow, a vacant voice. "I knew about it from my mother, but I've never heard him tell it."

Now I am slow to react, I suppose because I don't know how to react and maybe because I am saying to myself what I'm saying to myself again as I see the images: that it's not just the first time the Shearer is telling that story to his daughter, but probably the first time he's ever told it, at least the way he's just told it.

"Do you know why he was killed?" I manage to ask.

The Shearer is also slow to respond. He gives the impression of being disconcerted, although it's hard to guess why; perhaps because he doesn't fully understand how he has been able to tell what he has just told; perhaps because he feels strangely that it isn't him who has told it, but someone else.

"No," he finally answers, and for a second his eyes shine and he seems about to burst into tears. But it is just a second; when he speaks again he does so with his habitual dry sadness. "Back then people got killed over any little thing," he continues. "Over arguments. Out of envy. Because someone exchanged four words with someone. For anything. That's how the war was. People say now that it was politics, but it wasn't politics. Not only. Someone said they had to go after someone and they did. That was it. It was just like I told you: no more, no less. That's why so many people left the village when the war started."

From this moment for several minutes the Shearer gives the impression of talking almost spontaneously, free of restrictions or of inordinate restrictions, in the end even with some enthusiasm. He tells us that one day, shortly after his father was killed, he and his brother found out where his corpse was, went and buried him secretly, without any funeral or ceremony or anyone's help. He tells us that later he was called up and he had to fight the war in the army of those who had killed his father. He tells us that he fought the war in Ávila and somewhere in Asturias. He tells us that when he came back to the village he found his brother living with a woman—a generous woman who had taken him in—and that he went to live with his girlfriend and future wife, or that she came to live with him. "She got a lot of criticism for that," he says with a kind of fury. "You know what villages are like; and back then, I don't need to tell you . . . But she didn't care: she moved in with me because she wouldn't have me living on my own." And then he tells us that, even though he and his wife were very young, they fought a lot, that he learned his trade, that she raised their three children, that he felt proud of his work and having provided for his family. "Ask about me in town," he dares me. "You'll see what they say." After that sentence, the Shearer sinks into an exhausted silence, which Carmen rushes to fill talking about her mother and her father's work. He listens to her distractedly, moving the crutch and with his gaze fixed once again on the floor. It seems clear that he has decided the interview is over and I'm not going to get any more information out of him, at least for this afternoon, at least about Manuel Mena and the war. Strangely, I don't seem to notice, or maybe I haven't resigned myself to accepting his decision; in any case, the only thing I can dredge up to put to him is a fact formulated as conjecture and in a rather solemn tone. The phrase is:

"The war must have been terrible."

As soon as he hears these words, the Shearer glances towards where I'm sitting but doesn't say anything, as if he doesn't understand what he's just heard or as if he's just heard the observation of a child or a lunatic. It's Carmen who now comes to my aid. She says:

"May it never return."

Then it's obvious that I want to keep the interview going no matter what, because I change the conjecture into a question; the problem is that I don't change anything else, and the result is that I add another solemn obvious fact that now, for some reason, doesn't sound so stupid:

"The war is the worst thing that's ever happened to you, isn't it?"

It's at this moment that, glancing quickly at me again, the Shearer laughs for the first time, sincerely, and that I hear in his unexpected laughter his total inability to explain what he wanted or should explain to me and that I glimpse or sense in his crinkled-up eyes the intact joy of the boy who could never even imagine that one night his father would be murdered, the joy of the Shearer before the war who knew Manuel Mena. I don't know if I heard or sensed or glimpsed that then, while I listened to the Shearer in the front hall of his house, but I'm sure that I hear or sense or glimpse it now, years later, while watching the images that David Trueba filmed. Once this instant has passed, the Shearer lowers his gaze again and sinks back into his usual sadness. The silence that follows is again solid, and so long that as I watch it I am reminded of the limitless silences of *Big Brother*, of the limitless silences of *L'Avventura*. This time it's not Carmen but the Shearer who breaks it, looking at the camera with his dry, inexpressive eyes and murmuring as if the interview had ended for him a while ago:

"Okay, okay."

After another silence, much briefer this time, I state:

"You don't like talking about the war."

"No," says the Shearer. "Not a bit." And he adds: "Fuck it."

"You don't like it or it scares you?" I ask, half-seriously and half-joking.

The Shearer almost smiles.

"I don't like it and I'm careful," he answers.

"But nothing's going to happen now, Dad!" exclaims Carmen, recovering her cheerful lilt. "That was before."

"You didn't even talk about this with your wife?" I insist.

"Not even with my wife," says the Shearer, without abandoning his attempt at a smile.

"It's true, Javi," says Carmen. "My father never talks about the war. My mother did. I remember she told us that, during the war, they shaved the heads of the wives of the Reds and made them walk through the village. Things like that. But my father never told us anything. Never. Never. Never." And she tells us again, "It's the first time in my life I've heard him talk about these things."

❧ 6 ❧

On July 20, 1936, three days after Franco's army revolted against the legitimate government of the Republic in their garrisons in Africa and almost at the same time as rebel officers in Cáceres took power in the regional capital and declared a state of war in the entire province, the right in Ibahernando joined the rebellion and took charge of the village without the slightest resistance. We know quite well what happened in Spain when the war broke out. We know quite well what happened in Extremadura, including in Cáceres. But we barely know what happened in Ibahernando: no historian has been interested in finding out; the acts of the plenary sessions of the Council written up longhand by Don Marcelino—Manuel Mena's old teacher and then municipal secretary—allow the reconstruction of only a few events; the majority of the people who might be able to remember the rest are dead, and the minority who are still alive do not remember or barely remember. As with most of what pertains to this story, those terrifying days sank into oblivion as fast as they could.

But there are events that still resist disappearing into it. I have said that, when the military uprising happened, the right immediately took power in the village; I should clarify that they didn't do so on their own initiative, but at the insistence of the commander of the Civil Guard post, which obeyed orders from Cáceres; I should also make clear that, when I speak of the right, I am actually referring to the family of Javier Cercas, or an important part of his family. On July 20 the village council celebrated an extraordinary plenary in which the last Republican mayor, a socialist leader named Agustín Rosas, handed over power to a management board formed by four members; two of them were related to Javier Cercas: one on his father's side—his grandfather Paco Cercas—and one on his mother's side—his uncle Juan Domingo Gómez Bulnes, son-in-law of the village boss: Juan José Martínez. But immediately after that plenary session another was held, in which the four new members elected their chairman by secret ballot; the elected one, by three votes to one, turned out to be Paco Cercas. At the beginning of the war he was a well-informed farmer known as an upright man, endowed with a congenital authority and a congenital capacity to exercise it; he was also a man with an interest in politics: he had been a member of Republican Action—President Manuel Azaña's progressive party—had been a councillor as a representative of it, and at some point had sympathised with socialism; nevertheless, by the end of 1935 he was presiding over the Agricultural Association, the conservative countryside union, but after the general elections of February 1936 he was removed from his position on the village council by the civil governor and, before the war, imprisoned along with other conservatives or rightists of the village for the illegal possession of weapons. It should be said that the political evolution of Paco Cercas was not the least bit unusual during the Republic and, together with his personal prestige, perhaps constituted an incentive for electing him the first Francoist mayor. It should be added that he lasted barely a few weeks in the post.

During the days following the coup a hurricane of panic and violence swept over all of Spain. In Ibahernando those on the left took by far the worst of the cyclone, because the village had fallen into the hands of the right. The most reliable investigators maintain that over the course of the war and in the first postwar months, eleven murders were committed from political motives; Javier Cercas has counted thirteen, almost all at the end or the beginning of the conflict. It will be said that, compared with the number of murders caused by Francoist terror in other Spanish towns during the three years of war, it is not a very high number; it's true, but that truth did not alleviate the terror or spare the victims. Many of them were taken by force from their homes and shot without any pretence of justice; many did not know who was killing them: the material executors of the crimes often came from other places, although those responsible for them—those who pointed out the victims and ordered or encouraged the murders—resided in the village. I do not know whether the family or any member of the family of Javier Cercas was among them; I know that, even in a war (perhaps especially in a war), everyone is innocent until proven to be guilty, and that no honest person would be so abject as to condemn someone without any proof from the comfortable immunity of peacetime, much less when, as in this case, it is virtually impossible to reconstruct events with any precision eighty years on. Having clarified that, it seems impossible to exempt the family of Javier Cercas from any responsibility for the atrocities committed in those days: first, because it was the family holding power in the village and it is difficult to accept that all its members did everything in their power to prevent what happened; and, second, because on several occasions they did protect some leftists from the uncontrolled violence, either by taking them out of the village because they were in danger inside it or by handing them over to justice, as happened with one Republican who, in spite of falling out with some of them, had been their friend and belonged to their class or what they considered their class: Don Juan Bernardo, the doctor and local leftist leader, who was imprisoned in Trujillo and was tried and finally absolved by a military tribunal. As for the motives for the murders, they were of course political, but they weren't always only political and they weren't always clear: nobody really understood why at the end of the war they killed Don Miguel Fernández, the state schoolteacher, a man everyone in town considered a good person, unless his friendship with Don Juan Bernardo was enough reason to kill him; nobody entirely understood why at the beginning of the war—to be more precise: on November 26, 1936, on a part of the Trujillo-to-Cáceres road known as Puente Estrecho—they killed, along with three other villagers, a twenty-two-year-old woman named Sara García, though some conjecture that she had been killed because she was engaged to a young socialist leader who after the military coup had escaped Ibahernando for the same reasons other leftists had: to flee the climate of persecution that loomed over the village and join the Republican resistance that was being organised in Badajoz, a province where the coup had not triumphed.

So in Ibahernando it was only Republicans who were murdered in the rearguard; fear, however, was also felt by the Francoists, especially at the beginning. In fact, for them the initial days of the war were the most worrying. Between the end of July and the beginning of August, Franco had managed to land the majority of his Moroccan troops in the south of the country with the help of Hitler's air force, and from that moment on columns full of veterans of the African colonial wars commanded by Lieutenant Colonel Yagüe marched up from Andalucía towards Ibahernando, on their way to Madrid, putting the whole region to fire and the sword. Meanwhile, out-of-control violence had taken over the country, in Extremadura the front was not yet stable, and the Republicans from Badajoz were trying to recover the zones that the military uprising had put in rebel hands. That was the fear that spread among the village Francoists during the first days of the struggle: that the leftists who had fled after the coup would return and, supported by their fellow leftists from Badajoz, would retake the village and settle accounts with them. From the provincial capital they received emphatic instructions that, if the Republicans returned, they should do whatever they could to detain them until the troops of the Argel Regiment stationed in Cáceres came to their aid, and the new authorities chose to stand guard at all the main access routes into the village: on the calle del Agua, on Barrero, at the Pozo Arriba, and on the main road to Robledillo. Convinced that a Republican attack was imminent, the conservative families made the decision to entrench themselves twenty-four hours a day in the strong houses around the square, with the men all armed to the teeth and the doors and windows protected by sandbags. An event that occurred on August 2, a couple of weeks after the coup, seemed to endorse those extreme measures. At two in the afternoon on that day, a column of fourteen Hispano-Suiza trucks full of Republicans heading for Trujillo along the Madrid road burst into the village of Villamesías, cheering for the Republic, just a few miles from Ibahernando; the column, under the command of a Captain Medina and guided by a renegade priest known as Father Revilla, was composed of armed militiamen, including miners from Peñarroya and Puertollano. Obeying orders from Cáceres, the Civil Guards posted there and some local right-wingers put up enough resistance to allow three companies of the Argel Regiment under the orders of Commander Ricardo Belda to reach the village, and he had time to set up his machine guns on the outskirts and riddle with bullets that foolhardy detachment of militiamen who were driving around those roads at war like a gang of amateurs, without taking the slightest security measures. The result was wholesale massacre: in less than an hour the Republicans were annihilated and the road that led out of town was littered with more than a hundred dead militiamen.

The Battle of Villamesías constituted a small military success and a great propaganda success for the rebels, but it unleashed panic in Ibahernando, where over the days that followed the rumour circulated that some leftists from the village had been travelling in the thwarted Republican column. The panic, however, did not last long. On August 11 Yagüe's columns took Mérida; on the 14th, Badajoz; a little while later Franco set up in Cáceres and on the 25th, the heads of Yagüe's three columns—Tella, Castejón, and Asensio—met in Trujillo, scant miles from Ibahernando, along with the leaders of another two columns of reinforcements: Barrón and Delgado Serrano. For Ibahernando's right, the danger seems to have passed, although until the end of the war there is Republican resistance in Extremadura and the village continues to worry about a fairly close front, even if almost always dormant. But for the leftists of Ibahernando the danger persists: many are going to spend the rest of the war fearing that a murderous carload is going to stop outside their door as a sure herald of death.

Nor have some right-wingers who converted overnight into Francoists or Falangists (or, more frequently, both at once) completely outwitted the danger; for them the war then begins in earnest. At the end of September or the beginning of October twenty-five of them join the rebel army; Paco Cercas is one of them, leaving for the front having been in the office of mayor for just under two months. Javier Cercas's paternal grandfather is accompanied by two types of men: on the one hand, serfs, labourers with their own land or tenant farmers like him, almost all of whom were Republicans just a few years earlier, as he was, but now scared by the revolutionary drift of the Republic or what they consider the revolutionary drift of the Republic and especially by the atmosphere of violence they've been breathing in Ibahernando for months; on the other hand, serfs of serfs, landless day labourers addicted to order, very humble people frightened by the aimless or hopeless outrages being committed by other serfs of serfs like themselves and traumatised by the shattering into a thousand pieces of the peaceful coexistence in the village. The majority of the members of this expedition are of a certain age, starting with Javier Cercas's grandfather, who at that moment was already thirty-six years old and had to withstand his wife's tremendous anger when he announced he was leaving for the front: María Cercas shouted at him, asking if he was crazy, if he'd forgotten he was an old man and had three small children, and what the devil was an old man with three small children going to do in the war, she told him he was going to get killed, that young men had to go to war or those who weren't as old as him, that anyone should go but not him, asked him why it had to be him who went. Paco Cercas seized on that last question to stop the whirlwind with a single answer:

"Because if I don't go nobody'll go, María."

I don't know if it happened exactly like that, but that's exactly how an uncle of Javier Cercas's named Julio Cercas told it; he had heard his mother tell it many times and might have witnessed it without understanding a word, because he was just a newborn baby at that moment. As for Paco Cercas's reply, it's possible that it was an exaggeration, the only argument he could think of offhand to counter his wife's, but the fact is that some of the men who left for the front in those first days would perhaps not have done so without him and that, in the course of the episode of the war that was just beginning, Javier Cercas's grandfather exerted over his twenty-four companions, if not military authority, at least moral authority.

The group joined the Third Bandera of the Cáceres Falange, or rather were incorporated into the groups of volunteers that with time would end up constituting that Bandera. We know nothing or almost nothing about these earliest Francoist units, because nobody or almost nobody has studied them, as if they had never existed or as if they didn't interest anybody; the archives don't help either, at least in this case: in the Military Archives of Ávila they keep the Operations Diary of the Third Bandera of the Cáceres Falange, but only from September 1937, which is when it was officially founded. So, here and in other parts of this story of obscurities, we often have to feel our way and rely on hypotheses. Some things, however, seem certain.

The twenty-five volunteers from Ibahernando were a heterogeneous handful of men without the least preparation for war, badly dressed in civilian clothes and badly armed with hunting rifles, who, as soon as they were positioned in their improvised unit, were sent to Madrid with Yagüe's columns. Their commanders were professional military officers, but their role was secondary: essentially it consisted of advancing behind the colonial troops covering their rearguard and flanks, facilitating provisions and evacuations, and supporting the columns' progression, which was vigorous until they reached the outskirts of Madrid. Sure the capital was about to fall and that the war would last a matter of weeks, the twenty-five passed through Navalmoral de la Mata, Talavera de la Reina, and Navalcarnero, reaching Madrid in November and taking up positions on the Usera front, south of the capital. There they stayed for a while. It is doubtful that they ever entered seriously into combat; in any case, they had only one casualty to lament: a man named Andrés Ruiz. The campaign, otherwise, was brief, and at some point in that same winter, towards the middle or end of January 1937, they were all back in the village, discharged and with their particular war over. I do not know the cause of such an early return: it is likely that, as the war advanced and galvanised, and as the suspicion it was going to last longer than foreseen intensified, for many of the commanders the ineptitude of those aging, inexpert, and haphazardly armed peasants was increasingly obvious and they decided to relieve them with detachments of younger, better-armed and -trained volunteers; but there is also a possibility that their hurried return was another sign of the ingenuous pretensions of independence that some pure Falangists still nourished at the beginning of the war, obsessed with the ambition of not being gobbled up by the omnivorous Francoist conglomeration: at a certain point in the autumn or winter of 1936, Captain José Luna, one of the earliest Falangists and provincial leader of the party in Cáceres, retired several militia units under his jurisdiction from the Madrid front, without asking permission or giving anyone any explanation, alleging that some officers of the regular army mistreated his men, and the Third Bandera of the Falange could have been among them. It is also possible that both conjectures might not be mutually exclusive but rather complementary and that the military authorities neutralised or masked Luna's dangerous insubordination and the return of his discharged volunteers who they considered unfit for combat. The fact is that, during that return trip home from the trenches around Madrid, Paco Cercas took part in a strange incident about which he kept silent for the rest of his life, and which only came to light by chance many years later, when almost seventy years had passed and Javier Cercas's grandfather had been dead for two decades. No, not by chance: through Delia Cabrera, the granddaughter of the other protagonist of the incident. No, not Delia Cabrera: Fernando Berlín, the journalist to whom Delia Cabrera recounted the incident. Be that as it may, at the end of August 2006, Javier Cercas recounted it in an article titled "The End of a Novel," which goes like this:

It was the journalist Fernando Berlín who, more or less a year ago, dug up the events I am preparing to relate. At the time Berlín had created a segment on a radio programme where he invited listeners to tell their Civil War stories. One of the first listeners to call in was a woman: she was a little over forty and her name was Delia Cabrera; she called in to tell a story of her grandfather's, Antonio Cabrera.

The story is the following:

On July 18, 1936, Cabrera was the socialist mayor of

Ibahernando, a village in the region of Trujillo, in the province of Cáceres. Barely a month later the troops of the Army of Africa commanded by General Franco arrived there after having crossed the Strait of Gibraltar thanks to the Nazi aircraft and having razed hundreds of miles and villages and whole cities, leaving in their wake thousands of corpses. The village had fallen into rebel hands a few days after the uprising, so Franco's soldiers were welcomed with enthusiasm and, after stocking up on supplies and resting for a time, they took with them some local Falangists and obliged a few Republicans and sympathisers or members of left-wing parties to join the ranks of their service corps. One of those Republicans was Antonio Cabrera, who spent the rest of the war as a foot soldier in the army of his enemies. He was not a young man at the time, but he was strong, so he managed to survive those three years of inhumane forced marches all over the geography of Spain, dragging a mule loaded with supplies. The Republic's final defeat caught him in Talavera de la Reina, about ninety miles from his village; surprisingly (or maybe not: maybe they'd simply forgotten his Republican past, or considered that he'd redeemed himself in the war), they discharged him, told him he could go home, and for several days he searched for a means of transport in order to do so, until one morning he happened to meet someone from Ibahernando. Cabrera had aged, he was skinny and scraggy and exhausted, but his fellow villager recognised him; Cabrera also recognised this fellow from Ibahernando: although they were not friends, he knew his name was Paco, knew he was a few years younger, knew that in the early years of the Republic he'd been a socialist and before the war broke out he had joined the Falange, he knew his family. The two men talked. The man from his village told Cabrera that the following day a truckload of soldiers would be leaving for the region of Ibahernando, and Cabrera asked if there would be room for him. "I don't know," answered the villager, but he gave him a place and a time. When he showed up the next day at the agreed time and place, Cabrera saw that the truck was overflowing with euphoric victorious soldiers; he also saw, with apprehension, that some of those soldiers were from Ibahernando, and that they recognised him. For an instant he must have hesitated, he must have thought it would be more prudent to wait for another vehicle; but when Paco urged him to climb up, his impatience to return home was stronger than his caution, and he got in.

At first the trip passed without scares, but the increasing proximity to their native land turned their triumphal euphoria to intoxication and their intoxication to a quarrelsome boastfulness that found its perfect victim: those who knew Cabrera revealed to the rest that he had been a Republican and socialist and the village mayor, made fun of him, insulted him, made him celebrate the victory, made him sing "Cara al sol," the Falangist anthem, made him drink till he was drunk. Finally, when they were about to cross a bridge over the Tagus, some soldiers decided to throw Cabrera into the abyss. Horrified, at that moment Cabrera thought he was about to die, and he felt it was unjust or ridiculous or absurd to meet this fate after having escaped three years of war with his life, but realised he no longer had the strength to oppose his executioners. That was when, as the truck drove onto the bridge and he felt many ferocious hands lifting him up, he heard a question behind him: "What do you think you're doing?" Cabrera recognised the voice; it was that of his fellow villager Paco, who a second later added: "We told this man we were going to take him home, and that's what we're going to do."

That's how it ended: the soldiers let go of Cabrera and he arrived safe and sound in his village.

That was all: that's all that Delia Cabrera told Fernando Berlín. Well, not quite all. When she finished her story, Delia added: "The man who saved my grandfather's life was Francisco Cercas, everyone called him Paco and he was the paternal grandfather of Javier Cercas, the author of *Soldiers of Salamis*."

Soldiers of Salamis is a novel that revolves around a tiny episode at the end of the Civil War, in which an anonymous Republican soldier saves the life of Rafael Sánchez Mazas, poet, ideologue, and Falangist leader.

Shortly after Delia Cabrera told Berlín the buried story of her grandfather Antonio and my grandfather Paco, I spoke on the radio with her, with Berlín and with Iñaki Gabilondo, producer and presenter of the radio programme in which Berlín's segment aired. At a certain point in the conversation Gabilondo asked me if I'd been inspired by that story of my grandfather's to write *Soldiers of Salamis*. I said no. Then he asked me if I knew the story before Delia Cabrera had told Berlín. I said no. Then he asked me if my father knew it—I said no—or anyone in my family—I said no. Perplexed, Gabilondo then asked: "And why do you think your grandfather never told anyone that story?" For an interminable second I didn't know how to answer. I remembered my grandfather Paco shut up day and night in his shed, at the back of the yard of his house in Ibahernando, very old and sinewy and engrossed in his meticulous task of making useless miniatures of carts, ploughs, and other farming implements. I remembered an evening thirty-five or forty years ago, when I was a child: my grandparents, some of my sisters, and I were in a taxi from Collado Mediano, a town near Madrid where my uncle Julio lived, on our way to Ibahernando, and at some moment, when we passed Brunete and night was falling and I was dozing off on my grandfather's lap, he pointed towards the horizon and emerged from his silence as if he weren't emerging from his silence but as if he'd been talking to me for a long time: "Look, Javi," he whispered. "That's where the trenches were." I remembered another evening, more recent, but not that much, more or less in the years when Spain was beginning to emerge from the chasm of decades of a dictatorship that my grandfather had contributed in his way to digging and was peering out insecurely and fearfully at democracy: as on every summer evening, while my grandfather remained shut up in his shed, at the gateway of his house, relatives, friends, and neighbours all gathered to chat; that evening we were talking about politics, and near dusk my grandfather appeared at the gate, ready for his daily stroll, and as he stopped a moment to greet those of us who were there, someone asked him what he thought about what was happening in Spain.

Then my grandfather made a face or a slight gesture, which I couldn't decipher (something, I thought, halfway between a shrug and a cheerless smile), and before carrying on his way said: "Let's see if it turns out well this time." I remembered all that while Gabilondo waited for my answer, while I was wondering, like Gabilondo, why my grandfather had never told anyone that once he'd been brave and saved a man's life, and it was at that very moment when I understood that novels are like dreams or nightmares that never end, just transform into other nightmares or dreams, and that I'd had the implausible fortune of having one of mine end, because that was the real ending of *Soldiers of Salamis*. So, joyfully, with immense relief, I answered Gabilondo: "I don't know."

So much for Cercas's article. Or almost: I have left out superfluous passages, made the odd indispensable correction for accuracy, toned down some sentimental emphases; I chose not to omit, however, five glaring factual errors, which should not be attributed to its author's natural tendency to embellish, to his incurable *literato*'s predilection for imprecise legend over certain history, but to his negligence or his ignorance. First error: Antonio Cabrera was not the socialist mayor of Ibahernando in July 1936, when the war broke out; he was the mayor, but from 1933 to 1934, halfway through the Republic, and for almost three months of 1936: exactly from February 21 to May 16, 1936, when, shortly before the coup d'état, he was replaced by Agustín Rosas. Second error: on their march to Madrid, Franco's troops never passed through Ibahernando, but rather through Trujillo, and they didn't do any of what Javier Cercas said they did in the village; it is true, however, that the former socialist mayor was forced to accompany his enemies and work for them in the service corps, although he didn't do so for the entire war—this is the third error—but just for a few months, which explains why his return to the village would have coincided with that of Paco Cercas and his *compañeros*, at the end of 1936 or the beginning of 1937. Fourth error: there is no record that Paco Cercas, who undoubtedly knew the man whose life he saved much better than his grandson thought, was before the war a card-carrying socialist, or even that he then joined the Falange; there is, however, a record that he did so later, and even that on April 14, 1937, a few months after returning home, he was named leader of the local branch of the Falange. Fifth and final error: Paco Cercas did not fight in the Battle of Brunete, as Javier Cercas always believed, undoubtedly because he deduced it from the fact that, in that childhood twilight the article evokes, his grandfather was able to show him where the trenches were, and because he never made any effort to find out whether that deduction was accurate, and nobody ever refuted it; the reality is that Paco Cercas was only at the Battle of Madrid, and if he did know the trenches of Brunete it was because, many years after the war ended, he visited the ones preserved between Villanueva de la Cañada and Brunete several times with his son Julio, who lived near them, in Collado Mediano. In other respects, these errors do not exhaust the ignorance Javier Cercas has of his grandfather's life, or at least that he had when he wrote his article. At that moment he did not know, for example, that his grandfather had actually been the local leader of the Falange for quite a brief period: more or less two years, from the first half of 1937 until the first half of 1939. Nor did he know that, when the war ended, around the time his grandfather gave up the leadership of the Ibahernando Falange another war had been unleashed in the village, a political war between old and young, between pure Falangists and pragmatic Francoists, a merciless battle for power that the former, including his grandfather, ended up losing. He didn't know that until the end of his days his grandfather considered the victors to be a gang of unscrupulous upstarts, if not crooks, and that he never stopped professing an unconditional contempt for them. He had no idea that, before or after that defeat, his grandfather had not only left his position in the Falange but also the Falange itself, and that in his whole life he never again belonged to the only party there was. And much less did he know that his emphatic rejection of the Falange had turned into an emphatic rejection of politics, that he never held another political post, and that, while the victors of that war among victors of the war monopolised power in the village for the rest of the dictatorship, his grandfather left Ibahernando with his wife and children and, although he always kept his house in the village, he lived first in Cáceres and later in Mérida, renting parcels of arable land here and there which he worked from dawn to dusk to satisfy his determined desire to send all three of his children to university. He didn't know that, after his disillusionment with the Falange, he never allowed his sons to join that organisation or have anything to do with it, in spite of it being the first instrument of youthful socialisation during the dictatorship. He did not know in short that, as well as being disappointed by Franco, his grandfather grew disappointed with the ideas that led him to go to war (supposing that it was ideas and not a much more basic impulse that led him to war), although it is impossible to know how deep those two disappointments ran. Not knowing, he didn't even know that, in spite of being almost twenty years older than Manuel Mena, at some point in the war his grandfather had established a strong enough friendship with him that he was invited over for a meal every time he was home from the front on leave.

Manuel Mena was in Ibahernando when the war broke out. He was seventeen years old, had just graduated with brilliant results from the final year of his baccalaureate in Cáceres, and was preparing to start his first year of law school in Madrid. He was spending the summer holidays at his mother's house, with his three unmarried siblings and a niece and a nephew: Blanquita, who was five, the daughter of his brother Juan, and Alejandro, who was seven, and the son of his sister María, and with whom he was sharing a room. The year in Cáceres had ended up distancing him from his childhood friends, so his summer must have gone by between conversations with Don Eladio Viñuela, reading books and magazines borrowed from his library and walks with his mentor and with Alejandro, who went everywhere with him; he had also become inseparable from a kid his age, named Tomás Álvarez, who was the younger brother of the Ibahernando priest and who had been spending long stretches of time in the village since before the war. It is impossible that, no matter how isolated he might have been living in Ibahernando, Manuel Mena did not sense there the prewar atmosphere that was present throughout the country, that he would not have guessed such a situation could not last long and that he wouldn't have felt the imminence of the outbreak of violence or a military coup that everybody was feeling; there is no doubt that, when the army finally rose up against the government, he approved of the uprising and celebrated the end of Republican legitimacy in the village; nor is there any doubt that he decided to go off to war as soon as the failure of the coup triggered it.

His mother guessed that immediately and, perhaps knowing that she could not prevent him, tried to prevent him. For years the dialogues between mother and son during those early weeks of war constituted one of the largest chapters of the legend of Manuel Mena. They say that his mother repeated that he wasn't old enough to fight in the war and that she was a poor widow and still had two as yet unmarried daughters, and that he couldn't abandon her in those circumstances; they say that she reminded him that he was the family's great hope, that she and his brothers had spared him from working in the fields so he wouldn't get trapped in the village like them and could go out into the world and study for a university degree and would have a dignified future, and that he was going to risk all of that if he went off to the war; they say that she told him he was her favourite son and her shoulder to cry on, and asked him what would become of her if he were killed; they say she insisted, she begged, she implored, she coerced him with all the measures at her disposal. They also say that Manuel Mena remained serene and resolute and that, although he tried to assuage her concern, he never gave her the slightest hope that he might give in to her pleas. They say that Manuel Mena answered his mother that his obligation was to go to war, that he couldn't hide at home while others like him were risking their lives at the front, that he had to be equal to the task, had to measure up and not get scared, that he was going to defend her, his sisters, his brothers, his nieces and nephews, that he was only going to do what others were already doing, to fight for what's right, for his family, for his nation, and for God; they say that he told her: "Do not worry,

Mother: if I return, I'll return with honour; if I do not return, a son of yours will have given his life for the Fatherland, and there is nothing greater than that. Furthermore," he concluded, "if I get killed, they'll give you such a bonus payment that you'll never have to worry about anything." All this Manuel Mena said to his mother, but the phrase he most often repeated to her was not an anticipated attempt to console her but a request.

"Mother," he'd say, "I ask only one thing of you if I get killed: let nobody see you cry."

Manuel Mena finally left for the front one early morning at the beginning of October 1936, more than two months after the start of the war. I don't know if anyone saw him leave the village; I don't know if he went on his own or if someone else accompanied him on his flight. I do know that, before he left, he tried in vain to persuade his friend Tomás Álvarez to accompany him. I know that he left in secret, without asking anyone's permission or saying goodbye to anyone in his family: neither his mother nor his siblings, nor his nephews and nieces. Hours or days later, on October 6, he joined the Third Bandera of the Cáceres Falange as a volunteer, precisely the same unit that, months earlier, the village's first twenty-five volunteers had joined, among them Paco Cercas. I don't know if the fact is a coincidence. There are some who claim to have heard him (or someone close to him) on occasion talk about his presence at the Madrid front at the beginning of the war; there are some who maintain that Manuel Mena and other young volunteers like him were sent to Madrid to relieve Paco Cercas and the other old but early volunteers; there are some who maintain that was when and where he and Paco Cercas became friends. I don't know that either. This is the least certain stretch of Manuel Mena's life. The only thing we know about him is the little that is known about the events of the war in which his unit took part from October of that year until July of the following year, when he was transferred.

During those nine months the combat activity of the Third Bandera of the Falange was very infrequent. Supposing that they ever actually fought in Madrid, they returned very promptly to Extremadura, and were soon stationed in the zone of Miajadas, Rena, and Villar de Rena, in the province of Badajoz, where the Extremadura front had been established after the chaos of the early weeks of the war with the cemetery-like peace imposed by Yagüe's African columns making their way through the zone. It was an inactive front, which barely registered anything but inconsequential skirmishes until July of the following year, just when Manuel Mena left it. Everything indicates that in those first months of hostilities, vibrant with martial exaltation and collective enthusiasm, Manuel Mena was a soldier as eager for glory and battle as Lieutenant Drogo in *The Tartar Steppe,* a young idealist intoxicated with shiny speeches on the romanticism of combat and the purifying beauty of war; everything indicates that the passivity and lethargy that reigned over the Extremadura front where Manuel Mena spent that year waiting for the Republicans must not have been too different from the lethargy and passivity that reigned over the Bastiani Fortress, where Lieutenant Drogo spent his life waiting for the Tartars. This was not Manuel Mena's idea of war, this was not why he'd enlisted as a volunteer, so he must have begun very soon to look for a posting more in line with his expectations.

If that's how it was, it didn't take him long to find it. Franco's army suffered from a damaging shortage of officers and commanders from the beginning of the war; to mitigate this he improvised a corps made up of young university students who, after a short course lasting barely two weeks, were awarded officer rank. Almost thirty thousand provisional second lieutenants were created in this way over the three years the conflict lasted, almost two-thirds of the Francoist campaign's officer corps. Surrounded from very early on by an epic fame, in Francoist propaganda the provisional second lieutenant quickly became the prototypical hero: he was young, brave, idealistic, generous, and dashing, and, with his permanent readiness for sacrifice, he constituted the backbone of the rebel army. "Provisional lieutenant, corpse in waiting," ran the accurate saying: during the whole war more than three thousand provisional second lieutenants died, 10 per cent of the total. In March 1938, months before Manuel Mena fell in combat, José María Pemán, Francoism's official poet and honorary provisional second lieutenant, premiered a play at the Argensola Theatre in Zaragoza titled *Theirs Is the World*, in which he tried to immortalise the figure of the provisional lieutenant with verses that would soon be spreading by word of mouth:

Provisional . . . second lieutenant.
Sad and handsome
in his own fragility.
Like a flower in the wind,
like a crystal glass,
I am Spanish, and more so
for being provisional.

Here I am, offering you, Spain,
my twenty years, as if they were
twenty fresh dahlias,
and Death
the gardener.

At the beginning of July 1937 Manuel Mena enrolled in the Granada Military Academy, from which he emerged at the beginning of September with the rank of provisional second lieutenant; that's how long those preparatory courses lasted at that time: not two weeks, as they had at the beginning of the war, but two months. By then Manuel Mena had turned eighteen and had spent half a month at the front, two of the requirements demanded of those who aspired to that rank; the other was to have graduated from secondary school, which Manuel Mena had done the previous summer. After the tedium and inaction of the Extremadura front, he must have enjoyed military life in Granada, surrounded by students like himself and flattered by the city's residents, who stopped to admire the cadets and applauded them as they paraded along the Gran Vía towards the Academy or the training field as they sang:

> *When the cadets—come out of training*
> *all the girls—come out on their balconies.*
> *If you look up—you're going to see suspenders,*
> *you're going to be reprimanded—run, run, run*
> > *down to the sea.*

The Academy was located in an old Jesuit seminary surrounded by woods. The future officers were trained there under strict discipline and an invariable routine. Manuel Mena got up at dawn every day, and at six in the morning was already out doing field exercises, target and tactical practice in the hills that rise behind the Alhambra, with views of the city below and the Sierra Nevada above. At noon he returned to the Academy and had lunch with his comrades in a vast refectory with a pulpit meant for readings, which was never used. The morning classes were practical and imparted by German instructors who spoke very broken Spanish, while the afternoon ones were theoretical and imparted by Spanish instructors who taught tactics, logistics, procedural rules, military justice, morality, and religion. The cadets earned 320 pesetas a month; Manuel Mena once said that a veteran warned him when he received his first month's salary: "The first one's for the uniform, *pirulo;* the second, for the shroud." *Pirulo* was the name the veteran cadets reserved for the green ones, who they tortured during the first few weeks with hazing pranks; *padrecito* was the name the veteran cadets reserved for themselves.

The final days at the Academy were normally filled with great nervousness, because one of the rules of the institution was that nobody was allowed to repeat the course, so candidates who aspired to be officers had to pass all the exams on their first attempt; fortunately for the cadets, these exams were not excessively demanding, so most of them passed. Manuel Mena was religious without being sanctimonious, but it is more than likely that, once he had passed the course, he would have gone with his classmates to the sanctuary of the Virgin of Anguish to offer her their lieutenant stars and ask her for strength for themselves and their families, because cadets considered this visit almost obligatory. I don't think he would have requested the Ifni Riflemen posting, as it was a virtually unknown unit, but it is possible that he requested the Regulars, a corps created in Africa and formed essentially of native troops, to which the Ifni Riflemen belonged: the corps of Regulars was after all one of the most coveted by the second lieutenants; in any case, whatever he might have requested, in the end it was not him but the army who, according to its own needs, chose the posting. He undoubtedly swore allegiance to the flag during a ceremony with an open-air Mass, military music, patriotic speeches, and a parade, but I don't know where (it might have been in Granada itself, though it could also have taken place in any of the capital cities of Andalucía), and it is almost certain that General Gonzalo Queipo de Llano, commander of the Army of the South, would have attended. It is also almost certain that after the oath a banquet of brotherhood would have been held for the recently designated officers and their instructors, and that at night, after the party ended, Manuel Mena would have set off for Ibahernando to enjoy a week's leave before joining his new unit at the front.

I managed to rescue two anecdotes from Manuel Mena's first visit home as a second lieutenant; more than two anecdotes, they are two scenes, two moments, which, almost eighty years later, still survive in the memories of two of their witnesses. The first was seen by Blanca Mena, mother of Javier Cercas, in her grandmother Carolina's house during the happy afternoon when Manuel Mena arrived from Granada with his officer's diploma under his arm. At eighty-five years of age, Blanca Mena still retains an intact memory of the dining room exhilarated by the dazzling appearance of her uncle, by her grandmother Carolina's tearful reception, and by the hubbub of Manuel Mena's friends and acquaintances—Isabel Martínez, María Ruiz, Paca Cercas—who came from every corner of the village to celebrate the recently arrived hero, girls the same age as Manuel Mena who swirled around him like a chaotic harem, nervous and smiling, pestering him with questions about the Academy and Granada and the war while her grandmother tried to accommodate them and share with them the exultation at the return of her son; Blanca Mena remembered herself taking hold of his jacket in one hand and the handle or

sheath of his lieutenant's sabre in the other, delighted with that
tumultuous welcome, and remembered Manuel Mena with his
unpacked bedroll at his feet, tall, young, and as distinguished as
a prince, wrapped in his impeccable and very white uniform—
peaked cap with the officer's gold star, black tie, black chevrons
with gold stars and buttons, the jacket without a single crease
and the trousers straight, the golden set of buttons and shiny
shoes—lavishing smiles in the midst of the din, playing down
the importance of his months of instruction at the Academy, his
brand-new rank of second lieutenant, and the horror of the war,
and making jokes at which everybody laughed uproariously. As
for the second anecdote, it was Alejandro García, Javier Cercas's
uncle, who told it to the novelist not long ago. I have already
recorded that Alejandro García was Manuel Mena's nephew and
shared a room with him for years in his grandmother Carolina's
house; also that, when Manuel Mena returned from studying
in Cáceres or from combat at the front, he accompanied him
everywhere, holding his hand and as faithful as a dog: Alejandro remembered, for example, that he sometimes went with his
uncle to listen to the radio at the house of a man nicknamed
Rabbit, the only or almost only person in the village who owned
one, and that other times, at lunchtime, he accompanied him
to Don Eladio Viñuela's house, on the plaza, or to Paco Cercas's,
on Fontanilla, and that, following his instructions to the letter, he would return to pick him up after an hour and a half,
or after two hours, when the meal had finished or when he
estimated it would have finished. He must have done more or
less the same during that week of leave Manuel Mena enjoyed
in the village. Alejandro remembered two things about it. The
first is that Manuel Mena brought him a gift from Granada: a

plaster model of the Alhambra. The second is the anecdote I was referring to.

It happened two or three days before Manuel Mena returned to the front, now as an officer of the First Tabor of Ifni Riflemen. That afternoon Alejandro was playing in the doorway of his grandmother Carolina's house while Manuel Mena was reading in the courtyard. All of a sudden, Alejandro told me, he felt that something out of the ordinary was happening in the air or in the sky—as if the clouds had briskly covered the sun and had changed the colour of the afternoon, provoking a premature nightfall or a lambent foreboding of a cataclysm—and turned towards the west. What he saw left him astounded. In spite of the hours remaining before night, the sun seemed to be trying to hide behind the last rooftops of the village; its brilliance, however, had not disappeared, or not entirely: to the right there was still a brushstroke of yellow, unreal light, but most of the horizon was dyed red, a red less unreal than the yellow, pink at the left and very intense in the distance and in front of him, increasingly intense and invasive, just as if a storm of blood was gestating in the sky. All of a sudden, Alejandro snapped out of the spell and shouted to raise the alarm, which brought a handful of relatives and neighbours; among them, naturally, was Manuel Mena. Alejandro said that at first the group was dumbstruck by surprise, but soon people began to comment on the spectacle, to risk hypotheses, to argue; the only one who remained still and silent before the incandescent horizon was Manuel Mena. Alejandro approached him and took his hand. More anxious than intrigued, he asked:

"That's the war, isn't it, Uncle Manuel?"

"No," answered his uncle. "It's the aurora borealis."

"Did you notice?" David Trueba asked me. "Each time you mentioned Manuel Mena, the Shearer got nervous."

We'd left the Shearer's house a while ago and driven out of Ibahernando, crossing Pozo Castro and the square lit up at that hour by a couple of streetlights and the bright squares of the bar windows, through which I glimpsed men standing at the counter and seated men playing cards. Later we got into the deep darkness of the narrow road to Trujillo and took the highway to Madrid at the intersection by La Majada, the restaurant where we'd eaten lunch. We had planned to sleep in Trujillo, but it was not yet nine and we calculated that we could get back to Madrid at a reasonable hour, so when we got to the Trujillo turnoff we decided to stay on the highway as we passed the Cabeza del Zorro, the headland on which the town is built, with its medieval walls, towers, and castle floodlit in the darkness. Until then we hadn't said a word about the two and a half hours of conversation we'd just had with the Shearer, in the presence of his daughter and son-in-law, and I had attributed David's silence to a lack of interest in what he'd been filming; from his observation I deduced that the opposite was the case, so I immediately answered that I too had noticed what he'd noticed.

"He kept moving his crutch from one side to the other," I added.

"Not that it should surprise us," David said. "They kill your father like a dog, and you don't know who or why, and you have to bury him in secret without anyone saying a lousy prayer. How horrible. And then Manuel Mena goes off to war because he wants to, dies fighting like a man, and the whole town turns out for his funeral. In Ibahernando, Manuel Mena was a hero, and the Shearer's father was nothing, less than nothing, a Red who'd got what he deserved. Poor Shearer: almost eighty years without telling anyone that story, almost eighty years carrying that around inside him. I don't know about you, but I had the impression the whole time that I was in front of a man who's been ill for his entire life and doesn't even know he's ill."

"I had the same impression," I said. "And I also had the impression that he was talking about the war as if it were a natural disaster."

"Could be," David said. "Lots of people who lived through the war talk about it that way, especially in small towns. But I think the Shearer was doing it on purpose, as a cover-up."

"As a cover-up?"

"Your family was one of the right-wing families of the village, right? In other words: the people who had taken Franco's side; in short: the people who had killed his father. As well as the Shearer speaks of them, as much as he appreciates them, that's what they were. And you want him to say what he really thinks about the war and about Manuel Mena to a member of that family, which is what you are? But he's never even told his own daughters . . . ! That's why he talks with the hand brake on, man. And don't tell me it's been almost eighty years since the war, because for that man the war's not over; or at least

Francoism, which was, after all, the continuation of the war by other means. He couldn't have put it any plainer."

"Yes," I said. "I think that man knows more than he told us too."

"Not more: much, much more," he emphasised. "At least about the war and about Manuel Mena."

I agreed again and, perhaps fearing that David might change the subject, added the first thing that popped into my head:

"Didn't it seem like he might burst into tears at any moment?"

David took his eyes off the road to give me a look of incomprehension or surprise.

"Who, the Shearer?" David said; he quickly turned back to watch where we were going. "I'd bet my balls he never cries."

I thought of my mother, who'd cried so much when Manuel Mena died that she used up her lifetime's supply of tears, and understood that David was right.

"You're right," I said. "That man must have used up all his tears when they killed his father."

"For sure," David said, nodding. "And by the way, haven't you thought of something?"

In silence I wondered if the fundamental difference that divides people might not be the division between people who can still cry and those who can no longer cry; also in silence I wondered how many people had run out of tears during the war. Out loud I asked: "What?"

"That maybe the Shearer hadn't agreed to talk to you to tell you the story of Manuel Mena."

I tried to process David's assertion, but in vain.

"I don't understand," I said.

He clicked his tongue with an annoyed look on his face.

"Let's see," he began pedagogically. "That man has spent almost eighty years in silence, without talking about the war even with his daughters, and you really think he's going to start talking about the Francoist hero of the village just like that, willingly, and to top it off with you, the great-nephew of the village's Francoist hero? The hell he is. He agreed to talk to you to tell the story of his father, so the story of his father's murder won't remain untold, so you'll take on that story and tell it. He might not have been entirely aware of having done it for that reason, but he did. No doubt about it. Or wasn't it him who brought it up? And, by the way, who was talking about responsibility? Hannah Arendt? Well, take responsibility."

The highway was almost deserted. The moon wasn't up, and to the left and right the holm-oak woods were submerged in an almost hermetic darkness. Tall as giraffe necks or gigantic sunflowers planted at the roadside, the streetlights gave off a butane-coloured light, but there were stretches without lighting, or where the streetlights were not on, where the darkness completely colonised the asphalt and where only the headlights of our car seemed to fight against its tyranny and the few other cars that occasionally broke through the darkness, coming towards us in the opposite lane, before disappearing again behind us, or the even sparser cars that overtook us in the fast lane. David had set the cruise control at 75 miles per hour and was driving in a relaxed way, leaning back in his seat, holding the steering wheel at the bottom (or caressing it), with his gaze fixed outside, on the road, although the impression he gave was that he was not looking out but inward: not at what he was seeing but what he was thinking. He must have turned on the radio or put in a CD, because there was a melody playing very softly that sounded familiar but that I didn't recognise. We'd finished talking about the Shearer and were talking about Manuel Mena.

"People used to have a very different idea of war," my friend said at one point; combined with the brightness of the dashboard, the intermittent light from the streetlights created an unreal atmosphere inside the car, as if we were in a tank or an aquarium. "We've forgotten, but it's true. Actually, people have almost always thought wars were useful, that they solved problems. That's what men have thought for centuries, for millennia: that war is terrible and cruel but noble, the place where we get an authentic measure of ourselves. Now this seems fucking stupid to us, moronic ravings, but the truth is even the greatest artists thought like that. I don't know, you look at *The Surrender of Breda*, with the battlefield still smoking and all those people so gentlemanly, so dignified in defeat and so magnanimous in victory, and you want to be there even on the losing side: fuck, even the horses look intelligent and generous! On the other hand, you look at *The Third of May 1808* or *The Disasters of War*, and your hair stands on end and the only thing you want to do is run away. Of course, we know that Goya is much closer to reality than Velázquez, but we haven't known it for long; or perhaps it's simply that Goya paints war as it is, while Velázquez paints it as we wish it was, or as we imagined it was for centuries. Whatever the case, I'm sure when he went off to war Manuel Mena had an idea of it much less like Goya's than like Velázquez's, which is the idea of war young men have always had before going to war."

That was when David brought up a story by the Serbian writer Danilo Kiš, titled *To Die for One's Country Is Glorious*. He did so, I'm sure, because Manuel Mena's story reminded him of it, although I don't know exactly why it reminded him; he did so because the protagonist of Kiš's story is a young warrior who dies young and violently, like Manuel Mena, although perhaps he also did so because he wanted to tell me something he hadn't finished telling me or that he didn't dare tell me or had told me but not openly and which in that moment I didn't understand. I insist that I don't know. What I do know is that he loved the story and that years earlier he had thought of adapting it for the screen, which is why he'd read it many times.

"The story takes place in an undefined place and time," he began, choosing each word carefully. "Undefined on purpose, of course: we're in Europe, there is talk of an empire and Emperor, and there is an insinuation that both are Spanish, but there is also a mention of sans-culottes and Jacobins, who existed when there was no Spanish empire in Europe. Anyway . . . The protagonist of the tale, or rather the apparent protagonist, is named Esterházy, is a count, and is the same age as Manuel Mena when he died. More or less. Esterházy belongs to a family as noble and as ancient as that of the emperor who has sentenced him to hang for having been involved in a mass uprising. The action begins shortly before the sentence is carried out. One day Esterházy receives a visit in his death-row cell from his mother, a haughty aristocrat proud of the eminence of her lineage. They speak for a while, and the boy announces to his mother that he is prepared to die. That's what he says. Although it's possible his mother doesn't believe him. The proof is that she cheers him up and tries to instil courage in him so he won't despair, so he won't collapse and so he'll maintain his dignity in this terrible moment; more than that: she assures him that she is going to beg the emperor to pardon him, that she is ready to throw herself at his feet; and she tells her son that, if she obtains a reprieve, on the day of his execution he will see her dressed in white on a balcony, as they take him to the scaffold, and that will be the signal that he is saved and that the emperor's pardon will arrive in time." David paused here, as if he'd forgotten how the story went on or as if he'd just realised something that he'd overlooked until then. "The thing is that, during his stay in prison," he goes on, "Esterházy's main preoccupation consists of upholding aristocratic manners until the end; what obsesses him is that no one should see him collapse or show fear or reveal signs of weakness when the moment of death arrives. And so on the day of his execution the count rises at dawn, after a sleepless night, and does all he can to maintain his composure: he prays, smokes one last cigarette, allows them to tie his hands behind his back as if he were a highwayman, and climbs into the carriage that conducts him to the gallows. And, yes, during the journey to the scaffold there are moments when he feels fear is going to get the best of him, but the young man controls himself and overcomes them. That's what happens in one of the best scenes of the story, when Esterházy reaches a crowded boulevard, the rabble begins to shout and raise fists in hatred while he feels his courage deserting him, and around him the mob grows excited and cheers at his weakness. But everything quickly changes again, and the count straightens up and recovers the noble and brave aspect of the Esterházys. And do you know why?" Although it was obvious he wasn't expecting a reply to his question, he paused. "Well, because at the head of the boulevard he sees a blinding white spot on a balcony. It is his mother, in a white dress, leaning over the railing with the saving signal she had promised her son . . . So the young count understands he is not going to die, that his mother's entreaties had moved the emperor and at the last moment his pardon will arrive; so he mounts the scaffold and confronts death with the dignity expected from a man of his lineage. Nice, isn't it? The only problem is that in the end the pardon does not come. And Esterházy dies at the hands of the hangman."

David fell silent, as if allowing time for the conclusion of the story, or what seems to be the conclusion, to take effect on me.

"It's a great story," I said, sincerely.

"Yeah," David responded. "The best thing about it is its ambiguity, don't you think? Or its ambiguities, rather, because the story has several: one explicit, one apparent, and another real one. Kiš himself describes the apparent and explicit ambiguity in a sort of epilogue. There he says that the story he's just told has two possible interpretations. The first is the heroic interpretation, which is that of the poor and the losers; according to this one, Esterházy died bravely, with his head held high and fully aware he was about to die. The second is the prosaic interpretation, which is that of the victors; according to this one, it was all playacting on the part of his mother.

David turned to me for a moment and smiled only with his eyes. Or that's what it seemed like to me.

"But all this is a story, as they say, and never better said," he went on. "I mean that it's a lie, that the ambiguity is only apparent. Because we know that the heroic version of the story is the imaginative and legendary (in other words: false) version with which the poor and vanquished console themselves for their poverty and their defeat, or with which they try to redeem themselves, and the truth is that it was all a clever bit of playacting by the mother, that was what really happened even if it is the version the victors and official historians tell in order to prevent the birth of a heroic legend. Kiš is implacable, ferocious, leaves not a glimmer of consolation or hope: as well as having power, power has the truth. So that's not where the ambiguity of the tale lies, or its true genius. The ambiguity is in the mother, in the attitude or strategy of the mother, who is the story's authentic protagonist. Because her attitude does allow for two interpretations. The first is that she goes up to the balcony dressed in white and deceives her son by making him believe that the emperor has reprieved him because she loves him as only a mother can love and wants to spare him the agony of knowing his last few seconds of life will really be his last, because she wants him to die calm and happy, convinced until the last instant that the emperor's reprieve will eventually arrive. The second interpretation is that the mother deceives her son because she loves him, but not only because she loves him: she deceives him so he'll be worthy of his name and his lineage, so in the final moment he will not falter and will confront death with the integrity of an Esterházy.

"So he'll have a beautiful death," I interrupted. "*Kalos thanatos*, the Greeks called it. That's what the mother wants for her son."

"Exactly," David said.

"The Greeks thought that was the best possible death," I said. "The death of a noble and pure young man who demonstrates his purity and nobility by dying for his ideals. Like Achilles in *The Iliad*. Or like Count Esterházy."

"Or like Manuel Mena," David suggested.

Only then did I realise that my friend had not begun to talk about the Kiš short story in order to stop me talking about Manuel Mena. I said:

"Assuming he was a noble and pure young man," I added

rapidly. "Incidentally: can you be noble and pure and at the same time fight for a mistaken cause?"

David reflected for a moment before answering; when he did I had the feeling that he'd spent a long time thinking about this, perhaps ever since he'd adapted my novel about the war for the cinema.

"You can," he answered. "And do you know why?"

"Why?"

"Because we are not omniscient. Because we don't know everything. It's been almost eighty years since the war, you and I are over forty, so for us it's dead easy to know that the cause Manuel Mena died for was unjust. But was it so easy for him to know, when he was just a kid, who didn't have the perspective of time and didn't know what would happen afterwards, and to top it all had barely even left his village? Incidentally, was the cause Achilles died for just or unjust? It seems totally unjust to me: didn't poor Helen have every right to take off with Paris and leave Menelaus, who was a bore as well as an old fogey . . . You think that's reason enough to wage war, especially one as brutal as the Trojan War? I'm serious: we don't judge Achilles by the justice or injustice of the cause he died for, but for the nobility of his actions, by the decency and bravery and generosity with which he behaved. Should we not do the same with Manuel Mena?"

"We're not ancient Greeks, David."

"Well, maybe we should be, in this as in so many things. Look, Manuel Mena was politically mistaken, there's no doubt about that; but morally . . . would you dare to say you're better than him? I wouldn't."

In order not to answer his question I posed another:

"And if he was neither noble nor pure?"

"Then I'd take back what I said," he replied, emphatically. "But first you have to prove to me that he was neither one thing nor the other. Because otherwise . . ."

At that point we were overtaken by two speeding cars, one right behind the other; their red taillights raced away ahead of us until the darkness of the highway closed over them, as if the night had devoured them. David swore at the two drivers and said something about his son Leo or about one of Leo's friends. Then he asked what we were talking about.

"About *kalos thanatos*," I said. "The beautiful death, which was the Greeks' ethical ideal and the guarantee of immortality. But it all stemmed from the Kiš short story."

"Of course," David said. "Of the two interpretations of the story, right? Why the mother deceived her son when she appeared on the balcony dressed in white. In the first interpretation, the mother acts solely out of love, so her son won't suffer; in the second she acts out of love but also honour, out of family pride, to ensure that her son would be worthy of the Esterházy name. Which one do you prefer?"

Looking at the almost opaque blackness extending beyond the area illuminated by the car's headlights, with the white centre line running like an intermittent flash to our left, I tried to concentrate on David's question, but for some reason I once again remembered the phrase that had occurred to me that afternoon in La Majada ("I write so I won't be written") and I thought that Esterházy's mother had decided Esterházy's fate, that it had not been the young Esterházy who had written his hero's fate but his mother who had written him, and then I wondered if the same thing hadn't happened to Manuel Mena, if it hadn't also been Manuel Mena's mother, in spite of the fact that according to family legend she hadn't wanted her son to go to war, who had driven him to go, even if secretly or unconsciously, if it hadn't been her who, in order that her son would be worthy of his lineage of patricians of the village, had written his fate as hero. I thought that and then said to myself again, as I had done while we were eating in La Majada (except that now I told myself with a sort of pride), that by writing I had freed myself of the fate of Esterházy and Manuel Mena, that I had become a writer so I would not be written by my mother, in order that my mother would not write my fate with the fate she considered the highest, which was the fate of Manuel Mena. Perhaps a little ashamed of what I'd just thought, or of the pride with which I'd thought it, I went back to concentrating on the Kiš short story and on David's question. Then something occurred to me.

"There's another possibility," I ventured.

"What possibility?" David asked.

"It's not the mother who deceives her son, at least not on purpose," I said. "It's the emperor who deceives the mother."

David took less than a second to absorb my speculation, which led me to believe he'd considered it already. He asked:

"Are you saying that the mother went to beg the emperor to pardon her son, that she humbled herself to persuade him to grant it and that, even though he granted it, in the end the emperor did not fulfil his promise to pardon him?"

"Exactly."

"That's not a possibility," David said. "If it were, the emperor wouldn't be the emperor, and the mother wouldn't be an Esterházy: a woman who humbles herself before no one. Not even the emperor. Not even to save her son."

David said this last bit with a conviction that allowed no reply. I did not attempt to offer one. There was silence, and only at that moment did I recognise the music that had been playing the whole time on the radio or on a CD: it was Bob Dylan, or a good imitator of Bob Dylan. I thought David had no more to say about the story of the Esterházys; I was wrong.

"I don't know about you, but if there's one thing I detest in a short story it's those judgmental, conclusive endings that clear everything up," he said. "Kiš's story seems like it has one of those but it doesn't, because in reality it doesn't clear anything up. I like it so much that I know it by heart. 'History is written by the victors,' it says, and then goes on: 'Legends are woven by the people. Writers fantasise. Only death is certain.'"

David went on talking, although I no longer remember what about, in any case not the Kiš story but something the Kiš story or maybe the ending of the Kiš story suggested to him, and those four sentences remained floating around in the car like a diaphanous enigma and, while I listened to my friend's voice mixed in with the music of Bob Dylan or the Bob Dylan imitator and with the monotonous noise of the car gliding along the nocturnal and uneven asphalt, I distracted myself by thinking that it was true that we writers fantasise and that death is certain, but that it was also true that, even if Manuel Mena were a victor of the war, people have told nothing but legends about him and nobody had written his story. Did that mean that Kiš was not right and that sometimes the victors don't have history either, even if they're the ones who write it? Did that mean that after all Manuel Mena was not a victor, even if he'd fought on the winning side?

I was still thinking about Kiš's sentences when we stopped for a coffee at a roadside restaurant, a little way past the Talavera de la Reina exit. There, unexpectedly (or at least I didn't expect it: I had no reason to expect it), David began to talk about his broken marriage and his ex-wife, or perhaps he'd been talking about it for a while and I hadn't noticed until then. The thing is when we got back in the car he was still talking about it. He did so for a long time, and I listened to him turned sideways in my seat, to face him, as if observing the grey stubble that covered his cheeks and his two hands on the steering wheel and his gaze fixed on the road allowed me to forget Manuel Mena and concentrate on what my friend was saying. It had been several years since he and his wife had separated, but I'd never heard him talk about their separation like this, with that real serenity, without pain or without the pain showing through in his words. At one point he said:

"Do you know what I miss?" He waited for me to ask him what it was. "Being in love," he said. "It sounds like the lyrics of a silly summer pop song, but the fucking truth is that everything is much better when you're in love."

At another point, after describing in detail the happy new life his ex-wife leads with the well-built, reluctant Hollywood star, a thoughtful silence began.

"I can't understand it, Javier," he said finally; and, with the vehemence of one denouncing an enormous injustice, he exclaimed: "Can you just tell me what the hell Viggo Mortensen's got that I haven't got?"

Turning a little bit to his right, he looked at me for a second with perfect solemnity; a second later we both burst out laughing.

"Congratulations, man," I told him, unable to stop laughing. "You're cured."

It was past eleven and the traffic was getting heavier and heavier. Beside the road the solid patches of dark open fields were scarce now, dissolved in the growing suburban glow of hotels, restaurants, service stations, and darkened industrial estates; a profuse yellow brilliance illuminated the sky in the distance, like the coals of a colossal fire: it was Madrid. For a while we went back to talking about Manuel Mena and the Shearer.

"You can be sure of one thing," David concluded as we drove into the city on the Extremadura road. "That man is going to take a whole lot of secrets to his grave."

❧ 8 ❧

Manuel Mena reported to his first posting as a second lieutenant on September 25, 1937, and until the day of his death, twelve months later, lived with a hallucinatory intensity, accumulating the type of extreme experiences through which, as some survivors of war maintain in public, so many essential things are learned, and through which, as all survivors of war secretly know, nothing is learned except that humans can become much worse than we who have never been to war can ever imagine. During that time Manuel Mena saw front-line combat over much of the geography of Spain, fought in the worst battles, endured the elements at temperatures of more than one hundred twenty degrees above and ten degrees below zero, survived nightmarish marches through rocky deserts and sheer mountain ranges, repelled surprise attacks, carried out sudden attacks, took or attempted to storm towns or cities emptied by fear, inhospitable heights, fortified lines, and inaccessible summits, was wounded by enemy fire on five occasions, and saw an indeterminable number of men die. It is very possible, however, that his life ended before he'd ever slept with a woman, unless he lost his virginity on a visit to some brothel near the front; some people claim that he was in love with a beautiful, well-read, delicate, elegant, and intelligent girl named María Ruiz, daughter of the village's biggest landowner, but there is no evidence that she reciprocated, nor any certainty that this was not just one more of the fictions that swirl around his legend.

The last year of Manuel Mena's life can be reconstructed with certain precision thanks to the help of a few documents; they're not infallible—no document is—but, handled with critical imagination, they offer a reliable way out of the fog of legend and into the clarity of history. The most important of them is undoubtedly the Diary of Operations of Manuel Mena's unit: the First Tabor of Ifni Riflemen, belonging to the Group of Ifni Rifle Companies. The group was native to and took its name from the tiny West African territory, located opposite the Canary Islands, which in 1934 had officially become a Spanish colony. It was a shock unit comprised of North African and Spanish troops—most of the soldiers were African; most of the officers were Spanish—which over the course of the war the rebel commanders sent to the toughest fronts in order to settle awkward situations; the result of this commitment was that by the end of the conflict the unit had a casualty rate well over 50 per cent: almost four thousand wounded and more than a thousand killed. It is possible that, after dozing for months in the non-epic drowsiness of the Extremadura front, Manuel Mena wanted to experience the profoundly terrifying idealism of war at an exhausting and exposed posting; if that was the case, reality would have more than satisfied those desires.

Manuel Mena joined the First Tabor of Ifni Riflemen just at the moment when the unit, after having fought without a rest for almost a year, had been taken out of active service on the outskirts of Zaragoza. The expression "without a rest" is not hyperbole: since the beginning of the previous autumn Manuel Mena's comrades-in-arms had taken part in the decisive combats in the battle for Madrid, had entered Brunete, fought in Villanueva de la Cañada and defended Las Rozas, had taken the peak of Cobertera, had prevented the Pindoque Bridge over the River Jarama from being blown up in a surprise attack, had lost three hundred men in two days at the head of the Toledo bridge—among them seven of its thirteen officers—had fought on the Albarracín front and contained the Republican offensive against Zaragoza fighting at Zuera, San Mateo de Gállego, and Fuentes de Ebro. So, when Manuel Mena took up his post as second lieutenant at the end of September, the unit was exhausted and decimated. Along with the complete Group of Ifni Riflemen, the First Tabor then belonged to Barrón's 13th Division, known as the "Black Hand" because their insignia contains a black image of a hand against a red background, with a motto written in Arabic letters that reads: "Who entered Brunete?" The following two months were for Manuel Mena a period of adaptation to his new officer's life, and for the First Tabor of Ifni Riflemen an interregnum between hostilities that their commanders took advantage of to rest, to reorganise the battalion, and to instruct the new Spanish and Moroccan recruits who arrived to cover the losses occasioned in almost twelve months of continuous combat. It is more than likely that Manuel Mena participated in the training of these raw soldiers. It is also likely that he himself was instructed in the handling of Hotchkiss machine guns—the light M1909 as well as the medium M1914, the two types of these weapons the Francoists relied on—because he was immediately assigned to the Tabor's machine-gun company. It is even possible that during those days he might have participated in some secondary or auxiliary action with his own unit or with another. What is certain is that at the beginning of December, the First Tabor was in Alcolea del Pinar, in the vicinity of Guadalajara, preparing with the 13th Division and with the best of the Francoist army for the definitive attack on Madrid, which had been resisting since November of the previous year. Nevertheless, the operation—devised by Franco after the conquest of the north of the country—was never carried out, and at the beginning of January Manuel Mena was transferred again to Aragón with his unit to take part in one of the bloodiest battles of the war: the Battle of Teruel.

Manuel Mena's first battle with the Ifni Riflemen took place there. The battle had started two weeks earlier, when an army of 80,000 Republican soldiers cut off that rebel capital, which almost since the beginning of the war had been surrounded by Republican lines on all sides except one, the Jiloca Valley, where the road and railway ran that connected the city with Zaragoza and the rest of Francoist territory. The closure of the Republican ring had been carried out the night of December 15, when Líster's 11th Division broke through the front in the foothills of the Muletón and cut off the Jiloca Valley and Teruel's communications with the Francoist rearguard by coming down from the heights of Celadas, taking the village of Concud and joining up in San Blas with the 64th Division, which came in from Rubiales. It was such a fast and efficient manoeuvre, designed by the Republican High Command with two main objectives: one of propaganda and the other strategic. Inferior in all facets to the Francoist army, the Republican army had gone from defeat to defeat since the beginning of the war, unable even to conquer a single provincial capital, and its High Command thought that taking the small and badly defended Teruel could raise the ravaged morale of its side and attract international attention to its cause, encouraging hope that, with help from outside, the Republic could still turn around a war that increasingly seemed lost. That was the propaganda objective. As for the strategic objective, it consisted precisely in preventing Franco from attacking Madrid with his elite forces, among them the Ifni Riflemen, and in preparing the ground at the same time so the Republican army could carry out its most ambitious plan, known as Plan P, based on launching an offensive against the Extremadura front that would reach the Portuguese border and cut the Francoist zone in two. Otherwise, the whole success of the operation depended on reality confirming a rule and a complementary hypothesis elaborated by the Republican High Command over the course of the struggle: the rule maintained that Franco was not going to concede the tiniest amount of territory without immediately trying to recover it, moving the battle to wherever the Republicans dug in; the hypothesis ventured that Franco would not accept the loss of a provincial capital without throwing his best troops into the battle in an attempt to retake it. Both the hypothesis and the rule turned out to be right and, even though until December 21 Franco wondered whether to proceed with his initial plans to move again against the capital of the Republic, as his advisors urged, in the end he decided to postpone the attack, and on December 29 he undertook, with the troops originally destined to attack Madrid, a direct counteroffensive to go to the aid of besieged Teruel.

Five days later, on January 3, Manuel Mena disembarked at the railway station of Cella, in the middle of the Jiloca Valley, almost twelve and a half miles from Teruel. The station, or rather the stopping place, was a rectangular stone building beside a single track, isolated from any sign of civilisation and surrounded by hills bristling with enemy trenches. Teruel had not yet fallen into Republican hands, but since December 21 ferocious combat had raged inside it, house to house and hand to hand, with grenades and bayonets, through a mountain of rubble in the middle of which some thousands of troops of Franco's 52nd Division resisted desperately, without water or medicine or provisions, commanded by Domingo Rey d'Harcourt and crouching in the ruins of the buildings of the Bank of Spain, the seminary and the civil government, which surrendered that very day, as did the Santa Clara convent and hospital. I don't know if Manuel Mena had ever seen snow before in his life, but during the days previous to his arrival a fierce blizzard had fallen over the region of Teruel and temperatures had fallen to unheard-of lows, covering the valley of Jiloca in white; it is very likely that the majority of the members of the First Tabor of Ifni Riflemen, who, like Manuel Mena, had to await the rest of the 13th Division on that white plain lost in the middle of nowhere, had never seen snow.

Manuel Mena spent the night from January 3 to 4 there, around the Cella station, sleeping on the ground and trying to protect himself from the cold. He was not well equipped to withstand it—neither his footwear nor his clothing were winter issue, and he could barely cover himself with his regulation blanket and cape—so when darkness fell he dug or ordered others to dig a hole in the snow; then he spread a blanket over the uncovered earth and wrapped up there with two or three comrades in the hope that the natural warmth of the men lying beside him, the protection of the garments he managed to pile on top of them, and the resistance of his youth would allow him

to get a few hours of sleep and wake up without symptoms of
frostbite. I don't know how he got through that night. Or the
next morning. But at dusk on the following day the 13th Division finished disembarking all its forces at the Cella stop and,
without losing a minute, set off for the village and the Altos de
Celadas.

Manuel Mena went with it. The men began to advance in
order to approach along a path buried in the snow that soon
began to undulate gently up the slope, between abandoned
houses and sheepfolds. There was a glacial cold, an icy wind
was blowing, and, above the military column crossing the
immaculate white of the landscape like a phantasmagorical
caravan, the sky was low and uniform, the colour of chalk. To
the right was General Sáenz de Buruaga's 150th Division, which
had already taken the heights between Cerro Gordo and the
Celadas road and, even farther to the right, Saguardía's 62nd
Division, which on the evening of New Year's Day dominated
the plain, including the village of Concud; as for the 13th Division, that of Manuel Mena, it was supposed to take Hill 1207,
a plateau called La Losilla, which almost since the beginning
of the war the Republicans had reinforced with a system of
staggered trenches, which had been decisive for the 150th
Division to be able to take Alto de Celadas, strategically key in
the conquest of Teruel. I do not know whether, as he marched
through the valley of Jiloca towards the Republican positions,
Manuel Mena knew the mission his unit had been assigned;
undoubtedly he knew the following day, when General Barrón
assembled his officers in the village of Celadas, three miles
from La Losilla, and set out the plan of operations. That night
they again slept outdoors in refuges dug into the snow and,
when he woke up, Manuel Mena could see the snow-covered

and deserted fields around him, and in a second of unsurpass-
able astonishment might have thought that the 13th Division
had abandoned them before dawn, him and the two or three
comrades he'd slept beside, or that he was still sleeping and was
dreaming that dizzyingly empty whiteness, until he realised
that during the night another storm had passed and nocturnal
snow was covering the soldiers and their equipment like a spotless sheet. Later he would also discover, now almost without
astonishment, before resuming the march, how the cold had
solidified into a brown block the milky coffee in his canteen
and how, as one of his comrades would recall a long time later,
one incautious young man had turned his own head into a ball
bristling with stalagmites of ice by trying to comb his hair
with melted snow.

That very afternoon the 13th Division's assault on La Losilla
began. It was a frontal attack, because the Francoist command
wanted to break the siege of Teruel at all costs and prevent the
city's fall, which seemed imminent, and in the urgency of the
moment forewent the indispensible preparation of an artillery
attack to soften up a very solid Republican line, defended by
well-armed men of the experienced 39th Republican Division
under the command of Major Alba Rebullida, who in recent
weeks had further reinforced their position with fortifications
and barbed wire and had dug trenches, and machine-gun and
mortar pits. The Francoist attacks started from Peirón, a hill
facing La Losilla, on the counterslope of which the 15th Division had camped. They were, I insist, impudent, almost suicidal
attacks. The first fell to the 4th and 5th Banderas of the Legion
and was stopped by the Republicans at El Pozuelo, the hollow
that separated the Francoist positions from the Republican ones
and which was left strewn with corpses, wounded men, and

frustrated attackers who hit the ground and sought cover in that riverbed with no cover, offering easy targets in their green uniforms against the white snow, until nightfall allowed them to return to the base they had started from.

That was where Manuel Mena was wounded in combat for the first time. The episode took place on January 8. On the 6th and 7th the 13th Division had launched five new attacks against La Losilla, which had been repelled with heavy losses; it was like banging their heads against a brick wall—the Republicans not only were well armed, well fortified, and well deployed, but also enjoyed commanding views over El Pozuelo, the only place where the assailants could attack them—but the Francoists kept at it and at first light on the 8th it was the turn of the First Tabor of Ifni Riflemen.

I don't know exactly how the attack went. Nobody knows: there is not a single written account of it remaining in existence or a single survivor able to tell what happened; so at this point I must be quiet, stop writing, cede the word to silence. Of course if I were a *literato* and this were a piece of fiction I could fantasise about what happened, I would be authorised to do so. If I were a *literato* I could for example imagine Manuel Mena hours before the attack, curled up in his nocturnal refuge dug into the snow, kept awake by the glacial cold and by the certainty he's about to risk his life. I could imagine his fear and I could imagine him fearless. I could imagine him praying in silence, thinking of his mother and his brothers and nephews and nieces, knowing that the moment of truth had arrived and gathering strength to measure up and not be daunted, not to disappoint anyone, perhaps most of all not to disappoint himself. I could imagine him standing up in the dark, sure that he won't get any more sleep now, peering over the crest of Peirón

and glimpsing or imagining across from him, in the halting
light of the dawn that seems to be beginning to break beyond
La Losilla, over the peaks to Cerro Gordo de Formiche, the
Republican trenches stretching away to his right, silent and
sleepless, to the Alto de Celadas and perhaps further down as
far as Teruel, at that hour still enveloped in shadows. I could
imagine him waking up his men, ordering them to fall in on
the counterslope of Peirón, trying to get his gut, gripped by the
imminence of combat, to tolerate some food, preparing his soldiers for the fight, giving news to his captain or his lieutenant
and receiving final instructions for the attack. I could imagine
him crossing the crest of Peirón and immediately advancing
bent over, through the fresh dawn snow, towards the hollow
of El Pozuelo leading his men, swallowing his fear, first at a
brisk walk and then running, until the Republicans' shots that
begin to pepper the snow force him to dive to the ground and
find a safe or theoretically safe place to set up their machine
guns and start to fire on the trenches opposite to protect the
advance of the first line, perhaps sheltering in a foxhole dug in
the previous few days or behind a wall of stones improvised by
the attackers repelled the night before and still usable. I could
imagine him furiously battering or ordering his men to batter
the Republican positions for hours with bursts of machine-gun
fire, trying to protect himself against enemy fire or advancing
along the hollow without managing it or trying to find a better
position for their weapons on the side that leads up to La Losilla,
less than ten feet from the enemy's barbed wire. And of course
I would be able to imagine the moment he gets wounded: I
know for certain that he was hit in the right arm—although
I don't know if the shot came from a rifle or a machine-gun
or a mortar—but I could imagine the shriek of pain and the

simultaneous instant of panic, the tearing burn in the sleeve of his uniform and the blazing red of blood on the white snow, just as I could imagine some subordinate tying an emergency tourniquet to stop the haemorrhage—but maybe it was he himself who tied it—and I could imagine him lying for hours in the sparkling snow, enduring the unfamiliar pain of the wound, waiting until dark to be evacuated from that hell while bursts of machine-gun fire and rifle shots and mortar shells poison the air of the battle, as well as heavy artillery, shouts and insults that come down from the trenches to the hollow and rise from the hollow to the trenches, the sobs of the mortally wounded begging for help like frightened children and the deafening silence from the corpses on the snow.

All this I could imagine. But I shall not imagine it or at least I'll pretend not to imagine it, because this is not fiction and I am no *literato*, so I must confine myself to the safety of facts. I do not regret this, not too much: after all, no matter how much I fantasise I'll never manage to imagine the most important thing, which always escapes. And here the most important— or what right now seems most important to me—would be to determine what kind of feeling Manuel Mena experienced that night, when he was finally withdrawn from the battlefield after his first real experience of combat and when he was admitted to the division's field hospital and found out that all the awfulness he'd been immersed in for the last twelve hours had been futile because not only did the umpteenth attack on La Losilla fail but the great Teruel offensive had been called off, the last Francoist stronghold there had just fallen into Republican hands.

❦ 9 ❦

At the beginning of 2015, exactly a year after I'd learned of the Shearer's death from my mother, and two or three since I'd started collecting information about Manuel Mena, a film producer called to say she was preparing a television series about Catalans born in other parts of Spain and to propose that one of the segments should be about me. As usual when I'm asked to appear on television I remembered for an instant what a friend of Umberto Eco's told him on one occasion ("Umberto, every time I don't see you on television you seem more intelligent"), so I said no; the next instant, however, I remembered my mother and Manuel Mena and the Shearer and I said yes. With one condition: that we would film in Ibahernando and with my mother.

The producer accepted, and for three days at the end of June 2015 we were filming in Ibahernando. By that time I knew Manuel Mena's story quite well, I'd spoken to lots of people who knew him or knew things about him, I'd explored archives and libraries, I'd travelled to the places where Manuel Mena had fought during the war—around Teruel, Lérida, the Bielsa Valley, and the sites of the Battle of the Ebro, near the municipality of Terra Alta—and I had been in contact with professional historians, with amateur historians, with local experts, with historical associations and aficionados of local history, with the locals themselves. In spite of all that, I still couldn't see Manuel Mena; I mean Manuel Mena was still for me what he'd always been: a blurry, distant, schematic figure, without humanity or moral complexity, as rigid, cold, and abstract as a statue. Apart from that, at the beginning of my investigations I'd had a few shocks. I remember, for example, my first exchange of e-mails with Francisco Cabrera, a retired Civil Guard officer who possessed in his house in Gandesa, the capital of Terra Alta, an archive of documents collected over twenty years of almost exclusive dedication to the history of the Battle of the Ebro, and who had published several stout studies on the subject. I got his e-mail address from a friend and collaborator of his whom I'd met by chance in a Barcelona library, and I succinctly told him what I was looking for. Cabrera responded immediately, as if he'd been waiting for my question or as if his only job was to respond to questions like mine. "I regret to disagree with what you've so far been able to discover about your great-uncle," he wrote. "According to my database, he died on January 8, 1938, in the Battle of Teruel, and not September 21, 1938, in the Battle of the Ebro. I hope you won't be angry with me because my documents do not confirm what you thought you knew until now about the death of your ancestor." After that, beneath his reply, he added a page from a history of the First Tabor of Ifni Riflemen where the armed clashes Manuel Mena's unit was involved in from January 3 to 27, 1938, in the vicinity of Teruel, were summarised, and where Manuel Mena figured among the fatally wounded casualties of the combats during those horrific days.

More than perplexing me, the news provoked an instant of

vertigo. Immediately, however, I reconsidered. It had not been a long time since I'd begun my investigations into Manuel Mena and, although it is possible that I already knew he'd fought in Teruel, or that I'd heard people talk about it, I didn't know what he'd done in that battle; what I had undoubtedly seen, conversely, was Manuel Mena's death certificate, which was in the archives of the Ibahernando parish church and which I'd already thought to photocopy on one of my visits to the village. I went to look for it and it didn't take me long to find it: the document was dated September 1938, in the middle of the Battle of the Ebro, and not January '38, in the middle of the Battle of Teruel. Relieved in theory, but still anxious to get to the bottom of the misunderstanding, I explained to Cabrera what the death certificate said; Cabrera replied in short order. "Hello again, Javier," he wrote, phlegmatically. "I can confirm what I told you about the date of death for Second Lieutenant Manuel Mena Martínez (8-1-1938), in Teruel and not at the Ebro." He added: "See attached."

I opened the file he'd sent me and examined it. It was a fragment of an inventory of the casualties suffered by the First Tabor of Ifni Riflemen during the entire war; it was divided into five vertical columns: as clarified in a horizontal strip that ran across the top of the document, the first column reading left to right gave the victim's job, the second his number and the third his name; in the fourth and fifth it was specified whether the victim had been killed or wounded, as well as the date on which he'd been killed or wounded. I read through the list of names from top to bottom, and almost at the end I found that of Manuel Mena: on the left was his rank of second lieutenant; on the right, that he'd died on January 8, 1938. It seemed irrefutable proof that Cabrera was right. Now it all turns out

EMPLEOS	NUMERO	N O M B R E S	Muertos			Heridos		
			Día	Mes	Año	Día	Mes	Año
		Un herido de tropa				13	8	37
		Dos heridos más				14	8	37
		Tres heridos tropa				19	8	37
Sargento	4172	Brahim Ben Lahssen				25	8	37
otro	3830	Aomar Ben Mohammed	25	8	37	25	8	37
otro	3798	Buselham Ben Hamed					8	37
otro	3834	Brahim Ben Mohammed				25	8	37
3926	3926	Abdeselam Ben Mohammed				25	8	37
		Dos muetos y 22 heridos tropa	25	8	37	25	8	37
		Un muerto y tres heridos tropa	26	8	37	26	8	37
Sargento	3827	Mohammed Ben Embark				27	8	37
		9 muertos y 17 heridos tropa	27	8	37	27	8	37
		16 heridos tropa				28	8	37
		Uno de tropa herido				5	9	37
Sargento	3134	Maati Ben Hamed				10	9	37
		Tres de tropa heridos				12	9	37
		Tres de tropa heridos				13	9	37
		Uno de tropa herido				15	9	37
Sargento	3331	Brahim Ben Lahssen	23	9	37			
		Uno de tropa herido				28	9	37
		Uno de tropa herido				5	10	37
		Un muerto y dos heridos tropa	13	10	37	13	10	37
		Un muerto y dos heridos tropa	14	10	37	14	10	37
		Un muerto y un herido	15	10	37	15	10	37
Sargento	3127	Said Ben Abdeselam				18	10	37
		Uno de tropa herido				20	10	37
		Uno de tropa herido				23	10	37
O. Moro		Sid Hamed Ben Kad-dur				27	10	37
		Un herido de tropa				10	11	37
		Uno de tropa herido				12	11	37
		Un muerto y un herido tropa	18	11	37	18	11	37
		Un muerto de tropa	25	11	37			
		Un herido de tropa				29	11	37
						30	11	37
Sargento	3132	Mohammd Ben Abdeselam				30	11	37
		Uno de tropa herido				4	12	37
		Uno de tropa herido				6	12	37
		Uno herido de tropa				8	12	37
		Uno de tropa herido				10	12	37
		Dos de tropa heridos				17	12	37
		Uno herido de tropa				19	12	37
		Uno de tropa herido				23	12	37
Sargento	3720	Mohammed Ben Mohammed				24	12	37
Sargento	3727	Uno de tropa herido				25	12	37
		Brahim Ben Lahssen				26	12	37
		Uno herido de tropa				1	1	38
		Dos heridos de tropa				2	1	38
Sargento	3128	Mohammed Ben Kad-dur				2	1	38
		Uno de tropa herido				4	1	38
Capitan		Don Nicolás Baliño Carballo				4	1	38
		Uno de tropa herido				5	1	38
Capitan		Don Rafael Barros Manzanares						
Alferez		Don Leoncio Dominguez Perez	5	1	38	5	1	38
Cabo		Emilio Iglesias Prieto						
Sargento	3138	Lassen Ben Mohammed	5	1	38	5	1	38
		2 muertos y 30 heridos de tropa	5	1	38	5	1	38
		Un muerto y ocho heridos	6	1	38	6	1	38
Sargento	3333	Abdeselam Ben Mohammed	7	1	38	7	1	38
Teniente		Don Angel Gonzalez Coret				7	1	38
		4 muertos y 27 heridos de tropa	7	1	38	7	1	38
Alferez		Don Manuel Mena Martinez	8	1	38	8	1	38
		Un muerto y 14 heridos de tropa	8	1	38	8	1	38
		Un herido de tropa				9	1	38
O. Moro		Si Hamed Ben El Meki				10	1	38
		Dos heridos de tropa				10	1	38
		Dos heridos de tropa				11	1	38
		Uno de tropa herido				12	1	38
O. Moro 2		Si Hamed Ben Mohamed				15	1	38
		Tres heridos de tropa				15	1	38
Sargento	3336	Aomar Ben Tahar				17	1	38
		Cinco Heridos de tropa				17	1	38

to be false? I wondered. Now it turns out that Manuel Mena didn't die at the Ebro but at Teruel? Is it possible that his death certificate is mistaken and everything my mother has always told me about his death and his body's arrival in the village had not happened when she said it did but almost a year earlier? Of course, it was perfectly possible that whoever had drawn up Manuel Mena's death certificate had made a mistake or a series of mistakes, not to mention that my mother's memory had confused the dates; but if both things were true and the place and date of Manuel Mena's death were false, what other parts of the story were false as well? Was the whole story perhaps false? I was still trying to recover from my astonishment when another message appeared in my inbox from Cabrera. In this one the former Civil Guard officer had pasted a page from the Operations Diary of the First Tabor of Ifni Riflemen, corresponding to the first days of 1938, where an official certified that Manuel Mena had been wounded in the vicinity of Teruel. "It is possible that he was wounded at first and died subsequently, as recorded in the inventory of dead and wounded," surmised Cabrera. Only then did I react: incredulous, thinking that the death certificate could not be mistaken and Manuel Mena's whole story couldn't be false, I insisted, I begged my correspondent to consult the 20th and 21st of September of the same year in the Operations Diary of the First Tabor of Ifni Riflemen. "Very well," he answered, with some impatience. "This case has the makings of a novel." He was mistaken: a few minutes later he replied, attaching another page of the Operations Diary where it said that Manuel Mena had fallen mortally wounded on September 20, 1938, fighting in the Battle of the Ebro on Hill 496, and had died soon afterwards. "The inventory of casualties was mistaken," concluded Cabrera, without hiding his disappointment. "Instead of listing your great-uncle among the wounded at Teruel, they listed him among the dead. And then they expect you to trust in documents. Anyway: case closed, as Inspector Gadget would say."

I loved that Cabrera quoted a cartoon character (for a moment I imagined him watching television surrounded by a din of grandchildren and thinking, say, about the attack by the Montserrat Regiment on Punta Targa, Hill 481, defended during the Battle of the Ebro by the 60th Republican Division and one battalion of the Third), but the case was not, of course, closed; actually, it was only just beginning to be opened, at least for me. And that it had begun to do so with a document containing a flagrant error inspired a total distrust of documents, a very vivid awareness of their fallibility and of how difficult it is to reconstruct the past with any precision. The distrust was justified: it was not just that, as I often established, historians' texts were riddled with inaccuracies and falsehoods; it was that the documents themselves were.

I'll give another example. A historian of the Napoleonic wars says that a historian who doesn't bother to visit battlefields is like a detective who doesn't bother to visit the crime scene; investigating Manuel Mena, I discovered that the simile is correct. The Operations Diary of the First Tabor of Ifni Riflemen is not the only document that gives evidence of Manuel Mena's being wounded at Teruel; there is also a medical report written in Trujillo by a major in the medical corps named Juan Moret. I found it in the Ávila Military Archive, some time after the frenetic exchange of e-mails with Cabrera I've just described, and in it one can read, among other things, that Manuel Mena was wounded on January 8, 1938, on Hill 1027 of the Teruel Front. The date is correct, but not the place. To discover this

Hospital Militar de TRUJILLO

Diagrama hoja clínica de heridos de guerra y lesionados a los que se les considera como tales.

ARMA O DEPENDENCIA	Número del nomenclátor patológico	MOTIVO DEL ALTA
Infanteria.		Curado.

Hospital Militar de Trujillo Clínica Oficiales Número 1

REGIMIENTO	Batallón	Compañía	CLASE
Tiradores de Ifni.	1º Tº Amet	Alférez.

Estuvo sucesivamente en Zaragoza y Logroño.

SALA	HERIDAS QUE PADECE	ENTRADO		SALIDO		Nomenclátor
		Día	Mes	Día	Mes	
Ofic.	H.a.f.	18	1	10	II	

Diagrama hoja clínica del herido de guerra DON MANUEL MENA MARTINEZ.

Hijo de Alejandro y de Carolina Entrado el 18 de Enero de 1938
natural de Ibahernando, provincia Salido el 10 de Febrero de 1938
de Cáceres, profesión Estancias causadas
, edad 18 años. Empezó a servir
el de de del
reemplazo de

Diagnóstico Herida por arma de fuego en brazo derecho.

(1) Pronóstico Leve, incluído en el artículo de la categoría
Lugar del hecho de armas Cota 1.037 (Puente de Teruel)
Fecha del hecho de armas 8 de Enero 1.938
Terminación o concepto de la salida Alta por curación.

(1) Nota de puño y letra del Jefe de la Clínica.

Día	Mes	Año	Curso de curación	Pronósticos sucesivos
			Curac: asentica.	
			EL JEFE DE LA CLINICA	
			Juan Moret	
			=Rubricado=	ALFO...6 J O 4 5A
			E S C O P I A	
			EL COMANDANTE MEDICO DIRECTOR	
				O.K.

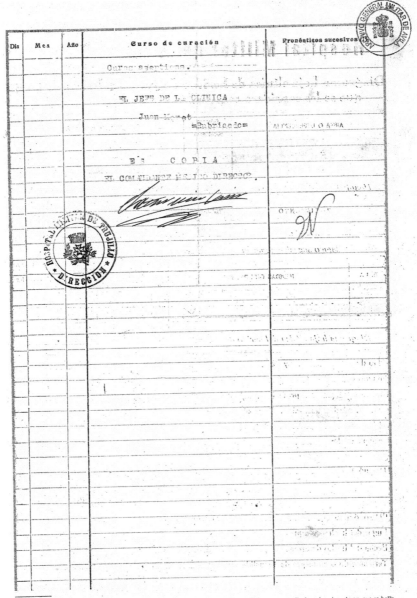

(1) Cuando se agrave un herido, el Jefe de la Clínica modificará el pronóstico, señalando el artículo y la categoría en que se halla comprendido por su agravación.

error I had to travel to Teruel and spend a weekend walking around and around the outskirts like a detective going over a crime scene. I did this in the company of Alfonso Casas Ologaray, a Teruel lawyer who knows every inch of the battlefields and who showed me on the ground that Manuel Mena could not have been wounded on January 8 on Hill 1027, as the medical report claimed; the reason is simple: Hill 1027 had fallen into Francoist hands days earlier, during the night of December 30 and early morning of December 31, due to the ineptness and haste with which forces of the 68th and 30th Republican Divisions relieved Líster's 11th Division, allowing Sagardía's 62nd Division to take that position with barely a hitch. In this way I understood that, actually, Manuel Mena was not shot on Hill 1027 but rather on 1207, better known as La Losilla, where on January 8 two heavy clashes had taken place, and the man who'd drawn up the report had accidentally switched the number of the place and instead of 1207 had written 1027: a tiny mistake, perfectly understandable and without apparent importance, except that it situated the battle in which Manuel Mena was wounded in an absurd place, several miles from where it really happened, which falsified that crucial point of his story.

Anecdotes like the one I've just detailed explain the wariness and suspicion that pestered me every time, over the years, between one book and the next, or at the same time I was writing other books, I took up again the pursuit of Manuel Mena's vanishing traces through the vanishing geography of the war, trying to step exactly where he'd stepped, to see exactly what he'd seen, to smell exactly what he'd smelled and feel exactly what he'd felt, collating with obsessive detail the information contained in books, documents, and memories relative to him or to his unit, as if in that personal story I could not trust anything

other than my personal experience. It's possible that this mania-
cal urge for veracity explains in part that, when the television
producer proposed filming a programme about me, I accepted
almost immediately, on the condition that we would film in
Ibahernando: for one thing, it had been more than a year since
I'd been back to the village; for another, I wanted to interview three people who had known Manuel Mena and speak to
another two who knew things about him and about Republican
and wartime Ibahernando. Now I think that something else
might have also influenced my decision. Three years earlier,
when David Trueba came to Ibahernando with me to film the
Shearer, my friend had unknowingly violated a self-imposed
prohibition, which had kept me from opening that private,
opaque, and shameful territory to anyone up till then, but the
violation had been confidential, had gone almost unnoticed,
and hadn't had any consequences, and it's possible that three
years later I was wondering whether a noisy gang of strangers armed with television cameras and prepared to broadcast
images of the village in every direction might not finish off the
prohibition once and for all, or would at least turn the prohibition into something else. Now I'm wondering if that's not what
happened.

They were slightly unreal days. The producer took a team
of six people there, all very young and led by the programme's
presenter, a versatile editor named Ernest Folch whom I'd
known for years; he was accompanied by a director of photography, a cameraman, a sound technician, a scriptwriter, and
a production manager. For its part, my team consisted of four
people: my wife, my mother, my son, and my nephew Néstor.
I was the one who asked them to come along. My wife comes
with me whenever she can; from the beginning I had the feel-

ing my mother would be indispensable: in our conversations before the trip, I had tried to explain to those responsible for the programme that, if they wanted to explain emigration from the rest of Spain to Catalonia by way of my biography, the secret protagonist of the programme should be my mother, because it was my mother who had deeply experienced emigration and who had become, because of it, I explained to them, a living variant of Lieutenant Drogo in *The Tartar Steppe,* settled into the perpetual waiting for an impossible return; those responsible for the programme understood this, or at least worked as if they'd understood it. As for my son and my nephew Néstor, they were both close to twenty years old, got along really well, had just finished their exams at university, and adored their grandmother: they both laughed at her barbarous postwar appetite and her granite-like Catholicism, both loved her idiosyncratic Spanish, the expressions she used, her incorrigible Extremadura accent, and, although neither of them knew who Manuel Mena was—which didn't prevent them from reminding me physically of him more with every day that passed, perhaps because they were both close to the age he was when he died—both called her Blanquita, which is what Manuel Mena called her, and both always left her with a raised finger and a warning: "Behave yourself, Blanquita!" All this turned them into the ideal white knights to look after my mother during those days, while my wife and I were busy with the filming and my investigations into Manuel Mena.

Both teams set up base in Trujillo: the producer's in a local hotel; mine in the Parador, a renovated former convent in the old quarter (we had decided for such a few days it wasn't worth opening up the Ibahernando house, which in any case is habitable only in the summer). As was expected, the presence of the six young strangers from the television crew exhilarated the village a little; the young people themselves seemed exhilarated: everything surprised them, everything intrigued them, everything fascinated them. As for me, ten days before embarking on that trip I had resolved to take a break from the novel I was writing to immerse myself in the sea of information about Manuel Mena that I had collected in recent years. The consequence of that immersion was that when I arrived in Ibahernando I was so steeped in Manuel Mena's story that during the filming of the programme I did not stop thinking about him for a single moment, nor did I stop putting myself in his shoes, sometimes identifying with him (and now I think the consequence of that consequence was the unreality of those days). I mean that, while the television crew was filming Ernest Folch and me walking along the white streets of the village through the residents' expectations, at times I must have been imagining myself to be Manuel Mena walking along those same streets almost eighty years before, with his bearing of an officer of the Regulars combined with his slightly lost air, pale, apart, and so young, trying to appear as cheerfully extroverted as ever but darkly swollen with violence and death, attempting to be faithful to the victorious, idealised, and romantic image a Francoist second lieutenant was obliged to project while he was struggling with an incipient and diffuse sensation of disenchantment, and I must have wondered, for example, if that adolescent who already knew or guessed that he didn't fit into his village before he went off to war wouldn't have been feeling an alienation multiplied by a thousand every time he came home from the front, as if he were returning from another world or rather as if he were returning to a world that was no longer his, and never could be. I mean that, while they were filming

Ernest Folch and me talking in the Field of Holm Oaks—a piece of land on the outskirts of town that still belonged to my mother—with the ruins of a sheepfold behind us and with the teams' cameras and microphones in front of us in the gleaming afternoon heat, I must have been wondering, for example, if during those fleeting returns to the village Manuel Mena would have felt better or worse than those around him: did he feel worse than the rest because he had killed people and had witnessed atrocious and degrading scenes and had participated or felt that he had participated in them, or that he hadn't prevented them? Or would he have felt better because he'd been able to risk the best he had for a cause he considered just, for something he considered superior to himself, and had more than done so, because he'd demonstrated that he was equal to the task and measured up and was not daunted, that he was capable of risking his life and of defending his ideals, his family, his fatherland, and his God? Or would he have felt at once worse and better than the rest? Would he have felt clean and bright on the outside and dark and filthy on the inside?

These were the sorts of questions I was undoubtedly asking myself, these were the sorts of things I must have been thinking. And it's odd: as far as I remember, over the course of the many hours of interrogation Ernest Folch submitted me to in Ibahernando I never once mentioned Manuel Mena, not even when we passed the street that bears his name; or perhaps it's not so odd: after all, the essential tends to be invisible, not because it's hidden, but because it's out in plain sight. Be that as it may, it was during those few days of filming that I thought I understood some things about Manuel Mena that up till then I hadn't understood. Two in particular. The first I have already insinuated, and it's that, from the end of his childhood or the beginning of his adolescence, Manuel Mena had suffered a growing alienation or estrangement from his village. At first the estrangement had been intellectual and had revealed to him, to a great extent under Don Eladio Viñuela's influence, that his real interests were far from those of the people of his village; later, during the year of his stay in Cáceres, the estrangement had been physical and had allowed him to glimpse a horizon beyond the minuscule horizon of his village, which had accentuated his intellectual alienation; finally, the estrangement had been moral, an estrangement provoked by the war that had revealed unknown aspects of himself and of the world and had carried him to a fleeting culmination of his previous estrangements.

That's the first thing I thought I understood during those days: that at the end of his life Manuel Mena was a stranger in his own village. The second thing I thought I understood is that, since war is an accelerated accumulator of experience, thanks to his time at war Manuel Mena had amassed in his nineteen years of life as much seniority as a normal man in fifty, and that perhaps on his last visits to the village, when he returned from the front on leave, his gaze was at once that of an old man and that of a youngster, that of a stranger and that of a local, and that gaze of his then must not have been very different from mine now. I will add that I have no doubt that only Manuel Mena or my obsession for Manuel Mena those days explains many of the answers I gave Ernest Folch before the cameras. At a certain moment, for example, Folch asked me what it had meant to me that when I was four my parents had transplanted me from Extremadura to Catalonia, and I'm sure I was thinking of Manuel Mena when I answered that it most likely meant that since I was a child I'd felt dislocated, a

guy who doesn't fit in Catalonia or in Extremadura, and that I
had always lived in both worlds with a feeling of strangeness,
feeling like an outsider in both places, as if each time I returned
from Catalonia to Extremadura or from Extremadura to Catalonia it was like returning from another world or rather as if I
was returning to a world that was no longer mine, and never
could be. At another point Folch asked me if I felt Extremeño
or Catalan, a question I'd been asked hundreds of times since
childhood, and I'm sure I was also thinking of Manuel Mena
when I heard myself answer as I had never answered before in
my life; what I answered was that for my whole life I had been
ashamed of coming from Ibahernando and that, although I left
Ibahernando as a little boy and had only occasionally returned
to Ibahernando and in Ibahernando I had always been an outsider and a native or a foreigner in my own village and I had
always fitted into Ibahernando as badly as I fit in anywhere
else, the truth is a person is from the place he had his first
kiss and where he saw his first western, and that I felt neither
Extremeño nor Catalan: I felt I was from Ibahernando.

The first two people I'd arranged to meet to talk about Manuel
Mena during that visit were my cousin Alejandro Cercas and a
friend of his named Manolo Amarilla. Alejandro was one of my
aunt Francisca Alonso and my uncle Juan's six children: the former had been a classmate of Manuel Mena's at Don Marcelino's
local school; the latter, first cousin to my father as well as my
mother, and perhaps due to this double kinship had kept up a
very close relationship with both of them. Alejandro and I had
not inherited it, in part because there is a thirteen-year age dif-

ference between us and in part because we lead very different lives. As with the majority of inhabitants of Ibahernando in the fifties and sixties, Alejandro had moved away from the village with his family; however, he had not moved to Catalonia, like me, but to Madrid, where since he was very young, in the last years of Francoism and the early years of democracy, he had distinguished himself as a socialist leader and held responsible positions in the party and in the Congress of Deputies, until in 1999 he was elected Spanish Representative to the European Parliament. He had held the post for several legislatures and, after having lived for more than a decade in Brussels, had just retired and moved back to live between Ibahernando and Cáceres, in the university of which he taught classes on the problems of European integration. In recent times we'd seen each other with some frequency, almost always in Brussels or in Ibahernando, and I had discovered without surprise that, although he'd moved to Madrid as a teenager, his relationship with the village remained intense and passionate, and that he knew many details about its history.

I remember the first time I asked him about Manuel Mena. It must have been shortly after I started collecting information about him, although I don't remember where, or even if it was in person or by telephone. However, I remember his reaction very well. "Whoa!" he exclaimed. "Are you sure you want to write about that?" "Who said I was going to write about Manuel Mena?" I rushed to answer. "Nobody," he said, and added with irony I might not have caught at the time, "It's just that I thought you writers only asked about things you're going to write about." Once the misunderstanding was cleared up, I wanted to know why writing about Manuel Mena seemed like such a bad idea. "I don't think it's a bad idea," he answered. "Maybe it's a really good one. I don't know. What I do know is that it's really complicated." "Why do you say that?" I asked. "What do you mean why?" he answered, switching in a second from irony to passion. "The war was horrible, Javi. Horrible. And in the villages even worse. You're left-wing, like me, and our family was on the right. If you dig into the story of Manuel Mena, you might find out things you don't like." "About him?" I asked. "About him or about whoever," he answered. "Then what do you do? Would you tell it?" "Of course," I said. "If I had to tell it, I'd tell it." "And your mother?" he asked. I didn't say anything. Alejandro took advantage of my silence to explain: "Look, Javi. I never wanted to know anything about my family; about my father's family especially, which is yours too, as you know, the ones who ruled the village. They seemed horrible to me. Now that I'm older, I think I understand them better, but—" "That's what I would need to try to do if I told the story of Manuel Mena," I interrupted. "What?" Alejandro asked. "To know," I said. "Not to judge," I added. "Understand," I clarified. And finally I concluded: "That's what we writers do."

That same day Alejandro confessed to me that his worst memory of his childhood was the silent wake of hatred, resentment, and violence the war had left behind; he also assured me that he had gone into politics to finish with that and so that nothing like it would ever happen again. Then he summed up what he'd heard about Manuel Mena (mostly from his father and his mother, who had known him), and from that day on we almost never saw each other or spoke without one way or another ending up at the war and Manuel Mena. Manolo Amarillo must have appeared very early in those conversations, because Alejandro always associated his friend with Manuel Mena, so he almost never talked about Manuel Mena without talking about Manolo Amarilla and without urging me to meet him. His name was very familiar. From Alejandro I learned that Amarilla had been born and raised in Ibahernando, that he was a long-time socialist activist like my cousin, that he had been a teacher at the school in Las Hurdes and in Cáceres, and that his wife, even though I didn't know her or didn't remember her, was my aunt, because she was the daughter of Andrés Mena, one of Manuel Mena's brothers. So it's not odd that after accepting the idea of filming the television programme in Ibahernando I called Alejandro and asked him if Manolo Amarilla would be in town and whether I could take advantage of my trip to see him. "Manolo's not going through the best moment of his life," Alejandro warned me. "He's just lost his wife. But I'm sure he'd love to see you and for us to have a chat. It'll distract him." It was only then that he told me that Manolo Amarilla kept a few mementos of Manuel Mena in his house, which he'd inherited from his father-in-law. "Among them," he specified, "a handwritten piece of text." I froze. "Why have you never told me this before?" I asked. "I don't know," he answered. "I didn't know it was that important. Didn't you tell me you weren't going to write about Manuel Mena?" Instead of replying to the question, I posed another: "And are you sure the text was written by him?" "Completely," he said. "I would say they're some notes for a speech to the Ibahernando Falangists. Or something like that." Alejandro talked about the text or what he remembered of the text. "Did you know that not a single paper written by Manuel Mena remains?" I asked again when he had finished. "Not a single letter. Not a single keepsake. Nothing.

They destroyed everything when he died. Everything except for one photograph." "Didn't I tell you?" Alejandro said. "You have to meet Manolo Amarilla." He gave me his friend's telephone number, I called him, we spoke a few times, and, when I'd agreed on the exact date with the television crew, I arranged to meet him and Alejandro in Ibahernando.

10

It took more than a month for Manuel Mena to completely recover from his first war wound. According to a report written in the Trujillo military hospital by Major Juan Moret of the medical corps, after suffering the impact of a Republican bullet in one arm on January 8, 1938, a few miles from Teruel, our man was attended to successively in the Zaragoza and Logroño hospitals before arriving at the Trujillo hospital, where he remained from January 18 until February 10, 1938, when he was discharged. I don't know what Manuel Mena's life was like during that parenthesis from the war, or what his state of mind was, although I'm sure that he received visits in the hospital from relatives and friends who would have come from Ibahernando to see how the hero's health was doing and spend some time with him; I'm also sure that, once his convalescence was over, he enjoyed some days on leave in the village, and that at some point he found out, perhaps with more melancholy than satisfaction, that Teruel had finally fallen into Francoist hands on February 22, a month and a half after he went into combat for the first time with the Ifni Riflemen to try to take it. Several trustworthy witnesses, among them Javier Cercas's mother, remember that the first few times Manuel Mena returned from the front on leave he did so accompanied by a North African orderly who followed him or tried to follow him everywhere— including on the walks he took with girlfriends at dusk along the Trujillo road—and that, in that village where nobody had seen an Arab for the last seven centuries, he caused almost as much dread as an extraterrestrial would have caused. This apprehension explains an incident that happened the first night the North African orderly spent in Ibahernando. Manuel Mena's family didn't really know how to treat him and, before they all went to bed, Manuel Mena's mother cautiously took her son aside and asked whether she should make up a bed for his companion in the hayloft or in the stable, beside the animals.

"How could you even think that, Mother?" Manuel Mena said, scandalised, according to what Blanca Mena remembers. "This man is just like me and will sleep where I sleep and eat where I eat."

José Cercas, father of Javier Cercas, also had a precise childhood reminiscence of Manuel Mena's furloughs during the war. According to him, Manuel Mena never spent a few days' rest in Ibahernando without coming to his house for lunch at least once, with him, with his two siblings, his mother, and his father, Paco Cercas, who was then the leader of the Falange in the village. José Cercas didn't remember them talking about the war during those meals, but he did remember that after lunch, Manuel Mena and his father would shut themselves up in his father's study and spend the afternoon talking and smoking while he and his sister Concha tried to catch snippets of their conversation through the closed door. Nobody remembers, however, Manuel Mena renewing during these fleeting stays in the village his disciple-friendship with Don Eladio Viñuela; it would have been an illusory memory, because by then Manuel Mena's mentor had been long since recruited by Franco's army and was working as a military medic in the village of Vitigudino, in the province of Salamanca. As for the rest, I don't know exactly how much time Manuel Mena spent in Ibahernando that winter once the wound in his arm had healed; but, however long he stayed, there is no doubt that by the beginning of March he was already back with his comrades of the First Tabor of Ifni Riflemen, which by then found itself in the rearguard in the vicinity of a village in the province of Teruel called Azaila, and that incorporated into the 13th Division, in turn incorporated into Yagüe's Moroccan Corps, they were preparing to take part in the great offensive against Aragon and Catalonia that Franco and his generals had designed for that spring.

The 13th Division did not set off until the 22nd, several weeks after Manuel Mena rejoined it. General Barrón's unit had been camped for some days in the village of Quinto, on the right bank of the Ebro, when he received the order to create a bridgehead to the other side of the river so the whole Corps of the Army could cross it. It was a manoeuvre as complicated as it was risky, especially at the beginning, because on the left bank awaited, solidly entrenched, the 26th Republican Division, Durruti's former column, and the divisionary leadership entrusted it to the 4th Bandera of the Legion, under the command of Major Iniesta Cano, and the First Tabor of the Ifni Riflemen, under the command of Major Villarroya.

The operation began at nine o'clock at night. If it hadn't been for the almost total darkness at that hour, Manuel Mena could have seen from the right bank how the bridge-builders laid out the pontoons and how the legionnaires rushed across them in silence, under a steady rain that wet their weapons and soaked their clothes. An hour and a quarter later the 4th Bandera had crossed the river without incident; after a few minutes' wait, during which all they could hear was the rain and the turmoil of the black, churning, fast-flowing waters of the Ebro, the First Tabor of the Ifni Riflemen began to do the same. The crossing concluded just after eleven, and on the left bank Manuel Mena's unit crouched in the dank silence of a reed bed while trying to regroup and reorganise themselves. Then they embarked on the advance with difficulty, splashing blindly through marshes criss-crossed with irrigation ditches, towards a place called Casa de Aznares (although on some maps it appeared as Casa de los Catalanes), until after a while, not far from where they were, a shot rang out. Then another. And another. And soon they were in the middle of a skirmish mixed with shouts, insults, and curses. Then they realised that the legionaries of the 4th Bandera had run into Líster's soldiers, but they received orders to stop and wait while the rifle shots blended in the darkness with mortar detonations and the rattle of machine guns. Although the clash intensified, they continued to wait, without joining it. After a while the silence gradually returned and they were ordered to try to sleep. They could not do so for more than a couple of hours, because before dawn Major Villarroya summoned his officers to inform them of the situation and to tell them that, since the 4th Bandera was effectively in front of them, blocked by the Republicans, they should make their way towards the right flank and try to overrun the enemy's positions there. At first light they launched the attack. The initial charges by the First Tabor of Ifni Riflemen were rebuffed, but after a while several Francoist planes appeared, which, after dropping a few bombs on their own positions, corrected their aim and began to bombard the Republican positions. When the planes left they were replaced by artillery fire from the other side of the river. Finally, two other Francoist units advanced south to surprise the enemy from behind, who before being surrounded abandoned their positions to the 4th Bandera.

The creation of that bridgehead on the left bank of the Ebro cost the lives of two hundred and sixty-five Francoists and two hundred and eighteen Republicans, but from that moment on and until they reached the gates of the city of Lérida, already in Catalonia, the 13th Division's advance was little more than a walkover. At the end of that first day of the offensive the Moroccan Army Corps had gone six miles deep into Republican territory while the opposing front crumbled, and on the following days its progression was meteoric: crossing the Monegros Desert with the First Tabor of Ifni Riflemen always in the vanguard—and with the 150th Division on their left and the 5th Navarra Division on their right—the 13th Division occupied Bujaraloz on March 25, Candasnos on the 26th, and Fraga and the banks of the River Cinca by the 27th; the following day the 5th Navarra Division took Mequinenza, and on the 29th Serós, Aytona, and Soses, where they linked up with the 13th Division, which on the 30th took Alcarrás. There everything got complicated. There, the Francoist vanguard began to be fired upon by enemy artillery, which slowed their progress, and when they arrived at a place called Partida de Butsenit, two and a half miles from Lérida, with the city and Gardeny Castle already in sight in the rusty light of dusk, they were attacked by Republican infantry and tanks, which forced their men to get down off the trucks, spread out, and create a front line all the way along the road to Collastret, towards Montagut and Serra Grossa.

The next day the Battle of Lérida began. Three days earlier its inhabitants had begun a massive exodus after being bombed by four squadrons of German Heinkel He 51s from the Sariñena aerodrome, and at that point the city was practically deserted; just the wreckage of demoralised Republican troops was left there, having been retreating in disorder for months, joined at the last moment at great speed by the 46th Division led by Valentín Gonzalez, El Campesino. He knew very well that, of the three key points to conquer Lérida, the fundamental one was Gardeny—the other two were Les Collades and Serra Grossa—a Templar castle at the end of a plateau that crowns the hill of the same name, which overlooks the city. Its strategic location explains why at the beginning of the war the Republicans had constructed on the slope, the peak, and the plateau of the hill a terraced system of dugouts, fortifications, barbed-wire fences, machine-gun nests, and evacuation routes that El Campesino now hastened to reinforce and arm with machine guns, mortars, tanks, and men, trusting in the hope of containing the Francoists there.

He did not manage it. During the night of the 30th the First Tabor of Ifni Riflemen camped on the Partida de Butsenit, and on the morning of the 31st began to advance in combat formation on Lérida following a path that zigzagged, between dry elevated strips of land, to the left of the road. They were at the head of the Second Regiment of the 2nd Brigade, with the First Regiment on their left and the 5th Navarra Division on their right, between the road and the bank of the Segre, and all day they managed to progress barely a half-mile to a mile, harassed unceasingly by Republican artillery firing from the other side of the river, and by the men of the 46th Division, who were putting up a fierce resistance. That night they slept out in the open, with the Republicans very near, and on April 1 they took the Creu del Batlle, a farmstead a hundred yards or so from

Gardeny that a few hours earlier had harboured El Campesino's headquarters. There, in the course of a nighttime meeting of officers including Manuel Mena, the command of the 13th Division decided that the next day, while the two Regiments of the 1st Brigade were attacking Les Collades, the 2nd Brigade would attack Gardeny: the Second Regiment would do so frontally, from the steepest and best-protected place, and the First Regiment would try to surround it from Camí de Gardeny, a more accessible zone to the north of the castle; they also decided that the First Tabor of Ifni Riflemen would fight in the vanguard of the Second Regiment, ahead of its other two battalions—the 262nd and the Victory Battalion.

It was another demented attack. From the early hours of the morning the artillery of the 13th Division pounded the Republican positions while these fired back with their heavy artillery at the Francoist positions, but the Ifni Riflemen did not emerge from their dugouts around Creu del Batlle until noon, when they launched their attack on Gardeny. What followed were six nightmarish hours. Manuel Mena placed his machine guns at the foot of the hill, trying to cover from there the ascent up the slope by his comrades, who attempted to take advantage of the pauses in enemy artillery, mortar, machine-gun, and rifle fire to gain a few yards crawling through burnt shrubs and seeking shelter in ditches and hollows opened in the red earth by the bombs, trying to scale inch by inch that clayey outcrop bristling with barbed wire and machine-gun nests where the toughest of the Republican defence was concentrated. Finally, towards three in the afternoon, the Republicans abandoned their trenches at the top of the hill for fear of being surrounded by the First Regiment, which had overtaken its left flank at Camí de Gardeny, and fell back towards the plateau and the castle, where they kept resisting, desperately supported by Russian tanks and sheltering behind a system of successive obstacles while the two Francoist regiments finished scaling the hill at the same time as invading the plateau, the cannons of the 13th Division crushed them, and a squadron of Heinkel He 51s strafed their positions with steep dives and low-level flights.

By mid-afternoon the castle had fallen, and Manuel Mena, still bewildered by the uproar, the blood, and the smoke of combat, contemplated from the ramparts undermined by the impact of the bombing, the city of Lérida at his feet, with the tower of the old cathedral on the left and the River Segre on the right. It was only a partial victory, so the calm lasted a very short time: two Republican battalions recently arrived from the Madrid front counterattacked around nine that night. They did so lighting the darkness with a flare and they did so with fury, while they sang at the top of their lungs the anthem of the 46th Division and tried to climb the hillside throwing hand grenades and firing automatic weapons. The counterattack failed in barely half an hour, and for the rest of the night all that was heard were occasional dispersed gunfights between the castle and the first houses on the outskirts of the city.

The conquest of Lérida was completed the following day. Towards noon, after several hours of heavy artillery preparation, the 13th Division rushed down on the city, the two regiments of the 1st Brigade surrounding it on the flanks and the two regiments of the 2nd assaulting it head-on. At that hour the machine guns of Manuel Mena's company were covering the regiment's descent from the Gardeny hill, with the First Tabor of Ifni Riflemen at the top, towards Academia and Alcalde Costa streets, where the city started and where its defenders had taken refuge around a gas station. Once the

Republican opposition was defeated at this point, the rest was easier. While Manuel Mena's machine-gun company escorted them, clearing the way and helping them to eliminate the sparse pockets of resistance, the soldiers of the First Tabor of Ifni Riflemen entered the ruined city down calle Alcalde Costa, taking every precaution to shield themselves from the desperate shots from terrified Republican snipers and soldiers clambering down from the old cathedral with the aim of getting themselves to the safety of the other side of the river before they were trapped in the city by the anticipated demolition of the highway bridge. Thus, advancing with maximum prudence, Manuel Mena crossed avenida de Catalunya and the Sant Joan Plaza and walked past City Hall and the military hospital and four churches that had been burned down at the outbreak of the war, and finally, having crossed the built-up area of the city from one side to the other, without firing a single shot he and the First Tabor of Ifni Riflemen took the final objective: the railway station, an intact neoclassical building with a big clock on its façade that at that moment read exactly three o'clock in the afternoon.

Lérida was practically theirs. After a couple of hours the 4th Bandera of the Legion and the Ifni-Sahara Tabor took control of the old cathedral and made prisoners of its garrison and, a short time later, two almost simultaneous blasts shook the city with a disastrous tremor: the Republicans had blown up the main bridge and the railway line to keep the Francoists from crossing the Segre and continuing their advance towards Barcelona. It was the end. Franco had just conquered his first capital of a Catalan province, and from that moment on the city and the River Segre marked the front line. As for the 13th Division, after having suffered more than a thousand casualties in the four previous days, they urgently needed a rest, and during the three and a half months that followed, until just before the most senseless battle of that senseless war began, all its units were sent to the reserves.

All except for a few chosen units, among them the First Tabor of Ifni Riflemen.

11

The meeting at Manolo Amarilla's house, to which my cousin
Alejandro and my wife also came, took place one afternoon
when Ernest Folch and the rest of the team were busy shooting
B-roll footage of Ibahernando and the surrounding countryside.
We had arranged to meet at five; at seven-thirty I had another
interview very nearby, in Ibahernando itself, with the only two
classmates of Manuel Mena's still alive: my aunt Francisca
Alonso, Alejandro's mother, and Doña María Arias, the village
schoolteacher.

I thought I would recognise Manolo Amarilla as soon as I
saw him, but I was mistaken. The man who opened the door
to my wife and me was about seventy years old; he was very
thin, with glasses, short grey hair, and slightly reddish skin,
and was wearing a checked shirt and worn blue jeans. After
a cheerless greeting (or with cheer so forced it almost didn't
strike me as cheerful), he led us through a well-tended patio to
a living room with walls decorated in the traditional style of
the village, with ceramic plates, antique bronzes, pictures, and
metalwork, some of which, as he explained in passing, were
his own work. Alejandro was waiting in the dining room, sitting at a brazier table drinking coffee. We sat down with him

and talked about generalities while my wife set up to film us and Manolo's daughter, a silent, smiling woman in her thirties named Eva, who worked as an economist in Madrid and who exchanged a few words with Alejandro and with her father, served us coffee. It was at that moment that I recognised him. I mean that was the moment when I remembered having seen Manolo Amarilla before, though I wouldn't have been able to specify the exact location or timeframe, and when I thought I hadn't recognised him when we came in, it was because it was as if he was hiding his face behind a mask; then I remembered what Alejandro had told me about his wife and I realised that the mask was not the mask of old age but of widowhood.

I immediately tried to centre the conversation on Manuel Mena. As soon as I mentioned his name, Manolo commented that, after the death of the second lieutenant, he had frequented his house with his wife or the woman who would later become his wife (who was also a niece of Manuel Mena's), and that one thing had always surprised him a great deal and that was that nobody ever spoke of him there.

"It doesn't surprise me," my wife said then. She had not yet started to record us but had the camera set up ready to do so. "If my son had died in a war at the age of nineteen, the last thing I would want to do is talk about it."

Her comment opened wide the doors of the conversation, and as soon as we began I sensed that Alejandro and Manolo had been talking about the years of the Republic and the war in the village all their lives, and I wondered whether, apart from their common socialist activism, it wasn't precisely this common interest that had knotted such a close friendship between the two. We spoke for quite a while about Ibahernando immediately before the Republic and then about Ibahernando during the Republic, about the turmoil of civic, cultural, and collaborative life at the time, about my great-grandfather Juan José Martínez and Don Juan Bernardo, and Don Eladio Viñuela and the community of Protestants, about the foundation of the Casa del Pueblo and about my grandfather Paco. In a comment on the unstoppable political and social radicalisation of the months leading up to the war, Alejandro said:

"I remember the first times I came back to the village as a socialist, in the second half of the seventies, when we socialists were just coming out of clandestinity." He was speaking with the contained vehemence he always reserved for these matters. "I was a kid obsessed with the war back then, and when I met any old socialists from the Republic I always said the same thing to them: what I don't understand is how you became enemies of people who objectively were not your enemies. That is, I'd say, the Republic had come to support you against those who were in charge, the large landowners, the oligarchy. But the Republic did not come to support you against the small landowners and tenant farmers; quite the contrary: the Republic had also come to protect them, and from the same people, besides. And I asked them: how is it that you didn't understand that your true enemies were, I don't know, the Duchess of Valencia, or the Duke of Arión, or the Marquis of Santa Marta, who lived in Madrid, and not the small landowners and tenant farmers of Ibahernando? How did you not understand that your class enemies were not those who were here, but those who were there, and that, instead of fighting against the ones here, what you should have been doing was allying yourselves with them to go and fight the ones from there?" He left the question hanging in the air and smiled with melancholy, as if laughing at himself in silence. "How innocent, no? How were people from here going to understand that, when half of them were illiterate and they had no horizon beyond the village, when the vast majority had never left here and only saw those from here and never those from there? That could maybe have been understood by the small landowners and tenant farmers, for them at least it might have been easier to understand it, especially if they made an effort to understand it and if they hadn't had the mentality of despotic and high-and-mighty young gentlemen; although, the truth is I'm not even very sure they could have . . . Anyway. The thing is that they didn't understand either, and instead of allying themselves with the poor almost as poor as them against the rich, they allied themselves with the rich against the poor who were even poorer than them. And they fucked up."

"This wasn't Madrid or Barcelona," Manolo chimed in with a slightly academic coldness, which contrasted with Alejandro's ardour. "In the village the confrontation wasn't between rich and poor, but between people who could eat and people who went hungry."

"That was the fundamental difference," Alejandro agreed. "But later there were others. There was also the difference between people of order, people who couldn't understand why someone would chop down trees and burn down olive groves and intimidate this person or another—"

"Yes," Manolo interrupted him emphatically, abandoning his detachment. "But don't forget that the people of order were arming themselves."

"I'm not forgetting it," Alejandro reassured him and, speaking only to him, added: "I've told you many times about my uncle Manuel." Now he turned to me. "My uncle Manuel, the person my mother was raised with, her second father, so to speak," he explained, before continuing: "One night he was on his way home, shortly before the war, and some men attacked him. Nothing happened: they pulled a knife on him, scared him. The next day my uncle went to the Civil Guard to report what had happened. And the captain said to him: 'I'm sorry. I can't protect you. Arm yourselves.' And that's what he did: they gave him a firearms permit and he bought himself a pistol."

"It's true that there were groups of agitators in the village," Manolo said; the mask was still there, stuck on his face, but, especially when he was speaking, his dulled eyes seemed to light up for moments and his almost-extinguished features became reanimated. "Youths who were no longer illiterate, who read at the Casa del Pueblo and who didn't back down before those who were in charge, who confronted them. And, of course, then the ones in charge didn't hire them, for being Republicans or leftists or for going to the Casa del Pueblo or for whatever reason. And the young men got even angrier and agitated more. And that's how the situation became so tense."

"That was the problem: that the village split down the middle, and coexistence became very difficult," Alejandro said. "Look, Javi: there's nothing that irritates me more than equidistant interpretations of the war, the 50 per cent ones, those that say that it was a tragedy and that both sides were right. It's a lie: what happened here was a coup d'état supported by the oligarchy and the Church against a democracy. Of course that democracy was nowhere near a perfect one, and in the end there were very few people who believed in it and respected its rules, but it was still a democracy; so the ones who were in the right politically were the Republicans. And that's it. But I also get very irritated by the sectarian or religious or childish interpretation of the war, according to which the Republic was an earthly paradise and all Republicans were angels who didn't kill anyone and all the Francoists were demons who never stopped killing; that's another lie . . . Look, I always understood very well that my paternal family, yours, was Francoist; at the end of the day they were the ones who gave the orders in the village; but for a long time I wondered why my grandfather Alejandro, my mother's father, a very poor man, a shepherd, a simple day labourer, had voluntarily enlisted in Franco's army and had left for Madrid with your grandfather Paco and with a few men from Ibahernando in the early days of the war. And now, after many years of asking myself that question, I understand that the answer is obvious: he was a man of order, he did not accept, could not understand, not bringing in the harvests or burning them, burning olive groves, invading estates, stealing animals, intimidating people. He thought it was wrong, it was simply intolerable to him. My grandfather Alejandro was a man who was traumatised by fear, disorder, and by the impossibility of coexisting in peace. Just like your grandfather Paco. Neither of them went to war out of political passion, because they wanted to change the world or bring about a national-syndicalist revolution; that's what you have to understand, Javi. They went to war because they felt it was their obligation, because they didn't see any other way out. And do you know what they got out of the war? Nothing. Others put on their boots, took everything, but not them. They didn't get anything out of it. Nothing at all. Your grandfather even had to leave the village to support his family, working bits of land here and there, from dawn till dusk, and my grandfather, you know, was a poor farmhand all his life. That's how it was, and in this village nobody will tell you any different because they'd be lying. But Manolo is completely right: Ibahernando is not

Barcelona or Madrid. Beyond the confrontations produced by the Republic's efforts to modernise the country and all those things the history books tell you, and they're true, what happens here before the war is something much more basic, like what happens in all the villages of Extremadura, Andalucía, and so many other places: it's a situation of extreme necessity that sets, as Manolo said, those who had nothing to eat against those who had something to eat, not much, barely enough, but they had something. And here is where it really does come to resemble a tragedy, because those who are going hungry are right to hate those who have enough to eat and those who have enough to eat are right to fear those who are going hungry. And each side reaches a terrifying conclusion: us or them. If they win, they'll kill us; if we win, we'll have to kill them. That is the impossible situation into which the responsible people of this country led these poor people.

Eva, Manolo's daughter, interrupted us at that moment to offer us another cup of coffee; we all declined, but we accepted the water she served us instead. She hadn't yet finished pouring when, impatient to continue, I brought up the murders committed in the village at the outbreak of the war. I mentioned the Shearer's father; they mentioned Sara García. By then I had already read and heard a lot about that murder, and I asked them if they knew why she was killed.

"She was engaged to a leader of the Socialist Youth, one of the men who left the village after the coup to join the Republicans in Badajoz," Alejandro said; then he swallowed saliva, but, to judge by the face he made, what he swallowed could well have been vinegar. "They say she was murdered to get back at him. They also say that a bastard she'd turned down was the one who did it . . . I don't know."

"She was very beautiful," Manolo said. "Have you ever seen a photo of her?"

Without waiting for my reply he stood up and came back a few minutes later with a handful of books and papers. Alejandro and I were talking about the village Falangists.

"Before the war there were none," Manolo joined in, sitting down again. "My father told me."

"His father was a military man," Alejandro told me.

"And an 'old shirt': his membership card of the Cáceres Falange was number seventeen," Manolo specified. "And he told me that he'd come to Ibahernando many times to try to convert people before the war. And nobody paid any attention to him. Here the right-wingers were for Gil Robles or Lerroux. They joined the Falange when the war broke out, as they did everywhere else. Look at this."

He showed me the war diary carried by his father-in-law, Manuel Mena's brother, during his time at the front—a not-very-thick notebook filled with neat handwriting—he spoke about the relationship between the two brothers, and then he told me what he knew of Manuel Mena. Finally he put in my hands two books that Manuel Mena had with him when he died on the Ebro front: the first was titled *Instruction and Tactical Use of Infantry Machine Guns* and was the work of several authors; the second was titled *Legislation of the National Government, 1936* and was by a certain José Pecharromán Colino. While I was leafing through the second, I discovered a pressed flower between its pages; holding it extremely carefully so it wouldn't disintegrate in my hands, I held it up to the camera.

"It's a daisy," my wife said, without stopping her filming. "It's probably eighty years old, isn't it?" Manolo didn't answer, and a dumbfounded silence took over the room while the four of us contemplated Manuel Mena's daisy. It was my wife who broke the spell. "Hey, Javi," she said in Catalan, "we should get going: it's almost seven-thirty and your aunt Francisca and Doña María are probably already waiting for us."

I asked Manolo about the handwritten text by Manuel Mena that Alejandro had told me about, and Manolo took out of the bundle of papers he'd just brought out four sheets of A5 paper written with a quill pen in slightly childish handwriting, which began: "Blue shirts of Ibahernando." Before reading on I asked him if I could photocopy them, and in reply he handed me a cardboard folder in the colours of the Republican flag.

"The photocopies are inside," he said. "I've also put in a photo of Sara; you'll see three women: Sara is the one on the right. And I put something else in there for you. Read it as well, and you'll see it's all even more complicated than you think."

Before we left, Manolo took us up to his study, a loft full of books and disorderly papers, illuminated by a big window that overlooked a brief expanse of chipped roofs. From somewhere he pulled out a pair of gaiters and suspenders of embossed leather.

"They were a gift for Manuel Mena," he said while I examined them. "From the family. They were made by a saddler in Trujillo. They had them ready for when he came back from the front, but he never came back."

"Didn't I tell you, Javi?" Alejandro said as we left his friend's house. "Manolo was happy with your visit. I haven't seen him that lively for a long time."

I didn't want to ask what Manolo was like when he wasn't lively, because we were soon arriving at Alejandro's mother's house, where the two elderly women who had gone to school with Manuel Mena were waiting for us. Alejandro promised he'd pass by the house in a couple of hours to say goodbye and left us alone with them. When he reappeared we were finishing our conversation. He walked us to the car while pumping us for what his mother and Doña María Arias had told us about Manuel Mena and the Republic and the war. When the three of us reached the car, Alejandro kissed my wife goodbye on each cheek.

"Shit," he said, almost relieved. "This talking about the war still turns my stomach." He stood pensively for a moment while my wife and I observed him, expecting him to go on. It was past nine-thirty at night, but the last rays of daylight still shone on the horizon; the swallows' cries tore into the silence of the streets like razor blades. Speaking only to my wife, he said: "Do you know why I went into politics, Mercè? Out of shame. I was ashamed that my family hadn't prevented what happened in this village."

"Could they have prevented it?" my wife asked.

"I don't know, but they were obliged to," Alejandro answered. "Or at least to have tried. They were the ones in charge, and those in charge are always responsible."

"Then this wasn't a tragedy either," my wife said, turning his own argument against him.

"I guess not," Alejandro admitted. "You're right. Whatever the case, I became a politician so this would never happen again."

Alejandro's phrase had the unmistakeable ring of truth, and at that moment I detested myself a little, because I knew that every time I'd heard him say it—and I had heard him say it many times—I'd thought that it was a politician's phrase, empty words for the gallery. I suddenly noticed Alejandro's appearance. He was wearing knee-length shorts, sandals covered in dirt, and a dark red T-shirt, which was also a bit dirty;

a beard speckled with grey seemed to want to devour a face tanned by the elements. For a moment, in the copper light of that extended twilight, it struck me that he looked like an old farm worker, and I wondered at what point in his life he had decided that his place was at the side of the poor and the losers of the war; I also wondered what Manuel Mena would have looked like if he'd reached his age.

"I'm not sure I agree with everything you said in Manolo's house," I confessed. "I have to think about it. But I am sure of one thing."

"What's that?" he asked.

"That in the war our family chose the wrong side," I said. "Not only because the Republic was right, but also because it was the only one that could have defended their interests. I'm not saying that in the circumstances it was easy to get it right, nor am I going to be frivolous and shameless enough to judge them now, eighty years after all that, with a present-day mind-set and comfort and when we already know the disaster that came afterwards." I remembered David Trueba and said: "They weren't omniscient. They didn't know everything. They couldn't have known. But they were wrong. Of that there is no doubt. They deceived themselves, or they were deceived: their side was the Republic."

"There's not the slightest doubt!" Alejandro exclaimed, opening his eyes very wide and visibly restraining himself so that, in the absolute quiet of the street, his exclamation wouldn't sound like a shout. "The proof is that our family didn't do any better after the war than before the war; on the contrary: they did worse. And over time much worse. Just like Ibahernando. Look." With a gesture that seemed to want to include the silence of the empty streets, the empty houses, the village crowded with ghosts, where the only living beings seemed to be the swallows that zigzagged in the twilight emitting whines of frightened or sick children. "Before the war all this was filled with people, there was life here, the village had a future, or could have had one. Now there's nothing. Francoism turned Ibahernando into a desert, swept the poor and the rich away from here, those who were able to eat and those who went hungry. All of them."

While Alejandro was talking I thought of my mother, who had always lived away from Ibahernando like a patrician in exile, thought of Eladio Cabrera, the caretaker of my mother's house, who lived in Ibahernando convinced that when he and his wife die, Ibahernando would be finished, and I thought that Alejandro had retired to Ibahernando so Ibahernando would not be finished; I also thought of my son and my nephew Néstor, who were more or less the same age Manuel Mena would always be, and I was glad that they were waiting for me and my wife with my mother in Trujillo. Then I thought: That's the saddest thing about Manuel Mena's fate. That, as well as dying for an unjust cause, he died fighting for interests that weren't even his. Not his and not his family's. I thought: That he died for nothing.

Alejandro and I said goodbye with a hug that he prolonged a second longer than normal, or I had that impression. When we stopped hugging he said as he turned to go:

"Write a good book, cousin."

My son and my nephew Néstor had been swimming and sunbathing in the Parador pool, and at suppertime had gone to pick up my mother at her sister Sacri's house in Trujillo, where the two of them had spent the afternoon talking. They told us this that night, while we had a light meal in the Parador restaurant and my mother made short work of a complete Extremadura menu, with a plate of *torrijas* for dessert. "Blanquita behaved herself very well," my son and nephew said. During supper we talked about something we had already talked about on the trip from Barcelona: the house in Ibahernando. My mother repeated that she didn't want to leave without having a look at the house and I answered that we'd go to see it the following morning, which was when we were planning to film there with the television crew. Then my mother said that one or another of my sisters had talked to her again about selling the house; it was something she said to me every once in a while, so that I would tell her again that, at least while she was alive, the house would not be sold. I repeated it.

"And when I die?" she asked.

We'll sell it, I thought, and then I thought, thinking of Alejandro and Eladio Cabrera and his wife: *Then the village will disappear.* My nephew Néstor came to my rescue: he said he didn't understand why we wanted that house where nobody could even live anymore; my son also tried to give me a hand.

"Grandma," he exclaimed, "not even Bill Gates keeps a house to use for two weeks a year."

My mother looked at him in astonishment.

"And who's he?" she asked.

Back in the room my mobile rang: it was Ernest Folch. Ernest explained that, for a number of reasons, they needed to postpone the morning shoot until the afternoon, and he asked me if the change would be inconvenient. I was busy the following afternoon with a meeting, but I answered that if he didn't hear from me, we'd see each other the next day in the afternoon in Ibahernando and, even though it was past eleven at night, I hurried to call my uncle Alejandro's house. He was the fifth person I wanted to talk to about Manuel Mena on that trip, and perhaps the most important, because he had lived his first years in my great-grandmother Carolina's house, as had my mother, and had shared his childhood and bedroom with Manuel Mena. I had already talked to him several times at length on the telephone; and on this occasion I spoke to his wife, my aunt Puri, who told me there was no problem in bringing the meeting that we'd scheduled for the afternoon at their house in Cáceres forward to noon.

That night I barely closed my eyes. On my investigations about Manuel Mena I usually took with me the translations of *The Iliad* and *The Odyssey* that I'd found in my mother's house on my trip to Ibahernando with David Trueba; I had already reread all of *The Iliad,* I'd made a start on *The Odyssey,* and that night I would have continued with it had I not, with my wife asleep beside me in the bed, begun studying the documents Manolo Amarilla had given me that afternoon. The first thing I read was Manuel Mena's handwritten text, which began: "Blue shirts of Ibahernando." It went on like this:

> I am going to speak to you with simple and moving phrases, if I can muster some, so you can see once again the significance of this movement and this organisation, which was founded on October 29, 1932, by the martyrs and liberators (as they must be called) Ruiz de Alda, Sánchez Mazas, and José Antonio Primo de Rivera.
>
> Days have passed, years, and our Spain, our Fatherland keeps going from bad to worse, not forgetting our Chief who taught:

Enslaved cannot be,
A people that knows how to die,

and took to the streets to save us all from the yoke that
oppresses us.

Since his good intentions could not be achieved by
any other means than revolution, this was the reason
our comrade José Antonio pronounced the following sentence: "Peace must come from war, but war must come
from the paths taken by good Spaniards."

Desirous as we all were to elevate Spain, to aggran-
dise her and serve her, the opportune moment arrived to
achieve it and this was July 18, 1936.

This is the hour to flaunt the blue shirt, this is the
hour to take off the mask and bare our chests to the
enemy, because the Falange does not want ambushes,
because the Falange does not want bon vivants: Falange
Española de la JONS wants "clean souls and repentant
hearts."

Let us not forget the words *Spaniards, the Fatherland*
is in danger, come to its defence, and in spite of missing
our Unique, Irreplaceable Prophet for a year now, the
Caudillo who wrote our doctrine with blood from his
own heart, we are not missing thousands and thousands
of new shirts to go to the battlefront, although hundreds
and hundreds of old, dirty shirts were called home. But
always singing "If they tell you I fell, I went to the post
I have up there."

After all this, we must not consent, nor can we consent, nor shall we consent, to the Falange being annihilated, because it is a healthy organisation, because it is

a pure organisation, and because it has known how, like no other, to help the Fatherland when it has needed it.

But keep in mind that for the Falange to progress it is necessary for you all to unite, because its programme recommends harmony between social classes. For José Antonio, "work in itself, like capital itself, has no worth; only work and capital in the service of the aim we want to achieve are worthwhile." Because, as he rightly said, "As the priest needs two hands to raise the divine form, two hands are needed to elevate society."

And now the only thing we need to ask of everyone is "that the blood spilled by our comrades on the various fronts serves as fertile material for the planting of our ideals" and "that spilled by our enemies as material corrosive to the rotten roots instilled in those hearts."

In this way and once and for all we shall make Men, we shall make history, and we shall make Spain One, Great and Free.

Arise Spain!!

At the end of the text there was a series of annotations or fragments of annotations; the longest (and the most interesting) read:

It is now time for the working and owning classes to unite, because, comrades: "Workers, businessmen, technicians, and organisers make up the entirety of production, and there is a capitalist system with expensive credit, with abusive privileges of shareholders and bond holders, without working, that takes the greater part of production and sinks and impoverishes employers, businessmen, and workers alike." José Antonio (May 19, 1935).

Here is another fragment: "[. . .] we must choose 'the best among the possible.'" And another: "We must work 'until we raise Spain to the stars, where those who taught us to die for our Nation, for Bread and for Justice, keep watch.' For Spain One, Great and Free." Here is the last one: "We fight alongside heroes as indeed they are: Aranda in Oviedo and Moscardó at the Alcázar de Toledo." At the bottom is Manuel Mena's signature.

I read those pages a couple of times. The first conclusion I reached is that my cousin Alejandro was right and that, rather than a letter from the front, it seemed like a speech or notes for a speech or a meeting addressed to the Falangists of Ibahernando. The second I deduced from the allusion to the death of José Antonio Primo de Rivera, which happened on November 20, 1936; Manuel Mena says it was a year ago, which means that the text was written and delivered (assuming it was actually delivered) in the autumn or winter of 1937, when doubts over José Antonio's execution in Alicante were dissipating in the Francoist zone and when Manuel Mena had acquired a certain authority in the village because he'd been at the front for a year and had just obtained the rank of second lieutenant and maybe joined the Ifni Riflemen, but also when he had not yet entered into combat with his unit and had not yet experienced the depths of war and when his political exaltation and bellicose idealism were still intact. The third conclusion was that that text was intended to infuse the village Falangists with spirit and attract new recruits to the party and new volunteers to the front, to encourage former Republicans and leftists to join the cause and preserve the purity and independence of

Camisas azules de Ibahernando:

Voy a dirigiros la palabra con frases sencillas y conmovedoras, si alcanzarlo pudiera, para que os deis cuenta una vez más de lo que significa éste movimiento y ésta organización que se fundó el 29 de Octubre de 1933 por los mártires y libertadores (que aún se les debe llamar) Ruiz de Alda, Sánchez Maza y José Antonio Primo de Rivera.

Habiendo pasado días, años y yendo nuestra ~~Patria~~ España, nuestra Patria de mal en peor, no olvidando nuestro lema que:

Esclavo no puede ser,

Pueblo que sabe morir.

se lanzó a la calle para salvarnos a todos del yugo que más oprimía.

Como sus buenas intenciones no podían alcanzarse de otra manera que con la revolución, ésta fué la causa de pronunciar nues-

tro camarada José Antonio la siguiente frase:

"La paz, ha de venir con la guerra,

Pero la guerra ha de ir.

Por las veredas que la lleven los buenos españoles"

Teníamos como estábamos todos de elevar a España, de engrandecerla y ennoblecerla; llegó un momento oportuno para lograrlo y éste fué el 18 de Julio de 1936.

Es la hora de estrenar la camisa azul, es la hora de quitarnos la careta y dar el pecho al enemigo, porque la falange no quiere emboscadas, porque la Falange no quiere vividores; F.E. de las J.O.N.S quiere "almas limpias y corazones arrepentidos."

No olvidándose las palabras de "Españoles, la Patria está en peligro, Acudid a defenderla." y a pesar de faltarnos El Único, El Insustituible, El profeta de hace un año, El Caudillo que escribió que con sangre de supio corazón nuestra doctrina, no faltaron"

Miles y miles de camisas nuevas,
para ir al frente de batalla; aunque
aunque cientos y cientos de camisas viejas, sucias y rojas,
tornaban a sus casas.

Pero siempre cantando "si
te dicen que caí, me fuí al puesto que tengo allí."

Después de todo ésto, no debemos consentir, ni podemos con
sentir, ni consentiremos que la Falange se aniquile, porque
es una organización sana, porque es una organización pura y
porque ha sabido, como ninguna otra, ayudar a la patria
cuando ésta lo ha necesitado.

Pero tengo presente que para que la Falange progrese es ne-
cesario que vosotros os unáis, porque su programa aconseja la armo-
nía entre las clases sociales. Para José Antonio "El trabajo en sí,

como el capital en sí, no tiene valor; solo vale el trabajo y el capital
en función el fin que se quiere conseguir, porque con razón decía"
Como dos manos necesita el sacerdote para alzar la forma di-
vina, dos manos necesitan para elevar la sociedad"

Y ahora lo único que debemos pedir todos es "Que la sangre derramada por nuestros camaradas en los distintos frentes, sirva de
substancia fértil para el semillero de los nuevos ideales" y "la vertida
por los enemigos de substancia corrosiva para las podridas raíces
que en esos corazones habían infundido"

De ésta manera y de una vez para siempre haremos Hombres, haremos Historia y Haremos a España;
Una
grande y
Libre.

¡¡Arriba España!!

no deben, ni saben, ni pueden darlas, debemos elegir
«Lo mejor entre lo posible »»»

Es hora ya que se una la clase obrera y patronal
porque camaradas:

«Los obreros, los empresarios, los técnicos, los organizadores, forman la trama total de la producción, y hay un sistema capitalista que con
el crédito caro, que con los privilegios abusivos
de accionistas y obligacionistas se lleva, sin trabajar, la mayor parte de la producción y
hunde y empobrece por igual a los pa-
tronos, a los empresarios, a los organizadores
y a los obreros »»»

José Antonio (12 mayo 1935)

Hay que trabajar
«««Hasta levantar a España a las estrellas, donde
vigilan los que nos enseñaron a morir por la
Patria, el Pan y la Justicia.

por
España Una, Grande y Libre

Luchando al lado de héroes como son:
"Un Aranda en Oviedo y
Un Moscardó en el Alcázar de Toledo"

the Falange: a few months earlier, in April 1937, Franco had dissolved or tried to dissolve the party by fusing it with Carlist traditionalism in the nationalist-Catholic slops of the single party, the Falange Española Tradicionalista y de las JONS, and in his text Manuel Mena seems to be appealing to the ideological foundations of the party of José Antonio to prevent that political alliance with the Carlists from deactivating its revolutionary potential. My fourth conclusion I gathered from the previous one, and it is the most relevant. In the text Manuel Mena appeared, in one part, like an adolescent infatuated with reading, keen to display his repertoire of historical-literary allusions selected from the patriotic vade mecum of the moment: two badly quoted lines from a very famous poem by Bernardo López García ("Ode to the Second of May"), a few words spoken or presumed to have been spoken by the mayor of Móstoles calling for a rebellion against the Napoleonic troops at the outbreak of the War of Independence, perhaps a verse from a biblical psalm (24:4), without doubt two lines from "Cara al sol," the Falangist anthem, and several lines selected from José Antonio's speeches. Furthermore, although he made the mistake of putting the foundation of the Falange a year early, in his writing Manuel Mena revealed himself as a pure devotee of José Antonio, not as a Francoist (in fact, the speech makes not a single mention of Franco), as a kid intoxicated by the pernicious idealism of the founder of the Falange and as a true believer in the harmony of classes preached by the revolutionaries of the far right and far left and in José Antonio's doctrine that consisted of uniting patriotism to extremism and social revolution in an impossible synthesis which nevertheless was the ideological concoction devised by the oligarchy to halt socialist and democratic equality. That was the fourth and final corollary I deduced from reading Manuel Mena's manuscript: that, read with care, those few words preserved thanks to Manolo Amarilla's passion for the past outlined a moral, political, and ideological portrait of the character that unexpectedly and partially brought him back to life.

The second document I studied that night was much longer than the first. It was a fifty-seven-page brief on court-martial no. 2,430, tried at the beginning of 1940 in Cáceres of a man from Ibahernando named Higinio A.V. As soon as I began to read it I was trembling. As deduced from the indictment, the story was the following:

On April 29, 1939, shortly after the end of the war, my grandfather Paco, who was then leader of the Ibahernando Falange, had sent a notification in his handwriting and bearing his signature to the military governor of Cáceres in which he declared succinctly that Agustín R.G., a neighbour imprisoned in the Trujillo concentration camp as a Republican prisoner of war, had confided to him that Higinio A.V. was the perpetrator of a murder in a village in the province of Córdoba during the war. My grandfather did not clarify that Higinio A.V. was also a neighbour from Ibahernando and that, like Agustín R.G., he was also in the Trujillo concentration camp as a prisoner of war. He only concluded: "This is as much as I can inform you in honour of the truth." Immediately following this in the brief is a declaration by Agustín R.G., dated a month later in Trujillo, in which he confirms his accusation and specifies: it was Higinio A.V. himself who had confessed the murder to him—the *paseo*, or "stroll," he called it, in the slang of the day—he'd committed it in Villanueva de la Serena, Badajoz, at some point in 1936 and in the presence of four other people, two of whom, he stated, were also incarcerated in the

Francisco Cercas Fernández (mayor) Jefe Local de
F.E.T. y de las J.O.N.S. de Villamesías

Tengo el honor de Informar á V. que
el vecino de esta Higinio Agudo Villar perte
neció en este pueblo á las Juventudes Comunis
tas siendo elemento muy rebolucionario, pen
denciero y siempre insultando á las personas
de orden y por referencias de Agustín R███
██ actualmente en el Campo de Concentra
ción de Trujillo sé que Higinio ████ ██
fué el autor de la muerte del padre políti
co de Salazar Alonso para el pueblo de los
Blazquez.
Es cuanto puedo Informar á V. en honor
á la verdad

Villamesías á 29-4-1939. Año de la Victoria
El Jefe Local
Francisco Cercas

Teniente de Investigación de Prisioneros
Gobierno Militar de
Cáceres

Trujillo camp. Next the two witnesses mentioned by Agustín R.G. endorsed his tale (only one of them added a detail: Higinio A.V.'s confession had occurred in the winter of '36, when he was on leave). Then came a series of declarations from various Ibahernando authorities—the judge, the municipal police, the Civil Guard—as well as the odd neighbour; in these was information on Higinio A.V.'s membership in the Communist Youth, his participation in "many abuses against people of order and properties that were committed" before the war, according to the brigade's report, and his escape to the Republican camp as soon as the war broke out; some repeated rumours of his participation in several murders, among them the one reported by Agustín R.G. All these reports are dated October 1939. In November—November 11—the accused made his declaration, in which he denied all the charges imputed to him, although he admits having been a member of the UGT, the socialist trade union, and having passed over "out of fear" to the Republican zone after the outbreak of the war. This was the last item in the examining magistrate's file. On December 4 the court-martial tribunal met for the first time in Cáceres; its first request was that Agustín R.G. and one of the two witnesses who had backed up his testimony in Trujillo confirm it in Cáceres. They both did so, eight days later: they once again accused Higinio A.V. of having committed the murder or, more precisely, of having claimed to have committed it. On January 27, 1940, the court-martial tribunal met for the second and final time and, after declarations from the prosecuting and defending counsel, sentenced the prisoner to death. The sentence was carried out: on June 8 of the same year, Higinio A.V. was shot by firing squad at dawn at a firing range on the outskirts of Cáceres.

Those are the events registered in the brief. I already said

I began to read them trembling, lying beside my wife in our room in the Parador; then, still with my heart in my mouth, I got out of bed and carried on reading standing up; finally I finished reading sitting at the desk, with a strange mixture of horror and relief. "So you can see that everything is even more complicated than you think," Manolo Amarilla had told me when he gave me a copy of the brief. At first, when I recognised my grandfather Paco's name on the first report, I thought Manolo was referring to him, and I remembered an article I'd written years before when I found out that during the war my grandfather had saved a socialist mayor from Ibahernando from being killed, and I said to myself in anguish that I was about to discover that in war the same man is capable of the best and the worst; when I finished reading the brief I understood that in this case, at least, I was mistaken. My grandfather had not reported a political crime but a common crime: the murder of a man, or rather the presumed murder of a man. In fact, he hadn't even reported a crime; he'd reported a report, that of Agustín R.G., he had recorded a request to investigate, which he would have been obliged to do from any point of view, beginning with the ethical one and ending with the judicial (he was not obliged, however, to register in the report his opinion of Higinio A.V., even if it was fair or even if he considered it fair: he was not obliged to say of Higinio A.V. that he was a "very revolutionary, troublesome element, who was always insulting people of order"): what my grandfather had done was an imperative of the penal code, as much that of the victors as that of the vanquished, as much that of Francoism as that of the Republic or of any democracy. Or, to put it another way, it's possible that my grandfather might have been unsure whether or not to deal with the report against Higinio A.V., out of fear of the consequences his action could have; but the fact is he was obliged to do it and that, if he hadn't done it, he would himself have been committing a crime: he would have become an accessory to murder.

Now, then, I wondered at this point, what about Agustín R.G.? Why had Agustín R.G. denounced Higinio A.V.? I didn't know anything about Higinio A.V., I'd never even heard his name mentioned, but I had read the name of Agustín R.G. in a multitude of documents conserved in the village archive and I often heard people talk about him, a man who according to the brief was then thirty-six years old (Higinio A.V. was twenty-seven) and who I knew had been an important socialist leader of the village during the Republic and had filled in for people at posts at the town hall and had acquired a universal reputation as a fair, honest, worthy, efficient, reasonable, and conciliatory politician. There was no doubt this man had known my grandfather Paco, or that when he presented his report he knew that he was the local head of the Falange, or that, perhaps out of fear for his family, he had managed to get my grandfather to go to see him in Trujillo to report what he knew and to get my grandfather to process the report; but why had he done that? Of course, Agustín R.G. was just as obliged as my grandfather was to report the murder or the presumed murder, but why had he not reported it to the Republican authorities at the time it happened, when he heard of it from Higinio A.V. himself? Why had it taken him almost two years to report it? Had it been out of fear of denouncing a very common practice at the beginning of the war in the Republican rearguard—though less so in the Francoist—the practice of the *paseo*, uncontrolled murders? Or had it been in order not to harm a comrade-in-arms? But, in that case, why denounce him now, when it was much more compromising for the accused? Did he do it because he could no longer bear that bloody secret on his conscience? Had he done it to earn the favour of the Francoist authorities? I knew that Agustín R.G. had returned safe and sound to Ibahernando around 1946, after years of forced labour, and that he had died of old age there: had he saved his own life with that report? Had he been looking for at least some reduction in his sentence or some sort of advantage at that moment of his fate, like that of so many other Republican prisoners of war, depending on the arbitrary cruelty of the victors? Perhaps he was seeking revenge against Higinio A.V. for personal or political differences (in theory Agustín R.G. and Higinio A.V., who in the brief admitted that he had belonged to the socialist union, shared political affiliations, but it was probable that Higinio A.V., nine years younger than Agustín R.G., belonged to the radicalised young socialists who joined up with the communists before the war: that would explain why, in the brief, several people said he was attached to the Communist Youth)? Or was Agustín R.G. pursuing all these things at once, or several of them? It struck me as impossible that Agustín R.G. would have invented the story of Higinio A.V., that he would have reaffirmed it on two occasions and that another two Republican prisoners would have confirmed its veracity, so I took it as true that Higinio A.V. had told them he had committed that crime; but had he committed it or had he just boasted about having committed it? The tribunal of Francoists who had rebelled against Republican legality who had tried Higinio A.V. had condemned him to death, with the criminal duplicity with which so many Republicans were condemned in those times, for the crime of "adhesion to the rebellion" and, although they had reinforced the reasons for the sentence with aggravating factors of "social danger and significance of events," the truth is that nobody took the trouble to investigate whether Higinio A. V. had actually committed the crime he was accused of. Had he really committed it?

For hours I mulled over these questions in our room at the Parador. Once in a while I'd go out onto the balcony to breathe the night air of Trujillo or to scrutinise through the window the light-speckled darkness or watch my wife sleeping in the bed. Once in a while I remembered what Manolo Amarilla had said about the complexity of things and what Alejandro had said about the impossible situations those in charge of the country had led its people into eighty years ago. Until at a certain moment I realised I could never answer those questions, that surely it was impossible to answer them, and that at least at this point in history, almost eighty years after the events, the questions were more eloquent than the answers. That was when I remembered the photograph of Sara. I took it out of the cardboard folder in the colours of the Republican flag that Manolo had given me and I looked at it. Actually, it was a photograph of three women, as Manolo had told me, a studio photograph; two of the women are standing and one is seated; I focused on the one on the right. I observed her with meticulous attention, almost with fierceness, from head to toe: I looked at her hair combed like that of a girl, her oval little girl's face, her eyes and her nose and her mouth, all those of a girl, her little girl's earrings and necklace, her unmistakable girl's dress—long and pleated and with a little girl's wide belt and buttons—her womanly fan clutched in her girl's left hand, her girl's long, white knee socks, her girl's shoes. I imagined her dead of a gunshot wound in a ditch. I felt like crying, but I thought of my mother and the Shearer, who could no longer cry, and I thought that I had no right to cry, and I contained myself. Or tried to. I looked out of the window. Dawn was breaking.

It is very likely that, once the Battle of Lérida was over, Manuel Mena enjoyed a leave of some days or weeks in Ibahernando; it's certain that by the beginning of June 1938 he found himself fighting again with the First Tabor of Ifni Riflemen, this time against the desperation of thousands of Republican soldiers who had been resisting Francoist attacks for three months in a stronghold lost in the highest reaches of the Pyrenees of Aragón, very close to the French border.

It was the so-called Bielsa pocket. As a result of the March Francoist offensive against Aragón and Catalonia, which had concluded in April in Lérida, the Republican 43rd Division had been isolated in the north of the province of Huesca. This was a flinty, basically communist unit commanded by Major Antonio Beltrán, alias El Esquinazau, The Slippery One, a local man who knew the area like the back of his hand and had conceived the stupid idea of holing up in the deep valleys and inaccessible peaks of the region of Bielsa until help from France would allow him to launch the decisive counterattack. But the help from France did not arrive, and during the month of March the 43rd Division was gradually withdrawing towards the east of Huesca, hounded by the Francoists of the 3rd Navarra Division, until on April 12 the circle closed on them entirely and El Esquinazau and his men became, for the propaganda of a Republic that privately was beginning to know it was defeated and was feeling an ever more urgent need for heroes, the protagonists of an unprecedented epic, a symbol of indomitable tenacity and resistance to the last against fascism. This explains why after six days the brave men were visited by the head of government, Juan Negrín, and the commander-in-chief of the Republican army, General Rojo, with the aim of raising their morale, giving them instructions and having press photographs taken of themselves with them; it also explains how, a month later, when they had been subjected to two months of daily torment from rebel artillery and occasional attacks from their infantry, Franco decided to finish them off, although it still took them another three weeks to transfer the elite forces that were needed to do so.

Among these was the First Tabor of Ifni Riflemen, Manuel Mena's unit. It had continued to be stationed in Lérida or on the outskirts of Lérida since the month of April, and one morning at the beginning of June its commanders received the order to leave behind the temporary tranquillity of the second line and head to Tremp, in the vicinity of the Pyrenees. There, over the following days, a special group was formed under the command of Lieutenant Colonel Lombana, composed of the best units of the Moroccan Army Corps and intended to extirpate the Republicans from Bielsa with the help of the 3rd Navarra Division, which had chased them up there but had proved unable to finish them off or expel them into France.

Mid-morning on June 6 the expedition left for Bielsa. It was a gruelling march. For two and a half days, several thousand men covered just over sixty miles of mountains on foot, along wheel ruts and impassable trails, struggling with the unseasonable spring cold of the Pyrenees, with over fifty pounds on each of their backs and a hundred mules carrying the machine guns, ammunition, medical equipment, and supplies and towing nine pieces of artillery of various calibres: two of 65, three of 105, two 155s, and two 105 mountain guns. So, after passing through Figols de Tremp, Puente de Montañana, Benabarre, Graus, and Castejón de Sos, they arrived at dusk on the 8th in the village of Sahún, in Benasque, one valley before Bielsa, surrounded by a crown of snow-capped peaks six thousand to ten thousand feet high. That night, after the soldiers had eaten, they loaded and readied their weapons and lay down to sleep for a few hours, while Lieutenant Colonel Lombana met with his officers in a house in the village. Manuel Mena attended the briefing. From what was said there that night he must have concluded that the following day's battle would be unequal, but not that it would be bloodless: the Francoists had gathered more than fourteen thousand combatants to face seven thousand less well-armed Republicans, lacking aircraft and running low on ammunition for their artillery; the only weapons the defenders could count on were the height of their morale, the strength of their discipline, their knowledge of the terrain and skill in taking advantage of it, as well as the defences they had erected during those months of siege in the natural heights that protected them. There is no doubt that Manuel Mena also heard, from Lombana, the plan of operations for the following day; it was simple: basically, it consisted of attacking the Puerto de Sahún, where the Republicans had established a solid defensive line occupied by one battalion of the 102nd Mixed Brigade, at the same time as the Moriones Group, part of the 3rd Navarra

Division, was attacking the Puerto de Barbaruens from their left, in the Sierra of Cotiella.

The battle broke out at dawn. At that moment the cannons of Lombana's Group began bombarding the enemy positions with the support of the Junkers Ju 52 and the Heinkel He 45s and the Heinkel He 51s of the Hispana Brigade, while the soldiers began to climb up to the Puerto de Sahún, with the First Tabor of Ifni Riflemen leading the way. At first, in the paltry light of dawn, they went up along a path across a gentle hillside planted with oaks, but after two or two and a half hours of walking uphill, with the sun now high in the sky, the path had turned into a stony mountain trail, the oaks into pines and the gentle hillside into an almost vertical slope and later into a rocky, snowy, and exposed meadow. It was here that they began to be shot at from the first machine-gun nests and when they had to face combat. This was prolonged for several hours without pause, during which they managed to have the Republican trenches within assault range several times and were driven back to their starting positions while calling for artillery and aircraft to intervene again to soften up the enemy's defences. Finally, early in the afternoon, the Republicans could endure that martyrdom no longer and the Francoists moved into their recently abandoned positions, taking only a few prisoners. A few oral and written testimonies of the end of that slaughter survive, so I don't need to resort to the fantasies of a *literato* to imagine what Manuel Mena saw: in some testimonies we can make out the last wisps of smoke dissolving in the crystalline air of the peak of Sahún and the weapons and supplies abandoned in panic by the breaks in the barbed wire; in another we spy extremely young corpses laid out on the dirty, churned-up snow; in another we glimpse the frozen sun of June in the immense cloudless sky. From all of them emanates the same certainty, and it is, just as much for the attackers as for the defenders, that the Republican defeat at that initial point of the Francoist charge predicted an immediate end for the Bielsa pocket.

The prediction was fulfilled. The following morning the First Tabor of Ifni Riflemen and Lombana's whole Group descended a snowy cliff into the Puerto de Sahún and marched towards the basin of the River Cinqueta, in the valley of Gistaín; there they joined the Moriones Group, which was arriving from the Puerto de Barbaruens, and for the next two days both detachments swept Republican soldiers from the heights of the valley and conquered, after violent clashes in which they suffered almost a hundred casualties, the villages of Plan, San Juan de Plan, and Gistaín. The two groups separated again on June 13: the Moriones headed up to the heights overlooking the village of Bielsa from the south, crossing the Sierra de Cubilfredo, to try to surprise the defenders on their flank, while Lombana's followed the course of the River Cinqueta towards the left side of the valley until, after several hours of marching past giant outcrops of bare rock during which they were continuously harassed by retreating Republican forces, they arrived at the Salinas crossroads, where the Cinqueta and the Cinca meet. They spent the night there, at the mouth of the Bielsa Valley, just over six miles from the village, and continued their advance through the following morning and afternoon, now beside the Cinca riverbed, always with the First Tabor of Ifni Riflemen in the lead, always taking maximum precautions in order not to be surprised by the soldiers of the 43rd Division who had stayed behind to cover their comrades' retreat. Towards dusk the advance parties got their first glimpse of the houses of Bielsa, and the troops received the order to halt and camp a couple of miles from the village, on the banks of the Cinca.

That night preparations were made as on the eve of a great battle. The battle, however, did not take place, or what took place could not exactly be called a battle. It is true that at dawn the Francoists fought for control of the bridges that led into the village tooth and nail with the Republicans of two battalions of the 130th Mixed Brigade and one from the 102nd, which had been left in charge of its defence; but it is also true that there it all ended: in view of the defenders' resistance, at twelve noon the Heinkel 45s and Heinkel 51s made their appearance in the sky over Bielsa and began to rain down on the village a deluge of bombs, which caused a colossal fire which illuminated the valley and the mountains that surround it all night long, while El Esquinazau gave the final order to retreat and the Republicans fled from the village of Parzán towards France, their way lit by the gigantic glow of the flames. I have evidence that the last Republican soldier crossed the French border at four in the morning on June 16, but I don't know how long Bielsa kept burning. I have evidence that Manuel Mena lost two comrades in those days, perhaps more or less close friends, two second lieutenants like himself—Centurión, one was named; the other, García de Vitoria—but I don't know whether they died during the conquest of the Puerto de Sahún, in the firefights in the valley of Gistaín or for Bielsa, or in any of the skirmishes the First Tabor of Ifni Riflemen were involved in; nor do I know whether he wept over their deaths, or if he was already so accustomed to death that he no longer cried. I know that Manuel Mena entered the village of Bielsa with the First Tabor of Ifni Riflemen, but I don't know exactly what he did. I also know that what he actually saw with his adolescent eyes, aged by famil- iarity with destruction and the nearness of death, was not the village of Bielsa but a cemetery of charred buildings in which not a sign of life remained. A stubborn legend maintains that for years after the fall of Bielsa a smell of burning lingered in the transparent air of the valley that not even the tremendous snowfalls of the postwar years could dissipate. I know, however, that it wasn't a legend, but a fact. Only that the smell wasn't a smell of burning. It was the smell of victory.

[13]

The next morning I got up at ten-thirty, my body ravaged by
lack of sleep and my mind clouded by the confusion that reading Manolo Amarilla's documents had produced. But I had
arranged to be at my aunt Puri and my uncle Alejandro's house
at twelve, so an hour later I left for Cáceres with my wife, my
mother, my son, and my nephew Néstor. Recently, ever since I
discovered the childhood relationship my uncle Alejandro had
had with Manuel Mena, I had spoken to him several times on
the telephone; he always told me more or less the same things,
as if his memories of Manuel Mena were fossilised or as if he
wasn't telling me what he remembered but what he had told
me on other occasions. In spite of that I was very interested in
talking to him, because I was cherishing the hope that a face-
to-face conversation and the comparison of his memories with
those of my mother would provide us with a surprise or two.

The hope was not unfounded. My aunt Puri and my uncle
Alejandro lived on the outskirts of Cáceres, on a street so new
it didn't register on the car's satnav, so it took us longer than
expected to find their house. When we finally found it, my son
and my nephew Néstor helped my mother out of the car and
then announced they were going to have a look around the city

until two, when they'd come back and pick us up to go back to Trujillo. They each gave their grandmother a kiss on each cheek and, while my son fixed her hair and clothes, ruffled by the trip, my nephew Néstor said:

"Behave yourself, Blanquita!"

It was my aunt who opened the door. She was a tiny, fragile, smiley little old lady, wearing a housedress and a pretty pair of silver earrings; behind her, expectant and almost solemn, my uncle waited. There were exclamations, greetings, kisses and hugs, and finally they showed us into a room furnished in the unmistakeable baroque style of Ibahernando dining rooms and inundated by the burning midday sun that poured in through a big window facing a vacant patch of ground, where some children were playing soccer on an expanse of yellow grass. We sat down on a sofa and three armchairs covered with throws, and my aunt served us coffee and water. Like my mother, my aunt and uncle displayed on their bodies the cracks and fissures of their more than eighty years; especially my uncle, a skinny, shrunken man in precarious health who spoke with a weak, raspy voice and looked anxiously out of eyes enclosed by deep circles. The three of them illustrated the inbreeding typical of the good families of the village: my mother was first cousin to both; my aunt and uncle second cousins to each other. They hadn't seen each other for years, and for a while I listened to them talk, until, ashamed of myself, I felt the same embarrassment I used to feel as a teenager in the presence of my family, the embarrassment that in the village they were or felt themselves to be patricians, but away from the village they were nothing: poor people with good manners, tiny untitled nobles trying to survive their exile with dignity; then I thought that in reality I wasn't ashamed of them but of myself, for having been ashamed of them.

Finally I reclaimed their attention with a few chimes of my teaspoon against my coffee cup. They fell silent, I reminded them that we had gathered to talk about Manuel Mena, I asked their permission for my wife to film our conversation, and from that moment on I tried to orchestrate a dialogue about Manuel Mena or about their memories of Manuel Mena. It was not difficult. For more than a couple of hours they talked, they interrupted each other and qualified and specified each other's statements, so I didn't have to do anything other than spur on their memory when it failed them, correct it when it misled them, or bring it back to Manuel Mena when he got lost in the labyrinth. Aware that he was the protagonist of the gathering, the one who spoke most was my uncle. He seemed to want to satisfy my curiosity, and for some time repeated things he'd already told me over the telephone, or that I'd heard him tell my mother, and he sketched a portrait of Manuel Mena as a calm, discreet boy without arrogance, without enemies, but also without friends. "Except for Don Eladio Viñuela," he clarified, and here he lingered to consider the doctor who had educated the village. My mother and my aunt joined him in his praises, and the three of them exchanged anecdotes about their time in Don Eladio and Doña Marina's academy. When they lost the thread I returned it to them. My aunt, who was not related to Manuel Mena at all and who, before we began to speak, had wanted to tell me that she hadn't known him, now timidly intervened; she said:

"I always heard your uncle was very good friends with the priest's brother."

"That's true," my uncle hurried to confirm. "They were good friends."

"I can believe it," my mother said. As always when she found herself with her cousins, her growing deafness seemed to diminish to irrelevancy, and she grew younger before our eyes; for a while she'd been fanning herself with a black lace fan, but she suddenly closed it energetically and pointed at me with it. "I've often told you about the priest's brother." I instantly remembered the story, or the legend. "Tomás, he was called. Tomás Álvarez. He and my uncle were the same age. He wasn't from our village."

"No," my uncle said. "He was from a village near Badajoz."

They all tried to remember the name of the village. My mother continued:

"Tomás spent long periods in Ibahernando, with his brother. That was when he and my uncle got to know each other. When the war broke out he came to live in the village, and my uncle Manolo tried to convince him to go with him to the front; perhaps the poor kid was scared. Anyway, whatever it was, he stayed behind. Then my uncle got killed and then Tomás did go off to the war. He said he was going to take his friend's place." She turned to my aunt and uncle and said with a mixture of irony and sadness: "The things boys do, you know . . ." She looked at me again and concluded: "The fact is, he was killed within a couple of months."

Suddenly remembering, I asked about María Ruiz.

"Who?" said my uncle.

"María Ruiz," my mother repeated, half-closing her eyes without conviction as she opened her fan again and waved some air against her face. "Uncle Manolo's special friend. That's what people said."

"Aunt Francisca Alonso and Doña María Arias told me that yesterday in the village," I said.

My aunt Puri shrugged.

"That's what they said," she agreed.

"I don't know anything about that," my uncle Alejandro said, with a sceptical air. "It's the first I've heard of it."

Then he explained, just as he had each time we'd spoken on the telephone, that he always remembered his uncle reading and studying. He still hadn't finished explaining when he was interrupted by a coughing fit. Concerned, my aunt poured him a glass of water and, as the convulsion subsided a little, her husband drank it down in three gulps while I remembered that as a young man he'd survived tuberculosis and that he'd been suffering from heart trouble for a while; I looked at his hands: they were covered in liver spots, and they were shaking a little. As he set the empty glass down on the table, my uncle asked what we had been talking about; his wife reminded him and I asked him if he remembered the titles of any of the books Manuel Mena read.

"No," my uncle said. "The only thing I remember is that in our bedroom we had the nine volumes of the *Encyclopaedia Espasa*. And he was always looking things up in it."

More or less at this point I began to ask them about the years of the Republic and the war and they began to tell me things that, with a few variations, I had heard my mother talk about. I asked my uncle if, when Manuel Mena returned to Ibahernando on leave, he talked about the war. He said no. "Never," he added. I asked all three of them if they remembered how many times Manuel Mena had returned from the front. They answered that they didn't remember, then, as if trying to compensate for his feeble memory, my uncle mentioned two things

I hadn't known: the first was that, when he died, Manuel Mena was about to be promoted to lieutenant for his commendable war record; the second is that he'd been wounded five times in combat.

"I've only found records of three," I said. "Once in Teruel and twice at the Ebro."

"Well, there were five," my uncle insisted. "It's possible he didn't request leave after one or two of them, but there were five."

"Are you sure?"

"Completely. His orderly told us when he came to the village after my uncle died."

"Did the orderly also tell you about his promotion?"

"I think so."

My mother started speaking at this point to thresh out her memories of the orderly, many of them borrowed from her grandmother or her aunts, all or almost all of them known to me. That day I realised, however, that Manuel Mena's orderly was not just a legendary character for my mother, but also for my aunt and uncle, who also held indelible memories of his stays in the village: my aunt, for example, said that, since he was a Muslim, he killed every animal he ate with his own hands; my uncle, that he refused to give letters to Manuel Mena's mother that had arrived for the second lieutenant: he had to hand them to him personally.

"But that was the first orderly," my uncle specified immediately after. "Later there was another. One who wasn't a Moroccan. A man from Segovia who was in the village after Uncle Manolo's death."

Uncle Alejandro said that the second orderly had been with Manuel Mena during the last moments of his life, had accompanied his corpse to Ibahernando, and had attended his funeral. We talked about Manuel Mena's funeral, of the arrival of Manuel Mena's body in the village, of the exact words Manuel Mena's mother spoke over his corpse and the exact words she had said to Manuel Mena the night before he left for the front. Then I asked the three of them to tell me how they had received the news of his death. To my surprise, neither my mother nor my aunt remembered anything; my uncle Alejandro, however, remembered it all.

"That day we were eating at my parents' house, on the square," he began, looking at me with his hands lying still on the throw that covered the sofa, his head leaning against the back. "There was me, my mother, my father, my aunt Felisa, and my uncle Andrés, who had just come back from the front. I don't think anyone else was there . . . No, nobody else. So anyway, when we finished eating, my aunt Felisa and I went together to Grandma Carolina's house, and when we got there we found it empty. We thought this was strange. Then someone, I don't know who, told us that everyone was at my uncle Juan's house." Without lifting his head up from the sofa back, he turned it towards my mother, and clarified: "At your father's house." He turned back to look at me: "And so we went there."

The house was packed with people, my uncle continued, but as soon as they went in they knew something terrible had happened, because the atmosphere inside was gloomy and everyone was trying to console his grandmother Carolina, whose face looked like death. He didn't remember who gave them the news, if someone actually did, or if anybody told them it had arrived by telegram. What he did remember is that, very nervously, he asked his aunt Felisa if he should go home and tell his parents and his uncle Andrés what had happened, and that his aunt said yes. And he remembered that he ran through the village as fast as his legs could carry him, and burst through the door of his house like a whirlwind with a breathless shout that made his parents and his uncle Andrés jump out of their chairs where they were still lingering after dinner:

"Uncle Manolo's been killed!"

More than narrate the scene, my uncle acted it out, suddenly sitting up straight on the sofa and imitating his childish shout from eighty years earlier while his sunken mouth opened wide and his hands came alive for a few seconds to mimic the dramatic quality of the moment; then, just as suddenly, he returned to his previous position and continued his story. The next day, my uncle remembered, a family expedition left for Zaragoza to collect Manuel Mena's corpse. And he also remembered something else: that just before the expedition left, a telegram arrived saying that Manuel Mena was only wounded. I had to compose an incredulous expression on my face before my uncle cleared up the mistake.

"It was an error," he said. "What happened was that the second telegram had been sent before the first, but had arrived later."

My uncle told us that the expedition to collect Manuel Mena's corpse returned accompanied by his second orderly, who stayed for a few days at his grandmother Carolina's house. This was the man who told them how Manuel Mena had died. My uncle reproduced his story in detail and, when he mentioned in passing that the bullet that killed Manuel Mena had hit him in the hip, I corrected him: I told him it had hit him in the abdomen.

"That's what the orderly said," my uncle agreed. "But it wasn't true."

"That's what it says on his death certificate," I explained.

"I can imagine," my uncle said. "But believe me: where the bullet hit him was the hip."

I asked him how he could be so sure and he told me the following story. Many years after Manuel Mena was buried in the old cemetery on the way into the village, a new cemetery was built a little beyond the lagoon, and they had to transfer the remains of the dead from one place to the other. The operation was simple, but laborious—they had to open the tombs, remove the remains, put them in sacks, take them to the other cemetery, and bury them there—and, when the time came to move those of his relatives, my uncle wanted to be present. So he discovered that what remained of his ancestors was placed in an iron-and-concrete sarcophagus; most of them were little more than dust, but some of Manuel Mena's bones were in very good shape, among them the hipbone, and he decided to take them home to study them. Or rather so that the husband of his daughter Carmen, who was a traumatologist, could study them, and after cleaning up and examining the remains, he came to the conclusion that the bullet that killed Manuel Mena entered from the side, perforated his hip, and lodged in his abdomen.

"That's how it was," my uncle pronounced. "Whatever the documents may say."

My wife's telephone had begun to ring before my uncle finished his anecdote and, while she answered it, my aunt went out of the dining room and my uncle and my mother started talking to each other. A little confused by the stampede, I thought that, no matter how much I'd discovered about Manuel Mena's story, not only was there much more that I didn't know than I knew, but there always would be, as if it was as difficult to trap the past as it was to trap water in your hands; I wondered if this wasn't what always happened or almost always, if the past is not deep down an elusive and inaccessible region, and I thought that was another good reason not to try to tell the true story of Manuel Mena.

My aunt came back into the dining room carrying a tray on which were a plate of potato chips, another of olives, and another of cubes of ham, and asked what we would like to drink. I looked at my watch: it was past two. When my wife finished her telephone call, she announced that my son and my nephew Néstor were waiting for us outside. I understood the interview was finished and tried to explain to my aunt and uncle that we had to go. It was impossible: it was no less impossible to convince my son and my nephew Néstor to come in and share my aunt and uncle's hospitality with us. Blocked between two intransigencies, we chose to make my son and Néstor wait in the car while we had a quick aperitif. My aunt was offering to refill our glasses when my wife's mobile rang again. It was my son and nephew again.

"This time we really do have to go," I said.

I stood up, my mother and my wife stood up as well, and I was still saying goodbye to my aunt when, suddenly sitting up again on the sofa, my uncle gripped my arm with an unexpected strength.

"Wait a moment, Javi," he begged me. "I have to tell you something about my uncle Manolo." My Uncle Alejandro's words put an immediate stop to our leaving, or perhaps it was the dramatic way he delivered them. "It's about the war," he said. "He said it, I've just remembered. I'm sure nobody else has told you this."

An abnormal silence fell over the dining room. My uncle Alejandro looked at me, his pupils dilated by curiosity, as if intrigued by his own memory; as he did so, two contradictory intuitions crossed my mind. The first was that my uncle was trying to bribe me, that his words were a ploy to keep us there with the bait of an insignificant or invented story, a decoy to alleviate a few more minutes of his solitude and prolong the pleasure of the conversation and the company. The second intuition was that my uncle had an enormous interest in my writing the story of Manuel Mena, perhaps because for him Manuel Mena was also Achilles, and because, in the way of humble people, he felt that stories exist only when someone writes them down. I don't know if the second intuition was mistaken; the first one undoubtedly was.

"You told me you never heard him talk about the war," I reminded him.

"And it's true," he said. He had just stood up with the help of my aunt and he was looking straight at me, his face inches from mine; suddenly he didn't seem so old, or so skinny, or so shrunken; his curiosity had turned into exaltation, and even his voice sounded more solid. "What I'm going to tell you is not something I heard him say, but it was he who said it. I was told this, and I'm sure it's true."

My uncle, in effect, hadn't been present at the scene. He didn't remember who told him; nor did he know when it happened, although from its contents we can deduce that it must have happened during one of the last furloughs Manuel Mena spent in the village. My uncle did know, however, that it had happened during a family lunch or dinner at his grandmother Carolina's house. Maybe it was a celebration, perhaps in an aside or small group that formed during the celebration. My uncle could not be more precise. According to the person who had told him the anecdote, what happened was that Manuel

Mena and his brother Antonio had got involved in an argument about some trivial matter, and the argument grew gradually more heated and changed topic even though it was ostensibly about the same subject, like in one of those classic family disputes when people seem to be talking about one thing when they're actually talking about something else; until at a certain moment Manuel Mena settled the controversy with the words that had just now surfaced in my uncle's astonished memory. Look, Antonio, said Manuel Mena (or my uncle Alejandro said that Manuel Mena said), this war is not what we believed at the beginning. Manuel Mena said the war wasn't going to be easy, that it was not going to be a matter of a little effort and a little sacrifice, were the exact words my uncle Alejandro used. He said it was going to be hard and it was going to be long. He said that many people were going to die. He said that many people had already died but many more still were going to die. And he said that he felt he had done his duty. He said he felt sure he had done his duty. To himself, to his family, to everyone. I've done my duty, Manuel Mena repeated. It's over, he said. I've had enough, he insisted. If it were up to me, I wouldn't go back to the front, he stressed. But he also said, in spite of everything, that he was going back. And do you know why? he asked his brother Antonio, squaring up to him, and the silence that must have met his question couldn't have been much different from the silence that met it now, almost eighty years later, in my uncle Alejandro's house, in my presence and in the presence of my mother, my aunt, and my wife. According to my uncle Alejandro, Manuel Mena answered his own question; what he said was: "Because if I don't go, the one who has to go is you."

"And he was right, Javi," my uncle Alejandro said. "According to their ages, the one who should have been at the front was not my uncle Manolo but my uncle Antonio, who was older than him. If he hadn't been called up it was because my grandmother already had two sons in the army, my uncle Manolo and my uncle Andrés, and by law she couldn't have more. But, if my uncle Manolo came home, the one who would have had to go to war was my uncle Antonio, even though he had a wife and children. That was the problem. You understand, don't you?"

The exaltation in my uncle's eyes had suddenly turned into anxiety or something resembling anxiety. I was as perplexed as I would have been if he'd just exhumed a chest full of gold that had been buried at sea for almost a century. For a second I looked away, towards the window: under the perpendicular June sun, the children had disappeared and now there was just the yellow expanse of grass in the vacant lot. When I looked back at my uncle I realised that what was in his eyes was not anxiety but joy.

"Are you saying that Manuel Mena was fed up with the war?"

"Exactly," my uncle answered. "Fed up." And he added: "If he could have, he would have come home. But he was trapped, and he couldn't."

All of a sudden I understood. What I understood was that Manuel Mena had not always been an idealistic young man, a provincial intellectual dazzled by the romantic and totalitarian sheen of the Falange, and that at some point in the war he had ceased to have the notion of war that young idealists have always had and had stopped thinking that it was the place where men find themselves and show their true worth. For a moment I said to myself that Manuel Mena had known not only the noble, beautiful, and ancient fiction of war as Velázquez painted it, but also the modern and horrifying reality that Goya painted, and I said to myself that the feverish condensation of his fleeting soldier's life had allowed him to travel in a handful of months from the exalted, utopian, and lethal impetus of his youth to the clear-eyed disenchantment of a premature maturity. I also understood that those words discovered by chance in the derelict memory of my uncle Alejandro did not refute the Manuel Mena I had imagined or reconstructed or invented over the years, but rather completed him: thinking of David Trueba, I understood that I'd just witnessed a small miracle; that resuscitated memory of Manuel Mena, along with the notes Manolo Amarilla had entrusted me with the day before and that I had deciphered in the middle of the night, were much better than any recording of Manuel Mena I might have found, much better than any home movie where I might have seen Manuel Mena moving and talking and smiling, I understood that those few words written by Manuel Mena and kept by Manolo Amarilla and that tiny piece of my uncle Alejandro's memory were a thousand times more valuable than a thousand animate images, they had a thousand times more evocative power, and only then did I feel that Manuel Mena was no longer a hazy, distant figure for me, as rigid, cold, and abstract as a statue, a mournful family legend reduced to a portrait confined to the dusty silence of a dusty loft of the deserted family home, the symbol of all the mistakes and responsibilities and guilt and shame and misery and death and defeats and frights and filth and tears and sacrifice and passion and dishonour of my ancestors, but had become a man of flesh and bone, a simple self-respecting *muchacho* disillusioned of his ideals and a soldier lost in someone else's war, who didn't know why he was fighting anymore. And then I saw him.

Outside, my son and my nephew Néstor were waiting for us.

"Did you behave yourself, Blanquita?" they asked my mother.

During the drive back to Trujillo I told them both the story of Manuel Mena.

This was the biggest battle in the history of Spain. For one hundred and fifteen days and nights in the summer and autumn of 1938, two hundred and fifty thousand men fought to the death the length and breadth of a barren, inhospitable, and wild terrain that extended along the right bank of the River Ebro on its course through southern Catalonia: a region called Terra Alta, a land of rocky hills, deep ravines, bare cliffs, villages of farm labourers and grain crops, vineyards, almonds, olives, and Aleppo pines and fruit trees, which that summer registered temperatures of almost sixty degrees Celsius in the sun and almost eighty years later has still not recovered from the furious firestorm that raged over this place. There, in several of the most decisive episodes of the struggle, Manuel Mena went back into combat.

It was a totally absurd battle; also totally unnecessary. At the beginning it didn't appear to be, or not completely, especially on the Republican side. As with the Teruel offensive, as with so many offensives of that war, the Ebro offensive had both a military and a propaganda objective for the Republic; in theory, the military objective was the most important, but in practice propaganda ended up taking priority. The military objective consisted of crossing the River Ebro, breaking through the front line, and then going as far south into Francoist territory as possible with the aim of reestablishing communications between Catalonia and the rest of Republican Spain, in the best of cases, and, in the worst, of alleviating the increasing pressure the rebel army was putting on Valencia (and therefore Madrid, since Valencia was the principal source of supplies for the capital). The propaganda objective consisted of a dramatic strike that would attract the world's interest to Spain and create the universal illusion that, in spite of Hitler's and Mussolini's massive support of Franco, in spite of the passivity of the Western democracies before that fascist onslaught, the magnitude of their own mistakes and of two years of defeats, the Republic could still win the war, or at least could carry on resisting; that was the final aim of Juan Negrín, the President of the Government, in unleashing the attack on the Ebro: to provoke a foreign intervention to force Franco to negotiate for peace or, failing that, to gain time until the forecast European war allied the cause of Spanish democracy to that of the Western democracies. The first aim was unreal, because Franco would not accept a victory that was not unconditional; the second was not quite as unreal, or at least it didn't always seem so in that summer when insatiable Nazi expansion was threatening to finish off Czechoslovakia and the shortsighted and fainthearted pacts of the European powers.

And so, on July 25, after meticulous weeks of preparation during which the Republic assembled its last great army of a hundred thousand men as well as the remains of their artillery, a great part of its air force, and numerous tanks, six Republican divisions under the command of Lieutenant Colonel Modesto crossed the Ebro at twelve different points. At that moment the First Tabor of Ifni Riflemen were camped not far from the river, in the olive groves on the slope of Montsià, between Ulldecona and Alcanar. Along with the entire 13th Division, they had been transferred from Lérida two weeks earlier due to rumours of activity on the other side of the Ebro, and since then had remained in the reserves of the 105th Division, which was guarding the front line around Amposta. By then, at the age of nineteen, Manuel Mena was already an old hand at war. He had a new orderly, of whom all we know is that he was from Segovia and that the Manuel Mena he knew was not very similar to the Manuel Mena they knew back in Ibahernando: according to what he himself would tell them weeks later in the village, that Manuel Mena was (or seemed to be) a humble, melancholic, solitary, withdrawn man, with no trace left of the enthusiasm of the early days of the war; in spite of that, the orderly also described him as one of those people who always took responsibility for what happened around them, an officer on whom his commanders and his soldiers always knew they could count, who was always in the front line, who never buckled. He had been wounded by enemy fire on more than one occasion and, in spite of not yet having been promoted to the rank of lieutenant, the day the Ebro offensive was triggered he commanded the machine-gun company of his Tabor, including six heavy machine guns, twelve regular machine guns, six mortars, and a staff composed of clerks and orderlies. Although the Republican attack had begun in the early hours of the morning, it was not until dawn that Manuel Mena's Tabor received news of the offensive, and it was not until eleven that two of their companies under the command of Captain Justo Nájera, among them that of Manuel Mena, left in trucks for the combat zone in Amposta, near the Mianés apex, where the almost four thousand men of the XIV International Brigade under the command of Major Marcel Sagnier had been stopped, after crossing the river, by the 105th Division and by an irrigation canal that ran six hundred and fifty feet from the riverbank, the existence of which the Republicans were unaware. The two companies of the First Tabor of Riflemen arrived there at around one o'clock in the afternoon, after leaving the trucks at mile 70 of the Valencia road, rushing to Mianés and crossing an open zone, battered as much by the Republicans trapped between the canal and the river as by those still lying in wait on the other side of the river and expecting to cross it, hidden among the trees and reed beds.

There began the real combat for the two companies of the First Tabor of Ifni Riflemen, once they managed to get themselves into a defensive position on the slope of the canal, on the enemy's north flank. Manuel Mena spread his company out behind the sloping side of the canal, and from that location his machine guns and mortars did not cease all afternoon, covering the Francoists' assaults and repelling the Republican counterattacks with the support of artillery and air force. A French volunteer from the Paris Commune Battalion of the International Brigade, who at that moment was on the other side of the canal, opposite Manuel Mena, described the skirmish in this way: "On the red sand, our overheated machine guns frequently jam, but our men in charge of the parts perform true wonders and their shots stop the enemy thirty feet away, forcing them to retreat. It is a violent and deadly combat we face in this small redoubt where we find ourselves entrenched. We all know it will be necessary to resist until nightfall; before that, we can expect no reinforcements. In front of us the enemy, at our backs the river; the situation is therefore quite clear and tragic." The description is very precise: in that bridgehead turned rat trap there were hand-to-hand combats and suicides of desperate soldiers and officers; apart from that, the Republicans did not manage to hold out until nightfall, reinforcements did not arrive and the Paris Commune Battalion was practically annihilated. At six in the evening, under a still-burning sun, a final Francoist assault with hand grenades meant the end of Republican resistance and sent hundreds of terrified International Brigade soldiers into the waters of the river, where many of them drowned. The Republicans left no fewer than a thousand corpses on the tiny river beach during the few hours of a thwarted landing. For its part, the six victorious Francoist battalions reckoned with 311 dead and 289 wounded. Among the wounded were Captain Nájera, who figures in the operational dispatch of that day as a distinguished officer; also commended as a distinguished officer in that day's dispatch was Manuel Mena, "for his daring and bravery."

Apart from a demented massacre, the International Brigade's attack on that section of the Ebro was also a failure, even if it was the only important failure of the great Republican offensive on its first day; besides, it was a diversionary manoeuvre, to a certain extent secondary: its real aim was to divert the Francoists' attention from the principal manoeuvre, which was taking place at the same time upstream and sought to take the capital of Terra Alta: Gandesa. Be that as it may, the offensive was so successful in its first days that it sparked euphoria among the downcast Republicans and led the President of the Republic, Manuel Azaña, to the illusory and ephemeral conviction that the unfortunate fate of the war had changed. In fact, during the initial twenty-four hours Modesto's men captured almost five hundred square miles of Francoist territory and, after taking Corbera d'Ebre, made it almost to the gates of Gandesa. Right at that point they were stopped by a Tabor of Ifni Riflemen, the Ifni-Sahara Tabor, and by the 6th Bandera of the Legion, both stationed on the Pico de la Muerte, on the Coll del Niño; but they were stopped with great difficulty, just short of a miracle, and the emergency situation of the Francoists necessitated that the 13th Division send that very day, without wasting any time, in support of those two elite units, two of the companies of the First Tabor of Ifni Riflemen who had just defeated the Republicans in the vicinity of Amposta. Neither of the two was the machine-gun company commanded by Manuel Mena, who was ordered to remain in the recently captured zone in order to secure it. For the Francoists, however, the situation continued to be very critical all along the front: they had to stop the triumphant Republican avalanche however they could and they needed their best troops at the key points of the enemy attack, so the following morning, once the situation in Amposta was completely under control, the two remaining companies of the First Tabor of Ifni Riflemen—among them Manuel Mena's—left for Gandesa.

They covered the distance by forced marches. In order to avoid the uncertainties of the front line they took a detour through Horta and then the Prat de Compte road with the aim of going down into Bot and from there entering Gandesa through the rearguard, but when they reached the outskirts of Bot they heard the clatter of machine-gun fire in the distance and approached to investigate. Before they went into the village by the valley of the River Canaleta, someone—a farmer, or maybe a Civil Guard—told them what was happening: a

Republican advance patrol from the Sierra of Pàndols had managed to infiltrate as far up as the Shrine of Sant Josep de Bot through the gullies of Font Blanca and the River Canaleta, and a few Francoist soldiers and Civil Guard officers were trying to frighten them off by firing at them from the village, only three hundred feet or so away from them; the same spontaneous local informant also conjectured that there couldn't be more than a couple of dozen poorly armed and undersupplied Republicans. At that moment, the episodic command of the two Rifle Companies fell to a lieutenant, and he and Manuel Mena could glimpse in the distance, on the summit of a slight hill against the backdrop of a circle of mountains speckled with vegetation, a building with white walls and brown roof tiles surrounded by cypresses: the occupied shrine. The two officers barely needed to deliberate before deciding that they were going to take it by storm immediately instead of continuing to Gandesa.

The decision turned out to be right. The Rifle Companies approached the sanctuary by following the trail of the valley, crossed the river, and spread out in combat formation: the machine guns and mortars of Manuel Mena's company joined the machine gun that had been firing for a while from the village, while the riflemen of the other company spilled out like a strange swarming stain rising up the hillside. A very widely circulated legend has it that the confrontation that then unfolded was epic, that it lasted for hours and resulted in numerous casualties; the reality, however, is that there was barely a confrontation, because the Rifle Companies vastly outstripped the Republicans in men and weaponry and because the Republicans fled as soon as they realised the Francoists were preparing to surround them; the reality is that there were just three deaths, all Republicans. This means that the skirmish held limited risk for Manuel Mena; it did not have real importance, but it did have symbolic importance: nobody could have known at the time, but that was the farthest point to which the Republicans would manage to penetrate during the entire Battle of the Ebro.

The episode at the shrine of Sant Josep de Bot was over by midday. Towards nightfall the two units of the First Tabor of Ifni Riflemen that had taken the sanctuary that morning arrived in Gandesa, joined the rest of the 13th Division, and, grouped with the 74th under the sole command of General Barrón, they enlisted in the defence of the capital of Terra Alta, entering the line north of the road from Gandesa to Pinell de Brai. During the days that followed the First Tabor of Ifni Riflemen fought day and night in the battles to defend Gandesa. On August 1, one week after the launch of the great offensive, the front began to quiet down and it now seemed clear to all that the Republicans would not enter the town; aware of their failure, as well as the fact that their men had lost the initial impetus and no longer benefited from the element of surprise, on the 2nd the Republican command's orders were to cease the attack, adopt defensive positions, and cede the initiative to the enemy. That was when, with the front stabilised, with the fields strewn with unburied corpses and the air saturated with the smell of rotting flesh, with the troops of both armies settled into a daily routine of ferocious attacks from dawn to dusk in delirious temperatures and ferocious nocturnal blind counterattacks, the battle changed tack; that was when it completely lost its precarious initial sense, especially for the Francoists. Nobody explained it better than Manuel Tagüeña, a twenty-five-year-old communist physicist who at that time was in command of the XV Republican Army Corps with the incredible rank of lieutenant colonel. Tagüeña reasons in his memoirs that, once across the Ebro and having taken an important strip of terrain on the opposite side of the river, the Republicans were tied hand and foot to their positions, and the most sensible and simple thing for the Francoists would have been to leave them there, corralled against the river, and launch an attack on Barcelona without letting up the pressure in order to prevent them from moving and getting help from their reserves. "The way for the occupation of Catalonia was free," concluded Tagüeña, "and the Army of the Ebro, if it didn't retreat quickly, would have ended up surrounded and captive." It did not happen like that. The reason is that Franco was the victim of an archaic, criminal, incompetent, obstinate, and pathological conception of the art of war, which his own generals and allies often couldn't understand: as had been proved earlier that year in Teruel, that conception obliged him to fight where the enemy proposed the fight and not to cede the slightest amount of terrain without immediately diverting forces to recover it; but most of all it obliged him never to settle for defeating his enemies: he needed to exterminate them. This explains why at that moment an exhausting battle of depletion began at the Ebro ("a clash of rams," as one of Franco's generals described it years later) on a piece of land with no strategic value and at an exorbitant price: to sacrifice whole divisions in vain, launching them over the following weeks, in a series of six nonsensical counteroffensives, against an enemy of inferior number and means but resolved to sell their skins at a very high price, much more able at defensive than offensive combat and fiercely entrenched in the most advantageous heights of the region.

The result can only be described as indescribable carnage. Perhaps we will never know the exact number of victims those apocalyptic weeks claimed. Many, beginning with the combatants themselves, have exaggerated the figures. It is not necessary to exaggerate; the truth is already exaggerated in and of itself. There were not, from the beginning to the end of the battle, fewer than one hundred and ten thousand casualties: sixty thousand Republicans and fifty thousand Francoists; there were no fewer than twenty-five thousand dead: fifteen thousand Republicans and ten thousand Francoists. Among those twenty-five thousand victims—a minuscule drop in an immense sea of dead men, many of them anonymous—was Manuel Mena.

On August 1, after a week of combat during which the men of the First Tabor of Ifni Riflemen did not know a minute of respite, Manuel Mena's unit was relieved from the front line of the Gandesa front; but after a couple of days of rest in the watchful comfort of the reserves they returned to the front. In the middle of the same month he participates with the whole 13th Division in the third Francoist counteroffensive by way of a demonstrative attack that would allow them to advance over Corbera d'Ebre while the 74th Division breaks through the front farther north, before Villa dels Arcs. The first days of September, during the fourth counteroffensive, are again frenetic. On September 3 they storm the positions defended by the Republican 27th Division in Usatorre and occupy Hills 349 and 355, the latter after four hours of artillery preparation. On the 4th they continue their advance to the north and east of Tossal de la Ponsa. On the 5th they repel several Republican counterattacks from Hill 360, with the 4th Navarra Division. On the 7th the resistance to their advance toughens, and on the 8th the Republicans finally manage to halt their offensive. That day (or the previous one) Manuel Mena is wounded. It is probable that this is his fourth time injured in combat, although, of all the wounds he received, so far we have the documentary evidence of only two of them; we barely know anything about this one: not where it came from, nor the exact circumstances of it, nor what kind of injury it was. We know only that the next day Manuel Mena is admitted to the Costa military hospital, in Zaragoza. We also know that his injury cannot be serious, because nine days later, at most, he finds himself back in the front line of battle, in charge of his company.

It is now September 18 and there are only forty-eight hours until Manuel Mena is wounded for the final time. That morning the 13th Division, which for almost a week has been bearing the burden of the fifth Francoist counteroffensive, receives the order to break the Republican front and take Hills 484, 426, and 496 to establish on them a line of defence. Barrón's men initiate the advance, but again and again they crash into a ferocious resistance, until the commander orders the First Tabor of Ifni Riflemen and the 4th Bandera of the Legion to look for a less exposed and more practicable way to penetrate Republican lines; after hours of reconnaissance, they find one in the Vimenoses or Bremoñosa Ravine. From there, struggling for every inch of terrain and dislodging the enemy from each trench with hand grenades and hand-to-hand combat, the next day they take Hills 426 and 460, and at dusk they arrive at the foot of Hill 496, known as the Cucut.

There death is waiting for Manuel Mena. It is a decisive position, a fundamental strategic point in a line of hills separated by the ravines of Valavert and Els Massos. That's why it has been bombed by artillery and aircaft since the previous day. And that's why it has been conscientiously fortified for weeks by the 12th Garibaldi Brigade, the unit of the 45th Division defending it (maybe alongside men of 14th Marseilles Brigade): using the abundant dry rocks on the ground, the International Brigades have constructed four successive lines of trenches among the Aleppo pines on the very pronounced slope, if they are expelled from one of them, they can retreat to the next and defend themselves from the next, and then the next and the next, up to the summit; also, to protect themselves from Francoist aircraft and artillery fire, they have excavated a series of shelters in the counterslope of the hill where they hide until the torment of the bombings ceases and they can return once more to the trenches and carry on fighting. All this explains why the Cucut is an almost impregnable hill, as the officers of the four companies of the First Tabor of Ifni Riflemen and 4th Bandera of the Legion who have been put in charge of taking it realise when they conscientiously study the terrain. Directing the operation is Iniesta Cano, natural leader of the two companies of Legionnaires; command of the two Rifle Companies is held by Captain Justo Nájera, and that of the machine-gunners company by Manuel Mena. Along with the rest of the officers of the units chosen, it is also these three who understand, after discussing the various options, that the only way to attack that hill is to storm it head-on in a direct assault.

There was no crueller battle in the Battle of the Ebro. Everything began at dawn. Towards 6:00 or 6:30 the longest and most destructive artillery preparation the Francoist command ever inflicted on any Republican position got under way, as Manuel Tagüeña wrote years later. The Legionnaires and the Rifle Companies had been chosen to carry out the mission because, apart from being accustomed to participating in extremely risky operations, they complemented each other, which explains why they often fought together. So towards 9:30, when Francoist aircraft and artillery had been pulverising the Republicans for an hour, after having adjusted their aim during the previous two, they set out. The Rifle Companies began to climb the escarpment, crawling carefully, staying low to the ground and making their way inch by inch between the smashed rocks and charred tree trunks, branches, and shrubs, through a very thick cloud of smoke and dust and deafening noise, while the International Brigade fired everything it had at them from above and the Legionnaires lay in wait behind them. The bombardment of the hill did not let up while they pressed up the slope, and on various occasions the Rifle Companies and Legionnaires were hit by friendly fire and had to request by radio that their gunners correct their aim. We don't know exactly when the first line of the Republican trenches was attacked, but without doubt it was carried out or at least initiated by the Legionnaires; it was their specialty: launching themselves head-on at enemy positions from about a hundred feet away to finish off any resistance expeditiously. By eleven-thirty they announced the conquest of the hill. It was, however, a premature announcement, because the fact is the combat lasted for another two and a half hours all over the slopes and summit of the Cucut, in the successive lines of trenches, with an end-of-the-world ferocity. It was not until 2:00 in the afternoon that they finally managed to dominate the whole hill, transformed by then into a smoking devastation of dust, ashes, and rubble where not a single tree was left standing.

But the battle had not reached its end; in reality, the worst was yet to come. The Riflemen and Legionnaires knew it, because the Republicans had rocked themselves to sleep in recent weeks with a watchword or motto they tried to apply rigorously—"Hill lost, hill retaken"—and they were sure this time would be no exception: after all, resigning themselves to defeat would be the equivalent of abandoning one of the dominant strongholds of the entire Battle of the Ebro. So, as soon as they took over the summit of the Cucut, the Riflemen and Legionnaires began to recycle at top speed anything left behind in the Republican trenches to defend themselves from the predictable enemy counterattack, raising improvised parapets on the counterslope of the hill out of stones and branches and anything they could find within reach. Reality fully confirmed their fears. The Republican counterattack began at dusk; it came from Hill 450, where the Republicans had sought shelter after their provisional defeat. From there they began to scale the back slope of the Cucut screaming, firing automatic weapons, and throwing grenades, covered by mortar shells and artillery fire, in a violent apotheosis of rage and desperation which the Francoists repelled with a violent apotheosis of rage and desperation. Uncountable numbers of men on both sides were killed or wounded. Many of them belonged to the two companies of Ifni Riflemen. A hand grenade split open Captain Nájera's abdomen. Another comrade of Manuel Mena's, Second Lieutenant Carlos Aymat, was also gravely wounded. Finally Manuel Mena himself fell, victim of a bullet that penetrated his hip, perforated the bone, and lodged in his abdomen.

What happened after that is confusing and our knowledge of it imperfect, because memories are even less reliable than documents and what we know of Manuel Mena's final hours depends, much more than on documents, on Manuel Mena's orderly's memory (or, more precisely, on the memory that Manuel Mena's orderly bequeathed to Manuel Mena's mother and siblings and that Manuel Mena's mother and siblings bequeathed to Manuel Mena's nieces and nephews and that Manuel Mena's nieces and nephews have bequeathed to us, so many decades after the events occurred). I will not ask what Manuel Mena's reaction was when he noticed a bullet had hit him. Nor will I ask if, thanks to his multiple experiences of being wounded by enemy fire in battle, he understands immediately that this wound is fatal, or if it takes him a while to understand this, or if he does not understand it at all, at least while he lies wounded on Cucut. Nor, of course, will I ask if he feels panic, if he swears, if he tries to measure up and be equal to the task and bear in silence the unbearable pain of his wound or if, aware of the seriousness, he collapses and groans and calls for his mother between tears and screams of anguish. Nor will I wonder how long he was lying there, on the charred top of the hill, bleeding and writhing, painfully aware of reality while the thunder of battle intensifies around him. I will not ask these things because I cannot answer them, because I am not a *literato* and I am not authorised to fantasise, because I must confine myself to the facts that are certain, even if the story we can gather from them is blurry and insufficient. This one is. But it is also true. Be that as it may, I can go no further: at most I can venture a timid conjecture, a reasonable hypothesis. Nothing more. The rest is legend.

His orderly was not with Manuel Mena when he was shot on the Cucut, but he affirmed that Manuel Mena lay on the summit of the hill with a bullet in his guts until the Francoists quelled the Republican counterattack and his men could bring him down to the battalion's first-aid post. That was where he joined him. And that was where the medics understood the gravity of the wound and sent them both immediately to a field hospital. It was not the closest hospital to the Cucut, which was in Batea, but the 13th Division's hospital, set up in Bot; who knows: perhaps if they had sent him to Batea he might not have died, because it would not have taken the three eternal hours it took to travel—first on the back of a mule, then in an ambulance—the thirteen miles separating him from Bot. He arrived in the village at night, bleeding but conscious, and as he entered he had the strength to see the streets overflowing with ambulances and dead and wounded men lying on stretchers or on the ground. It had been a black day: the hospitals of Bot could not keep up with all the victims. Manuel Mena was admitted to one of them and left in a room with his orderly; perhaps they were alone, perhaps he shared the room with other wounded men. We don't know how much time passed like this. At some point the orderly, exasperated by the wait and by Manuel Mena's weakness, left the room and asked an auxiliary nurse when they were going to attend to his officer, and the auxiliary nurse answered that they had to wait until the medical team finished the surgery on a higher-ranking officer, perhaps she mentioned the name of Captain Nájera, wounded in the same Republican counterattack on Cucut. They waited, Manuel Mena lying in a rickety old bed with his uniform soaked in blood, gasping, his fine hair messed up and stuck to his scalp and his face blackened and damp with sweat and the shine in his possibly green eyes increasingly rigid; his orderly, sitting beside him. At another moment, pale as marble, Manuel Mena asked for water; the orderly gave it to him. Then he asked for water again and his orderly gave him some more. Then he said:

"I am going to die."

After that Manuel Mena asked his orderly for two things: to

keep the money he had on him and to give his personal effects to his mother. Then he died. It was in the early hours of the morning of September 21, 1938.

That same morning Manuel Mena's body was transferred to Zaragoza by train; on that last trip he was accompanied by his orderly, who by then must have known that the previous night Captain Nájera had died as had another three of the 13th Division's second lieutenants, among them Carlos Aymat. Manuel Mena was interred the following day in the Torrero cemetery, in a wooden coffin with mouldings and wrapped in the Francoist flag. A little while later an expedition of four family members, headed by Manuel Mena's brothers Antonio and Andrés, arrived in Zaragoza. They had made a long and tortuous trip, avoiding the battlefronts across the interior of the rebel zone—from Trujillo to Salamanca, from Salamanca to Burgos, from Burgos to Zaragoza—with the aim of bringing the second lieutenant's body back to his native village. The authorities greatly facilitated their mission. So, after disinterring the coffin, opening it, and confirming that it contained the lifeless body of Manuel Mena, they set out on the return journey in two cars accompanied by the orderly and with the coffin in a zinc-lined box.

The arrival of Manuel Mena's corpse in Ibahernando was an event that for decades endured in the village's collective memory. Ibahernando is still overawed by that death: for the Francoist families, Manuel Mena was the model of the national hero, young, gallant, idealistic, hardworking, dashing, and killed in combat for the Fatherland; for all the families he was just a boy who hadn't even grown old enough to earn anyone's ill will.

Many remembered the funeral procession appearing in the distance that day on the Trujillo road, solemnly travelling the short eucalyptus-lined track leading into the village, leaving the green waters of the lagoon behind on the left and turning towards Poza Arriba on the curve by the old cemetery to then head past the Civil Guard barracks and up the calle de Arriba towards Manuel Mena's house, where people had been congregating for a very long time to await the arrival of the casket. Blanca Mena was not there: she had been confined by her family to her grandmother Gregoria's house, to spare her, at barely seven, the flesh-and-blood horror of seeing her dead uncle. She wasn't there, but she remembered the day very well, or some images of the day. She remembered herself at her grandmother Gregoria's house, crying in sorrow at the death of her uncle and crying in fury at not being allowed to witness the arrival of her uncle's body in the village. She remembered that her grandmother Gregoria's servants patiently endured the bottomless grief of her tears and that finally their patience ran out and one of them was put in charge of taking her to her grandmother Carolina's house. She remembered that, without stopping crying for a second or letting go of the maid's hand, she walked the deserted streets until they emerged onto the calle de Arriba, flanked at that moment by Flechas and Balillas waiting in formation for the appearance of the hearse. She remembered that the two of them walked very quickly between the double row of children dressed in the blue shirts and black shorts of the Falange and recognised among them José Cercas, the father of Javier Cercas, and that they looked at each other (according to Javier Cercas, his father also remembered that exchange of looks for his whole life). And she remembered very well that she arrived at her grandmother Carolina's house, on the calle de Las Cruces, just in time to witness a scene that was going to remain etched on her retina forever and on the retinas of everyone who was present.

The scene happened like this. Shortly after the arrival of Blanca Mena, the funeral procession made its way through the mourning crowd that packed Las Cruces. Manuel Mena's four relatives and his orderly got out of one car, and then the five of them lifted the coffin out of the other car and set it down in the courtyard of Manuel Mena's house. Only then did his mother come out, dragged or pushed by her daughters, who almost carried her. She was dressed entirely in black, her face and hands were white, she seemed consumed by suffering and could barely stand. Around her, people were crying, but she must have remembered the request her dead son had made of her every time he went back to war, or perhaps her sorrow was beyond tears, because she did not shed a single one. The only thing she managed to do, in the middle of the crowded silence that reigned over the street, was to raise her arm in a flaccid fascist salute and say with a thread of a voice that welled up from her entrails:

"Arise Spain, my son."

Blanca Mena did not attend Manuel Mena's funeral: at that time such ceremonies were reserved in the village for adults. During the following days, however, she visited her uncle's orderly frequently, or at least she often saw him. The orderly was staying in her grandmother Carolina's house and didn't leave her side for an instant, or perhaps it was her grandmother who didn't leave his side for an instant. Blanca Mena saw them whispering while her grandmother was cooking dinner or sewing or doing housework or chores in the yard, but she noticed that they stopped talking or changed the subject whenever she came near. Although she was sure they were talking about her uncle, she never knew exactly what they said. One day the orderly disappeared and they never heard of him again. More or less at the same time Manuel Mena's mother asked that, when she died, they would put her dead son's ceremonial sword in her coffin with her.

The family tried to forget. In spite of Manuel Mena incarnating the paradigm of the Francoist hero, his death in combat had very little repercussion outside of the village. On October 20 the *Extremadura*, the most important newspaper of the province, published a death notice; two and a half weeks later *La Falange*, the party's regional weekly, did the same. The text, signed by the local leader of the Falange, had been written by someone who, although he pretended to have known Manuel Mena, did not know him when he was alive and does not show a great interest in knowing him once he had died (in his idleness he even confuses which Bandera of the Falange he fought in during the first year of the war); unfailingly, he describes him as a "brave Falangist," a "courageous soldier," a "glorious hero," and, after inflicting these hollow, obligatory, and routine expressions on him, he treats him brutally by attributing an idiotic phrase to him: "You can only die once for your Fatherland!" As for the death notice, it was paid for out of the family's pocket, and did not neglect to record that he had given "his life for God and for the Fatherland." In Ibahernando Manuel Mena's memory is still, nevertheless, very much alive. Shortly after his funeral, on October 2, to be precise, the municipal government decided in a solemn session to consecrate a street to his memory. Months later Blanca Mena and her grandmother were sitting in the patio of her house when a man walked past them. Blanca Mena did not recognise him, but her grandmother abandoned what she was doing and stared at him. Blanca Mena was about to quietly ask who that stranger was when her grandmother shouted a question to him.

"Where are you going?" she asked, with a friendliness that seemed genuine to her granddaughter for a moment. The question rang through the whole street; the man stopped and turned to her with a faint smile. "Are you going home?" her grandmother Carolina asked again, although now Blanca Mena felt that, from one second to the next, her friendliness turned into a cutting sarcasm, full of pain. "You're going to see your mother, aren't you? How nice. I bet you're happy, aren't you?" The smile had fled from the man's face, and he was now looking at her grandmother Carolina paralysed with a mixture of perplexity and fright. Her grandmother Carolina spat: "Well, I can no longer see my son, because he is in the cemetery!"

The final sentence brought a sudden end to the man's paralysis, and without saying a word he lowered his head, walked away quickly, and disappeared towards La Rejoyada, or perhaps towards the calle de Arriba. Once he had gone, Blanca Mena asked who he was, and her grandmother Carolina answered that he was a Republican who had fought the war with the Republicans. Still shaken by the scene she had just witnessed, Blanca Mena reproached her:

"And why did you say those things to him?"

Her grandmother stared at her as if she'd just said something in an incomprehensible language.

"Ah, I suppose you think it's good they killed your uncle Manolo?" she asked.

Blanca Mena was not yet ten when her grandmother asked her that question, and almost eighty years later she didn't remember word for word the answer she gave her, but she did remember the general sense of her answer. What she said to her grandmother was that she did not think it was good that her uncle had been killed in the war, that she thought it was very bad, that she thought it was a horrible thing and she knew it was. But she also said that her uncle went to war because he wanted to. Nobody forced him to go to war. And the man who had just passed in front of them had nothing to do with his death.

That was all: all that Blanca Mena said to her grandmother and all that happened that day, or all that Blanca Mena remembers happening. The former Republican did not come near her grandmother Carolina's house again, at least, Blanca Mena never saw him there again, but for the rest of her life she could never cross paths with him in the village streets without feeling the shame and anguish she'd felt the day her grandmother had shouted at him as if he were responsible for Manuel Mena's death.

Blanca Mena also remembers another anecdote. When it happened, seven or eight years had passed since the end of the war and she was a fifteen- or sixteen-year-old adolescent who was now in love with José Cercas. One autumn afternoon, just home from school, she went to visit her grandmother Carolina. The door was not closed and the house seemed deserted; the first thing seemed normal, because in the village nobody closed their doors during the day, but the second did not. She looked for her grandmother in the kitchen, the dining room, the bedrooms, until she found her in the yard with her aunt Felisa and her aunt Obdulia. The three of them had just lit a bonfire and were watching it burn. She said hello to them, looked at the flames, and asked what they were burning. Her grandmother didn't answer her, but her aunt Felisa did.

"They're your uncle Manolo's things," she said.

Incredulous, Blanca Mena looked at the pyre: in effect, the fire was devouring clothing, books, papers, letters, notebooks, photographs, everything. She turned her horrified gaze to her grandmother, who seemed bewitched by the flames.

"But what have you done?" she asked.

She didn't remember if it was her aunt Obdulia or her aunt Felisa who took her by the shoulder.

"Come on, child." She sighed, whichever one it was, pointing at the fire. "What do we want all this for? To keep on suffering? We're burning it and let's have done with it."

Manuel Mena's mother died of cardiac arrest on August 29, 1953, a decade and a half after her son died. During those fifteen years, the Exterior Bank of Spain in Sidi Ifni had been paying her every month, from the account of the Group of Ifni Rifle Companies and with irregularities that often obliged her to write in complaint, a pension of three hundred and fifteen pesetas and ninety-six centavos, the current equivalent of approximately three hundred and fifty euros. We do not know if when she received those alms she remembered sometimes that before going off to war Manuel Mena told her that, if he died in combat, she would never have to worry about money again, but the truth is that is the price the Francoist State paid to the privileged families of Francoist officers, for surrendering a son to slaughter. On the day of Manuel Mena's mother's death someone remembered that many years earlier she had asked to be buried with her son's ceremonial sword; the family looked for it everywhere, but nobody could find it.

❦ 15 ❧

I no longer remember when or how or where I conceived the suspicion that Bot was the place where, according to family legend, Manuel Mena had died. I remember that it was a long time before I was sure it was true and a long time after my mother was hit by a car, and I understood that for her, Manuel Mena had been Achilles, and that perhaps he still was; I also remember that, when I asked my mother if the name of the village where Manuel Mena had died was Bot, her exiled octogenarian's face lit up.

"That's it!" she said, radiant. "Bot."

I'm lying. Actually what she said was Bos or Boj or Boh: just as twenty-five years of living in Catalonia had not enabled her to understand the Catalan word for "after you," *Endavant,* or at least not to confuse it with the Spanish expression *"¿Adónde van?"* (Where are you going?), half a century in Catalonia had not enabled her to pronounce the Catalan place name Bot, or at least not to pronounce it as Bos or Boj or Boh.

The fact is it still took me a few years to get to Bot. By then it had been quite some time that I had been following Manuel Mena's trail and that, like a detective prowling around the scene of a crime, I'd been to Teruel, to Lérida, and to the valley of

Bielsa; I'd also been to Terra Alta. By then I had visited the memorial consecrated to preserving the memory of the Battle of the Ebro in Terra Alta several times and I had realised that, unlike what happened in Teruel, in Lérida, and even in the valley of Bielsa, in that region the battle had left an indelible trace: during the postwar years many of its inhabitants made a living selling the scraps of shrapnel that covered their countryside, and even now many of them still bear the battle very much in mind, in a certain sense are still living with it and with its consequences, obsessed by it, some even unhinged by it. By then I knew the battlefields fairly well, I had walked in the same places Manuel Mena had walked, especially at Cucut, Hill 494, the place where Manuel Mena was fatally wounded, where there were still abundant remains of shrapnel in the ground and where time had not destroyed the Republicans' trenches and shelters (or even some of the much more fragile parapets improvised by the Francoists in the very short time between their conquest of the summit and the Republican counter-attack). Otherwise, from the start of my investigations I was aware that I wasn't searching for the singular trace, but the plural traces of the First Tabor of Ifni Riflemen, and that and no more was what I was finding: a multiple, shifting, slightly abstract, imagined and almost extinct trace. So it can be understood that the day I finally arrived in Bot I was almost sure I would find nothing less vague than that, and if that wasn't entirely the case it was because shortly before I had spoken by telephone with the man who, according to a widely held view, best knew the village's history.

His name was Antoni Cortés. The first time I called him I got straight to the point: I summed up Manuel Mena's story and told him that according to my mother he had died in Bot, although I had no proof of that. "It would be strange for your mother to be mistaken," Cortés said. "Didn't you say her uncle fought with the 13th Division?" "With the Ifni Riflemen," I specified. "Who were in the 13th Division." "Well, the 13th Division had their hospitals in Bot," he assured me. "So, if her uncle was attended in a hospital before he died, it was almost certainly here." Speaking very quickly, in fits and starts in a thick dialectal Catalan, Cortés told me that during the battle there were three hospitals in Bot, he mentioned a couple of books about it and about the Civil War in the village; then we were talking about what happened in Bot during the battle and, when I thought he'd told me everything he had to tell me, I thanked him for the information. "Don't thank me," he said. "For me it's a pleasure to talk about the history of my village. Do you know what the worst thing is that can happen to a person? To grow up and realise he doesn't know anything. It happened to me at the age of thirty-five, and since then I've done nothing but study. And now I'm retired. I still don't know anything, but I hide it better." "You hide it very well, sir," I said sincerely. "Bah," he said, just as sincerely, or that's how it seemed to me. "I hide it better when it comes to ancient history. That's what I'm really interested in, because it's what takes most effort to find out. We know everything about the Battle of the Ebro. And what we don't know we can soon find out." "About my mother's uncle as well?" I asked. "Of course," he answered. "Drop in here one day and you'll see."

I didn't believe him, I thought he was just talking for the sake of it or that he was trying to make himself sound interesting, and I hung up thinking I would not speak with him again. A few months later, however, I found documentary evidence in the Military Archive in Ávila that Manuel Mena had died in

Bot, and I called him again and made an appointment to meet him in his village when I had to make a trip to Valencia. Cortés said to meet him at noon in the plaza of Bot, so I could leave Barcelona at 9:30 and get to Gandesa two hours later; there I took a windy road that brought me to the village in ten minutes. This turned out to be an even smaller place than Ibahernando, a handful of brown houses clustered tightly around the bell tower of a brown church and surrounded by hills interspersed with rocks and pine trees. The church stood in the plaza and, as I parked outside its door, I saw that the only man in sight was walking decisively over to my car. He was dressed informally in worn jeans and a blue pullover, but his athletic carriage, his silver-framed glasses, and luxuriant grey moustache lent him the eccentric and polished air of a retired British colonel. It was Cortés. I got out of the car and held out my hand while thanking him for his hospitality.

"Don't thank me," he said, with a military handshake. "I don't like to be thanked. Also, I don't deserve to be: I'm delighted to help you."

I was about to thank him again but I held back and asked if he were a historian. He answered no, that he had been a butcher and then he'd worked at a leather company and then in a wine shop and later in a factory in Gandesa. There was not a soul in the plaza; the silence of the village was total.

"But let's not talk about me," Cortés said. "It's very boring. Tell me: what do you want to know about my village?"

I summed up the story of Manuel Mena again and hurried to tell him I'd located his death certificate, on which it stated that he had indeed died in Bot.

"You weren't mistaken," I told him.

"Neither was your mother," he said. "Do you remember the name of the doctor who signed the death certificate?"

"Cerrada," I said. "A Dr. Cerrada."

Cortés looked annoyed.

"Your uncle was an officer?" he asked.

"Second lieutenant," I said, nodding. "But he wasn't my uncle, he was my great-uncle."

"Why didn't you tell me earlier?"

"That he was my great-uncle?"

"That he was an officer." Cortés didn't give me time to apologise; he said: "Now I know where he died."

"He didn't die in Bot?" I asked, slightly disconcerted.

"Of course he died in Bot," he said. "I mean which house he died in."

I thought he was joking. I looked into his eyes; he wasn't joking.

"He died in Ca Paladella," he declared. "A house they turned into a hospital during the war." Pointing vaguely to his right, he said: "It's just here, right around the corner."

"How do you know? I mean: how do you know he died there?"

"Because that was the only hospital for officers in the village; that's where Dr. Cerrada worked. I'll tell you more: I know which room your uncle died in."

I heard myself ask again:

"How do you know?"

"Because in that hospital there was only one room for officers," he said. "And because my mother was a nurse there."

"What?"

"What you heard."

NOMBRES	EMPLEO	UNIDAD	NATURALEZA	FAMILIARES	HERIDO	DIAGNOSTICO	INGRESO	FALLECIDO	INHUMADO EN BOT.	OBSE...

"Your mother told you?"

"And she'll tell you whenever you want."

"Don't tell me she's still alive."

Cortés laughed.

"Alive and kicking," he said, grabbing my arm and forcing me to walk. "Come on, I'm going to show you the house where your great-uncle died."

Turning at the first corner, we walked a few feet down a street, and when we got to the next corner we stopped before a three-storey mansion built of large blocks of brown stone: on the ground floor there were several lattice-covered windows and a big wooden door under a semicircular arch, above which, carved into the stone, was a noble coat of arms; on the second floor were three large balconies, and the third was an open loft with a series of arched windows linked by a cornice with mouldings. It was more of a palace than a mansion.

"Here you have it," Cortés said, pointing proudly. "It's the only example of civil architecture in the village."

For a few seconds I stared at it in silence; then I asked:

"And you're sure it was here where—"

"Completely," Cortés interrupted me.

"It looks abandoned," I said.

"It doesn't just look it: it is." He explained that the house was the property of the richest family in Bot and had been up for sale for many years. "The descendants of the butler are the ones who show it to prospective buyers. They live in Tarragona, but if you want to see inside I can talk to them and get them to open it for us."

"Would they?"

"I think so."

"Well, I'd be very grateful if you'd ask them."

Cortés put his hands on his hips and scowled. It took me a second to realise I'd thanked him again.

"What I meant to say is that I'd be delighted if you were to ask them," I corrected myself.

Cortés moved his head from one side to the other, as if scolding me, and at last grudgingly stopped scowling. Then, suddenly, his lips, almost hidden by his moustache, spread into a frank smile.

"Well, do you want to talk to my mother or not?" he said.

"Right now?" I answered, perplexed again.

"Of course," Cortés said. "She lives just over here."

I walked beside Cortés and wondered what would be the next surprise he had in store for me and, as we went through the village without meeting anyone, my host told me that all his known ancestors were from Bot, that his father had died the previous year and had fought in the war and was from a Francoist family, while his mother was from a Republican family; he also told me his mother didn't like talking about the war.

Cortés's mother was a shrunken little old lady, as plump and wrinkled as a raisin. She answered the door herself; she was dressed completely in black and looked at us strangely, as if irritated or dazzled by the spring sunshine. Cortés had told me his mother had just turned ninety-one and was named Carme. Carme Manyà.

"Mother," Cortés said in an almost ceremonious tone, while I shook her suspicious, chubby hand. "This gentleman is a writer and wants to talk to you about the war."

The woman screwed up her inquisitive eyes even further, but did not ask us in. Feeling scrutinised and uncomfortable, not knowing what to say, I asked her if she remembered the Battle of the Ebro. Now I think that, especially after her son's

announcement, for a woman of that age born in Terra Alta the question was so obvious or so redundant that she must have thought that I could only be as ingenuous and inoffensive as my words.

"I believe I do." She laughed. Her brow cleared suddenly and I recognised in her expression a foretaste or a sketch of her son's expression. "Much better than what happened yesterday."

Only then did she let us in and, walking with difficulty but refusing her son's help, led us to a living room with thick walls of bare stone lit by deep windows, where we sat down. For the next two and a half hours the three of us stayed there, talking and drinking coffee. I told Cortés's mother what I knew about Manuel Mena's death and she told me that when the war broke out she was twelve, that she lived across from Ca Paladella, and during the Battle of the Ebro she had worked every afternoon in that improvised hospital together with a group of friends. Their job was not to attend to the patients, a task reserved for the professional nurses, but to cut bandages, put them in containers to be sterilised, make beds, wash dirty clothes in the river, and do whatever Dr. Cerrada ordered them to do; he was in charge of a fluctuating team of doctors and acted as head of the hospital. I asked her if they only looked after officers in that hospital; she said no, that they also looked after ordinary soldiers, but added that all officers were looked after there.

"In other words, you're absolutely sure that my mother's uncle died in Ca Paladella," I wanted to know.

"Absolutely sure," she said.

I looked at Cortés, who smoothed his moustache in satisfaction but didn't say a word, sticking to the subordinate role he had decided to play in that interview or that he always played in his mother's presence. He continued explaining that many more wounded soldiers arrived at the hospital than wounded officers, and that the officers had a room reserved for them on the first floor; I asked her if she knew which room it was and she answered of course, although she added that she didn't often go in there.

"So, in other words, you're absolutely sure my mother's uncle died in that room."

"Absolutely sure," she said again.

Marvelling at her reply, this time I didn't look at Cortés but kept looking at her, and at that moment she seemed identical to the remote little old ladies in mourning of my childhood summers in Ibahernando. I don't remember much more of the conversation except that, thanks to her, I was also able to clear up certain points about Manuel Mena's death (I understood, for example, the reason he had died while waiting for urgent surgery: because Ca Paladella had only one surgical team, which was insufficient on that ill-fated night for the 13th Division, with several officers wounded); I also remember that from a certain moment on I couldn't rid myself of the suspicion that this energetic and diminutive old lady unknowingly held in her memory the last living image of Manuel Mena, and the conviction that, if the suspicion were true, when she died that unconscious memory would die with her.

I said goodbye to Cortés's mother at the door to her house with a kiss on each cheek and told her I was very happy that she had agreed to answer my questions.

"I was told that you don't like talking about the war," I added.

"It's not that I don't like it," she said, waving one hand to get rid of an invisible nuisance while holding on to the door-frame with the other. "What happens is that I have only very

bitter memories of that time." Without a trace of drama, she explained: "Look, if they told me I had to choose between going through that again or dying, I would choose to die."

I said goodbye to Cortés beside my car and asked him to call me when we could visit Ca Paladella.

"I'll bring my mother," I promised. "She will be very pleased to see the place where her uncle died."

He told me he'd let me know as soon as he heard anything, and I was about to thank him, but stopped myself in the nick of time.

Cortés called me at the beginning of July, shortly before Ernest Folch and his team were going to film their television programme in Ibahernando, and told me he'd made an appointment to visit Ca Paladella. A few days later my wife and I drove to Gerona to pick up my mother.

"Well, Mamá" was the first thing I said after helping her into the passenger seat and doing up her seatbelt. "You're finally going to see Bot."

"Yes, son," she said, crossing herself as she always did at the beginning of a drive. "It's hard to believe: it seems like I've been waiting my whole life for this moment. If Grandma Carolina were alive ..."

During the trip my mother told us two things I'd never heard her tell before. The first is that on one occasion, when I was six or seven years old, I had gone with her and my father to the home of Don Eladio Viñuela, in Don Benito, a city in Badajoz where the doctor had moved with his family after leaving Ibahernando. It was a spur-of-the-moment visit. When we arrived, Don Eladio was not home, but his wife, Doña Marina, was, and we spent the whole afternoon with her having cakes and soft drinks and waiting for her husband, until night fell and we had to leave and I missed the only chance in my life to meet the man who had civilised Ibahernando. The other story had to do with Bot. My mother had always known that the village where Manuel Mena had died was in Catalonia and, according to what she said, when we moved to Gerona in the mid-sixties she thought of visiting it; in fact, during the first years she made a vague effort to find out where it was, but her all-consuming work as a housewife and mother of five, dispossessed of the patrician privileges of her village, obliged her to give up on the idea of finding it. For my part I told them, her and my wife, how I had discovered the exact place where Manuel Mena died, told them about Cortés's mother and about Cortés himself.

"He's a really nice guy," I warned them. "He hasn't stopped doing me favours since I met him, but don't even think of thanking him. He gets angry."

It was getting dark when we crossed the Ebro at Mora d'Ebre and entered the plateau that seventy-seven years earlier had been the scene of the battle. While I tried to give them an idea of its development, my mother looked out of the window as if she was not in the slightest bit interested in what she was listening to, or as if what really interested her was the succession of rocky, inhospitable, and desolate hillocks rising around us. We'd been driving for two hours and she seemed tired or bored. To distract her, as we passed by a signpost to Coll del Moro, I commented, almost in the tone of a tour guide:

"Look, Mamá: that's where Franco had his command post during the battle."

"Sainted Virgin of Perpetual Sorrow!" she lamented, indif-

ferent to my commentary: "Did my uncle Manolo have to come all this way to die?" With a single gesture she took in the whole landscape. "But this looks like the end of the world, son!"

That night we slept in the Piqué Hotel, on the way into Gandesa, where my wife had reserved a room; just one: my mother needed to sleep in company. After freshening up a little, the three of us went downstairs to the restaurant, and my wife and I had a few tapas while my mother did justice to a two-course menu plus dessert. She still hadn't finished her main course when I heard her say something I was surprised not to have heard her say during the whole trip: that one of my sisters had explained or insinuated to her that we had to sell the house in Ibahernando; arming myself with patience, I answered what I always answered: that she shouldn't worry, and that, as long as she was alive, we wouldn't sell the house. I saw the next question coming.

"And when I die?" she asked.

"And why are you so keen to die?" I said.

"Keen, me?" She was shocked. "Not at all, son. But one day Our Lord God will take me, and then—"

"Mamá, please!" I cut her off, irritated, and resolved not to allow myself to be blackmailed by her spontaneous tendency to catastrophic melodrama. "If you really want God to take you, make more of an effort . . ."

She looked at me without understanding; I pointed to the rack of lamb she was polishing off and clarified, implacably, as if I had been a victim of postwar hunger:

"It's just that, if you keep eating the way you eat, Our Lord won't even call you on the Day of Judgement."

Back in the room, my mother and my wife went straight to sleep and I sat down to read the translation of *The Odyssey* that I had taken from my mother's house in Ibahernando years before and that, since I finished rereading the translation of *The Iliad*, had accompanied me on my trips on the trail of Manuel Mena. I had been reading it for quite a while when unexpectedly I realised something I hadn't noticed before. What I realised was that the protagonist of *The Odyssey* was the exact opposite of the protagonist of *The Iliad:* Achilles is the man of a short life and glorious death, who dies at the youthful peak of his beauty and his valour and thus achieves immortality, the man who defeats death through *kalos thanatos,* a beautiful death that represents the culmination of a beautiful life; Odysseus, on the other hand, is the polar opposite: the man who returns home to live a long life blessed by fidelity to Penelope, to Ithaca, and to himself, although in the end he reaches old age and after this life there is no other. I was still under the effect of this revelation when I reached, towards the end of Book Eleven, the only episode in which Achilles appears in *The Odyssey.* Odysseus visits him in the house of the dead and tells him that he, who was the greatest of all heroes and defeated death with his beautiful death, the perfect man admired by all, who in the light of life was like a sun, now must be like a king in the realm of the shades and must not lament his lost existence. Then Achilles replies:

Illustrious Odysseus, don't try to console me for my death, for I would rather toil as the slave of a penniless, landless labourer, than reign here as lord of all the dead.

I read these lines. I reread them. I looked up from the book and for a while I thought of the hero of *The Iliad*'s regret. Then

I turned off the light and went to sleep wondering if, like him, Manuel Mena (the posthumous Manuel Mena, but also the Manuel Mena of his last days, the taciturn, absorbed, disenchanted, humble, lucid, aged, and fed-up-with-war Manuel Mena) would not have preferred to be a slave to some poor serf, breathing vital air, than a dead lord, wondering if in the realm of the shades he had also understood that there was no other life than that of the living, that the precarious life of the memory is not immortal life but barely an ephemeral legend, an empty substitute for life, and that only death is certain.

The next morning we parked in Bot's main square just before ten, and, as we were doing so, I saw Cortés talking to a woman at the door of a café. He said goodbye to her and walked over to us, and I introduced him to my wife and my mother. The first thing my mother did was thank him for his hospitality; the first thing Cortés did was get angry.

"But what's wrong with this family?" he asked, opening his impotent arms and looking to my wife for an explanation. "Can't they stop saying thanks or what?"

I feared the visit was going to fall through, but my wife and I managed to paper over the mess with a thick cloud of excuses and we all started walking towards Ca Paladella, my mother holding on to my arm with one hand and her stick with the other, Cortés recovering from his initial indignation while he explained that he had put the people who were going to show us the house in the picture about the reason for our visit. When we arrived at Ca Paladella Cortés knocked on the door and a dark-haired, middle-aged woman soon opened it, and we were still tangled up in introductions when another woman appeared, this one blond and somewhat younger, wearing glasses and a necklace of red glass beads; at her side was a teenage girl in a very short blue summer dress. The blond woman urged us to come in.

"It's just that if the village people see the house open, they'll want to come in and look around," she apologised.

Her name was Francisca Miró; the other was Josepa Miró (the teenager, whose name was Sara, was her daughter). As Cortés explained as we entered, they were both granddaughters of the last butler of the house, which had been built at the end of the seventeenth century or the beginning of the eighteenth by the village's wealthiest family and had been abandoned at the beginning of the war, although in the postwar years the owners used to spend a lot of time there.

"But for at least forty years nobody has come back to live in this house," Cortés said.

We were standing in the vast entrance hall with peeling walls, with light coming through a little cobweb-covered window and from a paraffin lantern. Two huge doors like the entrance opened from the hall: one led to the storehouses, which, according to Cortés, had been used as a mortuary during the war, when the house was turned into a hospital; the other allowed a glimpse of steps leading up to the darkness of the first floor. The feeling of abandonment was total: there was dust and newspaper everywhere, cardboard boxes, empty gas cylinders, old junk. Suddenly, while I was listening to the explanations Cortés and the Miró sisters were offering, I noticed that several people had come into the entrance hall, and I wondered if they were intruders or relatives or friends or acquaintances of the Miró sisters, taking advantage of the chance to visit the mansion. At some point my mother's voice broke through the various overlapping conversations.

"And this is where my uncle Manolo died?" she asked.

"Not here, señora," Cortés responded. "On the second floor. Let's go upstairs."

I thought my mother would be daunted when she saw the dark, dusty, cracked stairway she would have to climb, but she was not daunted. We left her stick in the entrance hall and began the ascent in a procession, with Cortés, Josepa Miró, and her lantern in the lead and my wife and the rest of the retinue in the rear. My mother went up heavily, resting on each step, with one hand on my arm and the other on the dirty iron handrail. When we got to the landing she was sweating. I asked her if she was alright and she said she was; I asked her if she was sure and she again said yes. Still following Cortés and Josepa, we turned left, crossed a dark parlour, and arrived in a living room or what seemed to have been a living room illuminated by a skylight. We were still there, listening to Cortés and looking around at the damage caused by forty years of neglect, when Cortés's mother appeared, tiny and dressed in mourning and accompanied by Francisca Miró. I said hello and introduced her to my mother.

"Mamá," I said, pointing to her, "this lady was working in this house when Manuel Mena died."

And who knows, I was about to add, perhaps she holds the last image of a living Manuel Mena. My mother's fatigued face was transfigured, and the two old ladies kissed each other on each cheek and began to chat as if they'd known each other for ever, my mother about Manuel Mena and Cortés's mother about her work as a nurse's auxiliary in Ca Paladella during the war; in spite of the fact that Cortés's mother was speaking in Catalan (and my mother's deafness), they seemed to understand each other perfectly. Cortés interrupted them: he asked his mother where the room for officers was; in reply his mother turned and, escorted by her son, was off like a shot into the darkness, with obvious risk to her balance. We followed her to a room on the same floor.

"It was here," she said. "The officers were here."

The Miró sisters' lantern barely chased away the shadows of a dining room that seemed stuck in the 1960s. Two shutters blocked the light from coming in through the only window. It smelled of dust and confinement.

"This is the room where your uncle died," Cortés explained to my mother. "It's been abandoned for many years. And, of course, you have to imagine that none of what you see here was here then."

My mother didn't say a word and turned to me with a lost look. To be sure she had understood, I repeated that this was the place where Manuel Mena had died and, with the help of Cortés and Cortés's mother, I tried to reconstruct for her some of the hypothetical details of her uncle's stay in that house. My mother listened to us and nodded while looking around the room: at the table covered in a velvet tablecloth with a brass soup tureen and a china plate, the carved wooden sideboards that occupied the ends of the dining room, the chairs and upholstered armchairs, the radio and record player of the time; the beam of the paraffin lantern seemed to focus on her face, damp with perspiration, suffering and waxy, projecting a spectral shadow on the wall. I thought she was dizzy and asked if she wanted to sit down; she said yes. I sat her down on a chair, dried her face with a handkerchief, sat down next to her. Meanwhile, Josepa Miró struggled with the shutters over the windows until she finally managed to open them; filtering through a broken blind, the scant light that entered the room lit up thousands of particles of dust floating in the cloistered air. I felt like I had already lived this instant, although I did not know when or where, and I realised that some strangers had come into the room and were observing us in intrigued or expectant silence and whispering to each other. I wondered again if they were friends or relatives of the Miró sisters, or if they were intruders. Meanwhile, Cortés and the Miró sisters offered to show us the rest of the house; I told them my mother would rather rest and the three of them left, followed by the other visitors. Her curiosity piqued, my wife joined them.

"Well, then, Mamá," I said, once they closed the door. "Now you see: here is as far as Manuel Mena got."

My mother nodded; alone with me, she didn't seem dizzy or faint, but nor did she seem to have recovered or to be in complete control of herself. Now she was scrutinising the opposite side of the room through the shadows, where the strips of light that pierced the broken blind and the half-open shutters lit up a patch of dirty, checkerboard floor with a damp patch on the wall. After a couple of seconds she pointed in front of her with a barely perceptible tip of her head and murmured:

"It's as if I can see him lying there . . ."

She kept contemplating the empty space in silence, and her withdrawn countenance reminded me of her perpetual countenance during her two years of depression, when an excess of lucidity revealed to her that she had spent a quarter of a century living in Gerona as if she lived in Ibahernando, that she had wasted her life waiting to go home, that this futile wait had been a misunderstanding and that this misunderstanding was going to kill her. "Well," I said to myself, trying to get that memory out of my head and remembering Lieutenant Drogo and *The Tartar Steppe*. "Here is where the legend of Manuel Mena began, and here is where it ends. Case closed, Inspector

Gadget." Case closed? For a moment I too saw Manuel Mena there, on the other side of the room, slumped and in agony on a rickety military bed, his uniform soaked in blood and the pallor of death invading his adolescent features. Then I turned back to my mother, who was still staring at the empty space, and I thought she was going to burst into tears, that she would cry again almost eighty years after Manuel Mena's body returned to Ibahernando from Bot and she used up all her tears crying for him, and it occurred to me that if I saw my mother weep for the first time in my life, there and then, the war would have finally ended, seventy-six years after it ended. But there were no tears, my mother did not cry: surrounded by two dark and wrinkled circles, her eyes were still dry. "This does not end," I said to myself. "This never ends." I looked again where she was looking and again thought of *The Tartar Steppe*, and of the end of *The Tartar Steppe*, again I imagined Manuel Mena lying and waiting for death as Lieutenant Drogo waited for death at the end of *The Tartar Steppe*. I imagined him like that and asked myself what I would have said to him if I had been at his side at that moment, if I had been in the place of his orderly. I answered myself that I would have tried to comfort him, that I would have done whatever I could to help him die well. I thought that I would have told him it was true that he was going to die, but that, as Lieutenant Drogo had understood on his deathbed, that was the real battle, the one he'd always been unknowingly waiting for. I thought I would have told him that it was true he was going to die, but that, unlike Lieutenant Drogo, he would not die alone and anonymous in the semi-darkness of an inn, far from the combat and glory, without having been able to test his mettle on the field of battle. I thought I would have told him that it was true he was going to die, but that he should die in peace, because his death was not an absurd death. That he wasn't dying fighting for interests that were neither his nor his family's, that he wasn't dying for a mistaken cause. That his final lucidity was a false lucidity and his disenchantment an unsubstantiated disenchantment. That his death had meaning. That he was dying for his mother and his siblings and nieces and nephews and for everything decent and honourable. That his death was an honourable death. That he had been equal to the task and had measured up and not been found wanting. That he was dying in combat as Achilles had in *The Iliad*. That his death was a *kalos thanatos* and he was dying for values greater than himself and that his was a perfect death that crowned a perfect life. That I wasn't going to forget him. That nobody was going to forget him. That he would live for ever in the volatile memory of men, as heroes live on. That his suffering was justified. That he was the Achilles of *The Iliad*, not the Achilles of *The Odyssey*. That in the realm of the dead he would not think it preferable to know old age as a slave of a penniless labourer than never to know it as lord of all the dead. That he would never be like the Achilles of *The Odyssey*, that nobody had deceived him, that he wasn't killed by a misunderstanding. That his was a beautiful death, a perfect death, the best of deaths. That he was going to die for his country.

"What are you thinking, Javi?" my mother asked.

Without looking at her I answered:

"Nothing."

My mother reached for my hand, held it, and pulled it into her lap. I noticed the feel of her fingers twisted by arthritis, with her wedding ring still on her finger, I noticed the wilted softness of her skin and her familiar scent amid the rancid, closed-up, damp smell of that room. I wondered how many more years her life would last and what I would do with mine when she died.

"Don't think anymore about it, Javi," she said. "Uncle Manolo felt obliged to do what he did. That was all. The rest just happened." After a pause she added, in a different tone of voice: "You can't know how much I wish you could have known him: he was so nice, always laughing, always joking . . . That's how he was. And that's why he felt obliged. No more, no less, no more or less."

I wondered if she was right and if it's all that simple. I let a couple of seconds pass. Then I said:

"I have to tell you something, Mamá."

"What's that?"

I thought: Uncle Manolo didn't die for his country, Mamá. He didn't die to defend you and your grandmother Carolina and your family. He died for nothing, because they deceived him and made him believe he was defending his interests when he was actually defending other people's interests and that he was risking his life for his own people when he was just risking it for others. That he died because of a gang of sons of bitches who poisoned the minds of children and sent them to slaughter. In the last days or weeks or months of his life he suspected it or began to see it, when it was already too late, and that's why he didn't want to go back to the war and lost the cheerfulness you'll always remember and turned in on himself and became solitary and sank into melancholy. That he wanted to be Achilles, the Achilles of *The Iliad*, and in his way he was, or at least he was for you, but in reality he's the Achilles of *The Odyssey* and he is in the realm of the dead cursing having to be the lord of all the dead in death and not a slave of a penniless labourer in life. That his death was absurd. Again I said:

"Nothing."

It was only then that I thought again of my book on Manuel Mena, of the book I'd spent my whole life postponing or the one I'd always refused to write, and now it occurred to me that I thought of it because I suddenly understood that a book was the only place where I could tell my mother the truth about Manuel Mena, or where I'd know how to or where I'd dare to tell her. Should I tell her? Should I tell that story? Should I put down in writing the story of the symbol of all the mistakes and responsibilities and guilt and shame and misery and death and defeats and fright and filth and tears and sacrifice and passion and dishonour of my forebears? Should I take on the family past that most embarrassed me and discuss it at length in a book? In recent years, while I scratched up information about Manuel Mena here and there, I had come to understand some things. I had understood, for example—I thought, thinking of David Trueba—that I was no better than Manuel Mena: it was true that he had taken up arms for an unjust cause, a cause that had provoked a war and a dictatorship, death and destruction, but it was also true that Manuel Mena had been able to risk his life for values that, at least at a certain moment, were for him more valuable than life, even though they were not or even though for us they were not; in other words: there was no doubt that Manuel Mena had been politically mistaken, but there was also no doubt that I had no right whatsoever to consider myself morally superior to him. I had also understood that Manuel Mena's story was the story of an apparent victor and an actual loser; Manuel Mena had lost the war three times: the first, because he had lost everything in the war, including his life; the second, because he had lost everything fighting for a cause that was not his but that of others, because in the war he had not defended his own interests but the interests of others; third, because he had lost everything for a bad cause: if he had lost everything for a good cause, his death would have had meaning, it would make sense now to pay him homage, his sacrifice would deserve to be remembered and honoured. But no: the cause for which Manuel Mena died was a hateful, irredeemable, dead cause, I thought, thinking of David Trueba and Danilo Kiš or of the end of the Danilo Kiš story David Trueba had told me: "History is written by the victors. Legends are woven by the people. Writers fantasise. Only death is certain." This is what had happened to Manuel Mena, I thought: that, even though the victors had written the history of the war, nobody had written his, everybody had preferred to tell legends or fantasise, as if they were all *literati* or as if they had guessed that in practice Manuel Mena was one of those who lost the war. Was that another good reason for me to tell his story? In that time I had also understood that it would be impossible for another writer to tell it, no matter how often I'd toyed with that idea, and that, if I didn't tell it, nobody would tell it. *Should I tell it?* I asked myself again. Or should I leave it untold, forever turned into a void, a hollow, into one of the millions and millions of stories that never get told, into a radiant never-written masterpiece—masterly and radiant precisely because nobody was going to write it—refusing to take it on, keeping it forever hidden like the best-kept secret?

My mother sighed without letting go of my hand; she still had her gaze fixed on the far side of the dining room, on the exact point where she'd decided that seventy-seven years earlier Manuel Mena had lain dying. I heard, very near, the sound of footsteps and laughter, and I thought of the intruders who had snuck into Ca Paladella; also, for some reason, I thought of ghosts. Then I remembered the Danilo Kiš story again and, maybe because I was sitting beside my mother, breathing in her scent with her hand in mine, it occurred to me that it was impossible that the Countess Esterházy had deceived her son on the day of his execution only so he would have a *kalos thanatos,* a perfect death that would crown a perfect life, and by doing so be worthy of his name and his patrician lineage: if she had deceived him—if she had appeared on the balcony dressed in white when her son was on his way to the scaffold amid the braying of the crowd—it had been so he could leave life without fear and without anguish, to help him die well with the deceiving security that before the execution the imperial reprieve would arrive. I thought this and I thought that, in the same way, it was novelistic ingenuousness to think that my mother had spent her life telling me about Manuel Mena because for her there was no higher destiny than that of Manuel Mena, because she wanted to write my destiny with Manuel Mena's destiny, because she wanted me to be equal to the task and measure up and be worthy of my name and my false patrician lineage. No, I thought again: the most likely thing is that my mother had spent her life telling me about Manuel Mena because with Manuel Mena or with Manuel Mena's death she had understood to the point of running out of tears that it was a thousand times better to be Odysseus than to be Achilles, to live a long and mediocre and happy life of fidelity to Penelope, to Ithaca and to oneself, even if at the end of that life another does not await, than to live a brief and heroic life and a glorious death, that it is a thousand times better to be a penniless labourer's slave in life than to be the lord of all the dead in the realm of shades, and because she needed or because it was urgent to her that I understood that. And I also thought that it was also ingenuous on my part (as well as presumptuous) to believe that the Countess Esterházy had written her son, and perhaps Manuel Mena's mother hers, and that whereas my mother had not managed to write me, I suddenly realised my puerile arrogance of believing that by becoming a writer I had prevented my mother from writing me, rebelled against my mother, avoided the destiny in which, knowingly or unknowingly, she had wanted to confine me; the truth, I thought, was precisely the opposite: that there had been no rebellion, that my mother had imposed her will, that I had not been the heroic and ephemeral and radiant Achilles but the long-lived and mediocre and loyal Odysseus, that by being Odysseus I had been exactly what my mother had wanted me to be and by becoming a writer I had done exactly what my mother had wanted me to do, that I had not written myself but had been written by my mother, I understood that my mother had wanted me to be a writer so I wouldn't be Manuel Mena and so that I could tell his story.

"What are you thinking, Javi?" my mother asked again.

This time I told her the truth.

"That maybe I should write a book about Manuel Mena," I said.

My mother sighed, and at that moment I thought there are a thousand ways to tell a story, but only one good one, and I saw, or thought I saw, with midday clarity, without a shadow of a cloud, the way to tell the story of Manuel Mena. I thought that to tell Manuel Mena's story I should tell my own story; or, to put it another way, I thought that in order to write a book about Manuel Mena I should split myself in two: I should tell one story on one side, the story of Manuel Mena, and tell it exactly as a historian would tell it, with a historian's coolness and distance and scrupulous veracity, confining myself strictly to the facts and disdaining legend and fantasy and the writer's freedom, as if I were not who I am but another person; and, on the other side, I should write not a story but the story of a story—that is, the story of how and why I came to tell the story of Manuel Mena in spite of the fact that I didn't want to tell it or take it on or bring it up, in spite of the fact that my whole life I have believed I became a writer precisely not to write the story of Manuel Mena. My mother said:

"What I don't understand is how it is that you have not yet written that book."

I turned to look at her; she looked back at me with a neutral expression.

"You're a writer, aren't you?"

"And if you don't like what you read?"

She answered my question with another question:

"Don't tell me now you write your books so I'll like them?" A glimmer of irony shone in her eyes: "Talk about locking the stable door after the horse has bolted."

We fell silent again. I kept hearing voices, footsteps, the odd bang, but they weren't coming from our floor but the floor above, or that's what it sounded like. In the midst of the shadowy silence of that abandoned palace we must have looked like two characters from the Antonioni film, or perhaps two outlandish contestants on an outlandish version of *Big Brother.* I heard footsteps approaching the room and thought about ghosts again. The door opened. It was my wife.

"You have to come upstairs and see the house," she said. "It's spectacular."

Cortés appeared beside her with an enthusiastic smile. My

mother stood up and took two headlong steps towards him, and he had to catch her so she wouldn't stumble. I could tell what was going to happen, but I didn't do anything to prevent it.

"You can't know how moving it is for me to be here," my mother said, taking Cortés by the hands. "I never imagined that one day I was going to be in the place where my uncle Manolo died." Unfailingly, she added: "Thank you so much."

The last phrase erased the smile from the face of Cortés, whose mouth opened below his moustache to protest and he looked at me with astonishment while, stifling a giggle, my wife took my mother's arm and led her out of the dining room. I begged for comprehension with my gaze, and he shook his head from one side to the other, defeated, and followed behind my wife and my mother.

Preceded by Cortés, we went up to the second floor. There, emerging from the shadows with the lantern, Josepa Miró joined us, and for a long time the five of us wandered around the darkness of the house. I have some precise, partial, and disjointed memories of that stroll. I remember an inexhaustible series of rooms and halls sleeping in a silent semi-darkness of polished doors and grandfather clocks stopped at arbitrary hours and stately wardrobes full of papers, old books, and embossed leather folders. I remember a decadent luxury of thick velvet curtains and green satin sofas and canopies of fuchsia silk and noble coats of arms and secret or seemingly secret rooms and kitchens and pantries full of rubble. I remember bedrooms with brass bedsteads with canopies and baldachins and hardwood cradles and bedside tables and skeletal bedsprings and empty umbrella stands and orphaned coat racks. I remember a chapel decorated with frescos representing the four evangelists, and I remember Josepa Miró and Cortés pointing out the scratched faces of the evangelists and explaining that they had been the victims of the anticlerical fury of the libertarians who seized the house at the outbreak of the war. I remember a chapel and benches and kneelers and church organs and saints mounted on pedestals or hiding in vaulted niches and marble and wooden crucifixes and tons of religious images. I remember tapestries that showed sumptuous hunting scenes (a pack of hounds pursuing a stag, a dog with a freshly caught rabbit in its jaws), and I also remember huge dusty mirrors and grand pianos and framed photographs and charcoal portraits and oil paintings of men and women who were surely dead and forgotten. I remember all of that and I remember my mother and my wife walking beside me, behind Cortés and Josepa Miró, who showed us the way with Josepa's lantern amid the ruinous splendour of that abandoned mansion, and I remember the silhouettes and the voices and the laughter of the increasingly numerous visitors or intruders whose paths we crossed, and who none of us greeted, not even Cortés and Josepa, as if they didn't know them or didn't recognise them or didn't even see them, as if they were ghosts and we were explorers lost in a sea of ghosts. But I especially remember myself feeling euphoric, almost levitating with stealthy joy at the certainty that at last I was going to tell the story I had spent half my life not telling, I was going to tell it so I could tell my mother the truth about Manuel Mena, the truth I could not or dared not tell her any other way, not just the truth of the memory and the legend and the fantasy, which was what she had created or contributed to creating and which I'd been hearing since I was a boy, but also the historical truth, the bitter truth of facts, I was going to tell that double truth because it contained a more complete truth than either of the other two on its own and because only I could tell it, nobody else could tell it, I was going to tell Manuel Mena's story so it would exist entirely, since only the stories someone writes exist, I thought, thinking of my uncle Alejandro, that's why I was going to tell it, so that Manuel Mena, who could not live for ever in the volatile memory of men like the heroic Achilles of *The Iliad*, should live at least in one forgotten book like the repentant and melancholy Achilles of *The Odyssey* survives in a forgotten corner of *The Odyssey*, I would tell Manuel Mena's story so that his wretched story of a triple war loser (of a secret loser, of a loser disguised as a winner) would not be entirely lost, I was going to tell his story, I thought, to show that within it there was shame but also pride, dishonour but also integrity, misery but also courage, filth but also nobility, fright but also joy, and because in that story there was what there was in my family, and maybe in all families—defeats and passion and tears and guilt and sacrifice—I understood that Manuel Mena's story was my inheritance or the mournful and violent and wounding and onerous part of my inheritance, and that I could not keep refusing it, that it was impossible to refuse it, because in any case I had to take it on, because Manuel Mena's story formed part of my history and therefore it was better to understand than not to understand it, to accept than not to accept it, to discuss it at length than to leave it rotting inside me the way that mournful and violent stories rot inside someone who has to tell them and leaves them untold, to write the book about Manuel Mena my way, I finally thought, what I had always thought it was, taking charge of Manuel Mena's story and my family's story, but I also thought, thinking of Hannah Arendt, that this was the only way to take responsibility for both, the only way also to alleviate and emancipate myself from both, the only way to use the writer's destiny my mother had written for me or had confined me to so that not even my mother would write me, to write myself on my own.

I thought all this as I wandered almost blindly with my mother holding on to my arm and my wife making sure we didn't stumble, the three of us following the light shining from Josepa Miró's lantern through the gloom of Ca Paladella, and at a certain moment I said to myself that, since I was going to tell Manuel Mena's story and take responsibility for the bad part of my family legacy, there was no reason for me not to take responsibility also for the good or not so bad, that if I was going to take on that mournful and violent and wounding and onerous piece of my inheritance there was no reason for me not to take on my whole inheritance and that I was authorised to tell my mother the truth once and for all: that I was not Stephen King or Bill Gates, and that when she died I would get rid of the house in Ibahernando. Standing at the door of a room Cortés and Josepa Miró had just entered, I announced to my mother that I had something important to tell her. She stood still and silent.

"It's about the house in Ibahernando," I prepared her, trying to prepare myself.

From the threshold of the room my wife beckoned us in, but my mother ignored her gestures and gave me a complicit squeeze on my forearm.

"Oh, then I know what it is," she said, and, without giving me time to ask, added: "You're not going to sell the house in Ibahernando. And that, when I die, you'll keep it."

Perplexed, I looked for her face in the darkness but didn't find it; I didn't start to laugh either. I just thought of Odysseus and of Ithaca and, almost grateful, I lied:

"You've read my mind, Blanquita."

We heard Cortés calling us, and followed my wife into a

relatively large room that had perhaps once been an office, or looked like it had, with a curtain behind which was an alcove in which all I remember is a double bed without a mattress and a ceramic washbasin. There, Cortés explained—or as Cortés's mother had just explained to him—they had set up the operating theatre of Ca Paladella, the room where seventy-seven years earlier Manuel Mena was about to be urgently operated on. While Cortés was repeating his mother's explanations about the place, I could not help wondering what would have happened if Manuel Mena had not died in Ca Paladella, if that night in September 1938 that campaign operating theatre had been free and Dr. Cerrada could have operated on him and saved him. I heard noise outside, in the hallway and the adjoining rooms, only now it didn't seem like an isolated murmur of steps or voices but the swarming buzz of a crowd or a forest of ghosts. Then I was assaulted by a thought. *He didn't die,* I thought. *He's not dead.* A cold chill ran up my back. I tried to get this thought out of my mind, but I could not, as if it wasn't my own. *He's not dead,* I thought again. *He's here.* And I thought: *He's here, they're all here, none of the dead who died in this mansion died. Nobody has gone. Nobody goes.* Cortés was still talking, but I wasn't hearing him anymore, and bit by bit the euphoria and stealthy joy in which I'd felt myself lifted turned into something else, or maybe it was me who felt he was turning into someone else, a sort of happy and mediocre and old Odysseus to whom that expedition through the shadows of that big empty house in search of the lord of all the dead had just revealed the most elemental and most hidden, most recondite, and most visible secret, which is that we don't die, that Manuel Mena had not died, that's what I thought all of a sudden, or rather what I knew, that my wife and my son and my nephew Néstor would not die, and I would not die either, with a shiver of vertigo I thought that nobody dies, I thought that we are made of matter and that matter is not destroyed or created, it just transforms, and that we do not disappear, we transform into our descendants just as our ancestors transformed into us, I thought that our ancestors live on in us as we will live on in our descendants, it's not that they live metaphorically in our volatile memories, I thought, they live physically in our flesh and our blood and our bones, we inherit their molecules and with their molecules we inherit everything they were, whether we like it or not, despise it or not, accept it or not, whether we take it on or not, we are our ancestors as we will be our descendants, I thought, and at that moment I was overwhelmed by a certainty I'd never felt, now I think I could have felt it at any other moment, or better yet that I should have felt it or at least intuited it, but the fact is that when I felt it for the first time, I was in that former operating theatre in that abandoned mansion of that village lost in the middle of Terra Alta, beside my mother and my wife and Cortés and Josepa Miró, I felt that I was at the summit of time, on the infinitesimal and so fleeting and extraordinary and daily peak of history, in the eternal present, with the incalculable legion of my ancestors beneath me, integrated in me, with all their flesh and their blood and their bones turned into my bones and my blood and my flesh, with all their past life turned into my present life, taking them all on, converted into all of them or rather being them all, I understood that writing about Manuel Mena was also writing about myself, that his biography was my biography, that his mistakes and his responsibilities and his guilt and his shame and his misery and his death and his defeats and his fear and his filth and his tears and his sacrifice and his passion and his dishonour were mine because I was him as I was my mother and my father and my grandfather Paco and my great-grandmother Carolina, in the same way that all those ancestors who gathered in my present just like a crowd or innumerable legion of dead people or a forest of ghosts, just like all the bloods that flowed into my blood coming from the unfathomable well of our infinite ignorance of the past, I understood that telling, that accepting Manuel Mena's story was to tell and accept the story of all of them, that Manuel Mena would live on in me as all my ancestors lived in me, I thought that too, and in the end, drunk on lucidity or on euphoria or on stealthy joy, I told myself that this was the final and best reason to tell Manuel Mena's story, the definitive reason, if Manuel Mena's story had to be told it was most of all, I said to myself, to reveal the secret I had just discovered in the realm of the shades, in the profound darkness of that forgotten ruined palace where his legend began and where, I saw it then as if written in a radiant never-written masterpiece, I was going to finish my novel, that transparent secret according to which, although it might be true that history is written by the victors and people weave legends and writers fantasise, not even death is certain. *This does not end,* I thought. *It never ends.*

AUTHOR'S NOTE

Some of the people to whom I am indebted appear in the pages of this book with their first and last names, but there are many more who do not appear; at the risk of forgetting some, I shall mention the following: José Luis and Ramón Acín, Leandro Aguilera, Josep Mª Álvarez, Francisco Ayala Vicente, Messe Cabús, Julián Casanova, Enrique Cerrillo, Julián Chaves Palacios, Luciano Fernández, Pol Galitó, Antonio Gascón Ricao, Roque Gistau, Jordi Gracia, José Hinojosa, Anna Martí Centelles, Jorge Mayoral, Enrique Moradiellos, Sergi Pàmies, José Miguel Pesqué, José Antonio Redondo Rodríguez, Joan Sagués, Margarita Salas, Manolo Tobías, David Tormo, and the children of Don Eladio Viñuela and Doña Marina Díaz: Marina, José Antonio, Julio, José María, and José Luis. To all of them, thank you. I also want to thank my old friend Robert Soteras, who accompanied me halfway around Spain following the trail of Manuel Mena and the First Tabor of Ifni Riflemen.

A NOTE ABOUT THE AUTHOR

JAVIER CERCAS is a novelist, short story writer, and columnist for *El País*. His books include *Soldiers of Salamis*, which was awarded many prizes, including the *Independent* Foreign Fiction Prize, and sold more than a million copies worldwide), *The Tenant* and *The Motive* (the latter now a film directed by Manuel Martín Cuenca), *The Speed of Light* (short-listed for the 2008 IMPAC Award), *The Anatomy of a Moment* (winner of Spain's National Narrative Prize), *Outlaws* (short-listed for the 2016 Dublin International Literary Award), and, most recently, *The Impostor* (winner of the European Book Prize). In 2015 he was the Weidenfeld Professor of Comparative Literature at St. Anne's College, Oxford, and a book based on the lectures he gave there is published under the title *The Blind Spot: An Essay on the Novel*. His books have been translated into more than thirty languages.

A NOTE ABOUT THE TRANSLATOR

ANNE McLEAN has translated Latin American and Spanish novels, stories, memoirs, and other writings by many authors, including Héctor Abad, Julio Cortázar, Gabriel García Márquez, and Enrique Vila-Matas. She has twice won the *Independent* Foreign Fiction Prize, with Javier Cercas for *Soldiers of Salamis* and with Evelio Rosero for *The Armies*. She shared the 2014 International IMPAC Dublin Literary Award with Juan Gabriel Vásquez for his novel *The Sound of Things Falling*, and in 2016 and 2004 won the Premio Valle Inclán for her translations of *Outlaws* and *Soldiers of Salamis* by Javier Cercas. In 2012 Spain awarded her a Cruz de Oficial of the Order of Civil Merit.

A NOTE ON THE TYPE

This book was set in a typeface called Walbaum. The original cutting of this face was made by Justus Erich Walbaum (1768–1839) in Weimar in 1810. The type was revived by the Monotype Corporation in 1934. Young Walbaum began his artistic career as an apprentice to a maker of cookie molds. How he managed to leave this field and become a successful punch cutter remains a mystery. Although the type that bears his name may be classified as modern, numerous slight irregularities in its cut give this face its humane manner.

Composed by North Market Street Graphics,
Lancaster, Pennsylvania

Printed and bound by Berryville Graphics,
Berryville, Virginia

Book designed by Betty Lew